Crime and Suicide in the Nation's Capital

Gloria Count-van Manen

The Praeger Special Studies program—
utilizing the most modern and efficient book
production techniques and a selective
worldwide distribution network—makes
available to the academic, government, and
business communities significant, timely
research in U.S. and international economic, social, and political development.

Crime and Suicide in the Nation's Capital

Toward Macro-Historical Perspectives

Praeger Publishers   New York   London

PRAEGER SPECIAL STUDIES IN U.S. ECONOMIC, SOCIAL, AND POLITICAL ISSUES

Library of Congress Cataloging in Publication Data

Count-van Manen, Gloria, 1922–
    Crime and suicide in the Nation's capital.

    (Praeger special studies in U.S. economic, social,
and political issues)
    Includes bibliographical references and indexes.
    1. Crime and criminals—Washington, D.C.—History.
2. Suicide—Washington, D.C.—History.   3. Crime
prevention—Washington, D.C.   I. Title.
HV6795.W3C68   1977   364'.9753   76-24347
ISBN 0-275-56860-1

PRAEGER SPECIAL STUDIES
200 Park Avenue, New York, N.Y., 10017, U.S.A.

Published in the United States of America in 1977
by Praeger Publishers,
A Division of Holt, Rinehart and Winston, CBS, Inc.

789   038   987654321

© 1977 by Praeger Publishers

Printed in the United States of America

IN MEMORY OF THOSE WHO HAVE HARNESSED
INTELLECT IN THE SERVICE OF HUMANITY

By predilection, I cannot interpret man's behavior easily in terms of any "one factor" theory. This is one of the reasons for my decision to attempt to test alternative views on crime causation, the findings of which are reported here. A second reason is my growing dissatisfaction with the state of U. S. criminology. The discipline remains today one of diverse predications, without significant movement toward a resolution under investigative fire of either theoretical priority or of integration. It remains a field, thus, ripe for the flourishing of opinion and of myths. Every few years a new criminology volume is published that, in essence, contains interesting ideas on the old. The field, then, stagnates with numerous perspectives of truth, frequently the product of particular university schools of socialization.

There seem to be a number of handicaps characteristic of our times, which have worked to forestall definitive assessments of the empirical solidity of competing ideas of reality. Among these is the low status within the discipline of multicausal approaches. Occasional serious examinations of macrostructural variables tend toward observation of the impact of one variable only on deviance levels, without tests of alternative hypotheses. Thus, one author reports a high correlation of business cycles with crime; another reports a low correlation; and someone else reports high correlations, as well, of alienation with crime. Others report high correlations of the police force with crime, and still others, low ones. While such specializations within specialization provide at least minimal insurance that the researcher knows what he or she is about (and thereby precludes, as well, the frequency of peer attacks, if only since the number of vulnerable flank exposures is thereby reduced), the practice does not provide the student or the policy maker with reliable guidelines.

Chapter 1 identifies the problems of the discipline and of policy on crime control more fully. Chapter 2 is an attempt to identify a few central theories that relate to the nature of the larger society and to crime levels. Chapter 3 examines the directions provided by cumulated research that have probed these theories. It is clear that varying research designs and techniques, while healthy in themselves, work to confound the cumulation of knowledge. It is difficult to ascertain which association should be regarded as real and explanatory.

The research reported here, then, represents an attempt to assay the relative importance of a few central macrostructural themes. The research design is described in Chapter 4. Through the use of a longitudinal case history of Washington, D.C., each variable is subjected to repeated tests within one research design, both by the use of three time periods and by experimentation with a number of measures on each variable. Thus, the findings constitute a progress report that is both substantive and methodological. It is hoped that the work may encourage additional efforts along these lines, and that it may offer at least some tentative guideposts for these.

The results do not give simple answers to the question of theoretical priority. Some weight is found for those views labeled as economic and anomic or social disorganization, as being stronger focuses for the regulation or control of crime levels than the element of the criminal justice system tested here, the police. In fact, within the context of the givens of our society, the latter is turned upside down from much thinking, and is regarded as another of the social forces contributing, in instances of some Class I crimes, to higher crime levels. In some epochs, it is found that economic forces are stronger; while in other epochs, ecological changes (interpreted here as leading to anomie and social disorganization) are stronger. While this complex design moves toward the resolution of some problems—for example, the location of extant archive sources of data for multiple hypothesis testing—it raises other problems. It points up, for example, existing inadequacies in statistical techniques for dealing with problems associated with multivariate analyses of time series.

The question can be asked, Why is the kind of study reported here unique in criminology? In addition to the ideas suggested previously, relating to specialization and high risk from peer attack, there are a number of additional factors that seem to be at work. One of these is the ritualistic abjuring of the use of official crime data, usually referred to as the crime index. The impact has been to forestall experimentation with selective use of some of these measures, as well as other archive sources. Yet it is only through such use that criminology has the potential of becoming a truly sociological enterprise, in the sense of achieving a balanced integration of macrostructural and microstructural approaches. For whatever just or unjust reasons, the field has remained dominated by social psychological theoretical approaches that support rehabilitative action programs and that continue to dominate thinking and funding efforts.

Favored explanations of crime and deviance in the discipline, as will be documented in Chapter 1 fit into existing biases of our culture. A notable example of these is supplied by subcultural theories of violence and of gang delinquency which continue to enjoy credibility in criminology and which are widely circulated in the mass media, in spite of a growing cumulation of empirical findings that fail to support them. There are a number of alternative explanations consistent with knowledge accumulated here (see Chapter 8).

It is possible, as well, that there has been a coordinated alliance between the power structure of criminology and the power structure of our society and of funding agencies. For nothing less than a diagnosis of the state of society is needed in order to achieve an understanding of why crime rates fluctuate, in order to aspire to the goal of prevention. Any such diagnosis must raise difficult questions. The time is long overdue for tests of competing ideologies that dominate professional and nonprofessional thought. Toward this end, the development of an empirically based macrocriminology is fundamental.

In my initial efforts to translate major structural theories into working hypotheses, it became evident that there are some unexpected conceptual overlaps. Ideas have been boundaried intellectually* and politically by labels of vocabularies and ideologies of their protagonists. The translation of theory into operational hypotheses showed that varying species of theory lead, unexpectedly, to similar hypotheses; while similar theoretical rubrics sometimes lead to varying hypotheses! When faced with the job of empirical test, then, the confining rubrics of difference, such as radical versus conservative, functional versus conflict, and so on, began to dissemble. There can be no pretense that there are not differences in varying theories, but it is suggested that there is the possibility, indeed the actuality, of common borders and concerns, as well.

In particular, then, the writer finds herself at odds with a number of instances of the rhetoric of criminology that have interfered with, rather than clarified, this work. It seems as if it were necessary to go back behind the starting lines to refresh verbal meanings. One such case is the concept system, at once overused, underused, and misused: its overuse—the criminal justice system, which is not a system, which is not justice, which is not the source of social control of crime; its underuse of meaning—the total social system, of which the criminal arresting-trying-sentencing-punishing process (with other misleading verbiage) is a part, along with other economic and social factors in the regulation of crime levels; and its underuse—the system of alternative deviant social responses as an interacting

---

*For an excellent summary of these intellectural compart-mentalizations, see Nanette K. Davis; Sociological Construction of Deviance: Perspectives and Issues in the Field (Dubuque, Iowa: Wm. D. C. Brown, 1975), pp. 8-11.

process. Examples of the latter are displacements from robbery to burglary, or from heroin to wine use, and vice versa. Examples of misuse are the foreordained associations or castigations such as conservative, functional, and so on. The writer opts for the central meaning of the concept of system to be that of interdependence. It is the writer's personal conviction that it is, in fact, a wedge for the empirical consideration of change.

A word should be said about the background of the writer, as it may affect this undertaking. My university and professional experience has been interdisciplinary, crossing the boundaries of sociology, psychology and psychoanalysis, and economics. By inclination and socialization, I was initially a social psychologist. My Ph. D. training at the University of Chicago included a substantial program in both psychology and sociology, including a one-year training program in counseling. Much earlier, I had studied psychoanalytic theory with Harry Stack Sullivan and others at the Washington School of Psychiatry. A minor in economics at the M. S. level was used in employment as a social economist at the U. S. Department of Labor, Bureau of Labor Statistics. The Ph. D., with a specialization in crime and deviance, was earned at the University of Chicago, where my dissertation was undertaken on the subject of family socialization patterns. At this time, I worked in high crime areas of the city of Chicago, as an employee of the programs of the mayor of Chicago and of President Kennedy. It was my disillusion with the results of psychological counseling approaches to rehabilitation some years ago that eventually pushed me in the direction of becoming a macrostructural sociologist.

The research effort reported was supported, in part, by the Faculty Research Program in the Social Sciences, Humanities, and Education at Howard University; the District of Columbia Office of Criminal Justice Plans and Analysis; and a Ford Foundation Grant to the Department of Sociology and Anthropology at Howard University. The Department of Sociology, as well, allowed release time from teaching to allow for the writing of the volume. Mr. Cecil Josiah, Ph. D. candidate in the Department at the University, collected most of these data and carried on computer procedures. Much gratitude is owed to him. Mr. Arthur J. Simpson, formerly an instructor at Howard University, collected data on business conditions, just before his untimely death. He was interested in writing his dissertation on the topic, business cycles and black homicide. Mr. Milton Sorota, formerly chief of the Operations Branch of the District of Columbia Police Department, was most cooperative in supplying needed data. Dr. Charles Moore and Mr. Mitchell Brown of the Computer Services Section of the University were helpful throughout the period of the study. Dr. James C. Su resolved the apparent difficulties of the SSPS computer program on multiple regression in dealing with the problems of missing data, by working up a special adaptation of the IBM multiple regression program. I an indebted to him for this. Finally, Mr. Jesse O. De Jaynes consistently cooperated far beyond the call of duty. He effectively typed the manuscript and called attention to editorial discrepancies. Dr. James F. Scott, Chairman of the Department of Sociology at Howard University, found a number of ways to encourage the writer during numerous times of difficulty.

Thanks must be expressed, as well, for comments on some chapters of the manuscript read by Dr. Theodore Ferdinand, Department of Sociology, Northern Illinois University: Dr. Richard Quinney, Department of Sociology, Brown University; Dr. Lien-fu Huang, Department of Economics, Howard University; and Dr. Tom van Valey, University of Virginia.

CONTENTS

Chapter	Page

LIST OF FIGURES

Crime and Suicide in the Nation's Capital

INTRODUCTION:
THE NATURE
OF THE PROBLEM

THE SUBSTANTIVE PROBLEM
UNDER INVESTIGATION

The anomaly of the crime problem is that—as criminal justice budgets mount drastically; as calls for increased punishment and police enforcements are made—the crime rates continue to wind their own way. The public, the law, treatment agencies, and the discipline of criminology have focused their attention, in common, on the individual criminal. Each person is held responsible for his or her own acts, and it is he or she who is at fault and must change. While the writer does not deny the role of the individual in accountability for action, this volume falls within the purview of a long tradition of thought attempting to identify the elements in the social environment that determine an individual's life chances, that narrow his freedom and provide constraints to his action.

The search for a basic anatomy of the social environment has constituted a mental battleground, epitomized by divergent perspectives on reality called to mind by the great contributions of such observers as Karl Marx, Sigmund Freud, Emile Durkheim, Max Weber, and Pitirim Sorokin. What factors, theoretically and in fact, determine the size of the crime problem? Economics? Or the state of society's moral malaise? Or the power relationships among vying groups? Or does the police force actually control the size of crime rates? What structural elements, in short, are the true arbitrators of the size of crime rates?

The research to be reported here constitutes an empirical examination of competing theoretical frameworks (see Chapter 2) for the sources of structural regulation of crime and suicide rates in a case history of the capital city over the relatively extended period of 1890 through 1970. Although criminology has given theoretical allegiance to such structural perspectives, it is interesting that the findings of studies of this nature are largely unavailable to students in criminology texts. This tendency may be attributed to various possible motives of criminologists, ranging from an interpretation that they are allied with the power elite, to their suspiciousness of archive data use, to the relative lack of funding available for research that might raise questions about the state of the body politic. This neglect is at least partially due, as well, to the apparent state of the results of such accumulated research: They appear to be contradictory and confusing, even though any one author may arrive at fairly clear conclusions. Chapter 3 will therefore briefly review the state of structural empiricism, pointing to some of the reasons for the contradiction—possibly more apparent than real. The social engineering consequence of this informational hiatus has been that criminologists have not had much to say about the guidance of social policies for the prevention of crime at the national, state, and city levels.

Operationally, the question under exploration here can be translated into the following: Is it feasible to make an empirical multivariate test of competing structural perspectives on the antecedents of changing crime rates in a longitudinal study of one city? Or, again, which structural variables explain most of the variance through time? Empirical testing is, of course, limited pragmatically by the availability of data. A long and patient search through numerous archive sources has made feasible a complex series of tests.

This study unfolds as one which, to the best of the writer's knowledge, does not have a precedent in criminology research design— that is, the application of multivariate procedures to time series data. The study may thus be considered exploratory insofar as this design (1) constitutes a pragmatic search for the identification of social indicators (measures of the state of society over a continuous time period) from existing archive sources that may serve to measure, indirectly or directly, structural themes; (2) erects specific hypotheses drawn, but not necessarily specified, from existing theoretical orientations for time tests; and (3) raises a number of technical methodological questions in which criminologists are not experienced and which must be the subject of future work.

Previous designs for structural research can be described as (1) multivariate and cross-sectional, or one-point-in-time studies; (2) multivariate and longitudinal with qualitative measures of independent variables and quantitative measures of dependent variables; (3) univariate, with longitudinal measures of one independent and one dependent variable. In the last category, for example, are studies of the effect of business cycles upon crime, delinquency, or suicide rates. Historical and multivariate studies, (2) above, generally

utilize qualitative measures or discrete events for independent
variables, such as the timing of national wars or of national depressions, with graphic documentation of crime rates, and impressionistic
comparisons of trend movements. Cross-sectional structural studies,
(1) above, work with numerous measures of both independent and
dependent variables, with variation in findings and in theoretical
emphasis from one study to the next. These are generally able to
explain most of the statistical variance. Summary statements on the
state of structural research are made at this point to further elaborate
on the nature of the problem, and documentation is provided in Chapter
3. A number of related questions, then, remain unsettled. For example,
which structural factors appear to be paramount, or to explain most
of the variance? Which appear to be spurious? Which may act in the
role of catalyst? Are there real changes in the effects of these forces
or factors on specific crime rates over time?

Technical problems arise in this research, stemming
essentially from the state of development of statistical tools and
knowledge. It is likely that the solution of these problems will remain
open for some time to come. It is hoped that the writer will be able
to work on some of these, with the collaboration of other specialists.
In the meantime, many of the central findings of this study will be
reported here. These technical limitations of the research, as well
as others, will be discussed in greater detail in Chapter 4.

Macrostudies

The terms macro and aggregate are applicable to structural
studies, but are more commonly referred to in the field of econometrics
than, as yet, in criminology. Macro has been defined by one author
in the former field as "magnitudes reflecting the summation of all
similar . . . units in a region, a nation, or a sector," while the
study of individual units is commonly called micro (Merrill and Fox
1970). Thus, the term is applied here to relationships and interactions of data totals or aggregates for the central city of the District
of Columbia. As far as the writer knows, specification of the cutting
points between micro- and macro-units within criminology have not
been identified. The peer group and the family, it would seem self-
evident, would be considered micro-units or small units. A neighborhood, county, or police district is certainly not a micro-unit, but it
is uncertain that it should qualify as a macro-unit, as do such entities
as cities, states, regions, and nations. It might be recalled that
neighborhood boundaries, or police and/or census tracts, have been
utilized in much of the ecological research in crime and delinquency.

Social Structure

At least three elementary concepts are central to the above statement of the problem and the task set—those of social structure, social control, and social force. All have some diversity in usage, and therefore the intent applied here will be specified. There is some core agreement on the meaning of social structure. Blau (1960) has suggested a twofold criterion for the dimensions of the term's meaning, namely: "networks of social relationships in which processes of social interaction become organized" and "common values and norms embodied in a culture." The problem involved here relates, then, to how the chances for abrogation of legal norms (for Class I crime and suicide) in one city are affected by social elements that change the nature of social relationships. Acts of crime are, of course, social relationships themselves, and are—in turn—affected by changes in other social networks. The factors affecting social relationships manifest themselves in the form of institutions and organizations, as well as in individuals. These forces may or may not be congruent with institutional and organizational life. For example, the state of the economic system is hypothesized to affect crime rates, while the economic system itself constitutes both an institution and numerous organizations. On the other hand, population increases and decreases could be classified as a social force, a changing structural element affected by other structural changes and, in turn, affecting changes in other social phenomena, including crime rates. Population and ecological arrangements do not, however, constitute either an institution or organization. The chances for value consensus or dissensus (anomie) in society are likely to be affected as well, it can be hypothesized, by changes in structural forces such as those mentioned.

Social Control

As was mentioned earlier, many lay people, politicians, and even some social scientists connote the control of crime with the criminal justice system. The clarity of the social science concept is diminished by its multifaceted dimensions and usages within varying contexts. The social psychological meaning signifies socialization, small group processes, and internalization of controls through vocabularies that include superego and conscience development. Within deterrence theory, social control tends to refer to the effects of punishment, formal and external controls, upon the individual criminal as well as upon noncriminals. In this volume, the concept is used in still a third sense, within the context of macrostructural regulation

of crime rates, or the internal controls of the body politic. These
are classified as internal insofar as they refer to factors at work
within society, with or without self-conscious knowledge and policy
regulation, but as providing the true and basic sources for regulation
of the size of crime rates. This last sentence constitutes the under-
lying assumption of this work and the thesis under test.

Social control, in this sense, relates well to the Durkheimian
notion of social fact, with the idea of these forming constraints upon
individual behavior. Further, only the use of aggregate data, or
totals of large social units, are thought to be appropriate for uncovering
structural principles. For example, it is possible to learn something
about economics and crime through a random sample of individuals and
their social class position and the frequency of their criminal acts.
It is less feasible, however, to learn about the effects of the relationship of changing economic currents to crime rates. Or, again, although
a sample of individuals can be categorized arbitrarily as black or
white into at least socially meaningful categories, a sample could not
reveal structural principles of the effect of changing population composition ratios upon crime rates of a city. Societal principles may be
reflected in individual facts, or facts collected about individuals, but
there is the possible danger that crucial structural relationships may
remain undiscovered with the use of samples of individuals. Durkheim
was correct: only studies of aggregates, or of social facts, can locate
these and bring about the assurance that structural principles are,
indeed, under scrutiny. "Society is a reality sui generis: it has its
own peculiar characteristics which are not met with again in the
same form in all the rest of the universe." (Nisbet 1965, p. 33).

Social Force

The concept of social force, like that of ecology, was
borrowed from the natural sciences, but it is currently less fashion-
able than verbiage on the former. The physical science connotation is
"anything that changes or tends to change the state of rest or motion
in a body" (Britannica World Dictionary). This concept, then, implies
a notion of equilibrium and change, ideas that find parallels within
the province of sociology in the related concepts of social structure
and social system. One historian has defined concepts of social
forces as "human energies which, originating in individual motivations,
coalesce into a collective manifestation of power" (Gustavson 1955,
p. 28). But human motivations, in turn, are affected by social conditions. Park and Burgess, in their early textbook, devoted an entire
chapter to the concept, with a similar usage, emphasizing changes
in processes, "in terms of interactions of tendencies. These tendencies

are what science calls forces . . . and are objectively embodied in
. . . institutions, organizations and persons" (Park and Burgess
1924, p. 436). There is, then, nothing mysterious about the use of
the concept of social force, and it is closely related to that of social
structure. What is the nature of the social environment that affects
socially structured relationships, those leading to street crimes and
suicide?

CRIMINOLOGY AND SOCIAL POLICY

What have criminologists had to say about crime control
policies? Although they have given counsel on prison and parole procedures and on policies that should be pursued at the neighborhood level,
the informational hiatus mentioned earlier works to prevent conclusive
statements being made that would have implications for city, state, or
national policies that might be pursued at the preventive level.

There is more clarity of statement, interestingly, at the
individual, small group, and neighborhood levels. For example,
criminologists have long taken the position that most criminals and
delinquents are psychologically normal (Thrasher 1926; Cohen 1955).
Nevertheless, counseling practices remain the predominant modus
operandi for rehabilitation, constituting an almost magic-like word
that ritualistically is thought to be able to right all wrongs, to change
values and attitudes of those who err. Never mind that the diagnosis
may be wrong, and that the medicine doesn't work.

At the subcultural (an ambiguous concept) level, sociologists
have varied in statements with policy implications. Cohen (1955) and
Miller (1958) have defended variant values as healthy reactions to
common problems, or as systems that have their own independent
integrity, while Wolfgang (1967) has recommended that the violent
ethos attributed to the black subculture should be integrated out in
the predominant, presumably nonviolent, larger culture. Others,
such as Thrasher (1926) and Clark (1965), have warned that the
breaking up of gangs and of minority subcultures could be potentially
disastrous and that, on the contrary, it would be better to strengthen
subcultures. Subcultural theories have been disappointing in that
these have not furnished an etiological base (Erlanger 1974) for the
prediction of differential rates of crime.

Numerous writers have recommended changing social
environments in ways that will open up opportunities. Cloward and
Ohlin's well-known perspective was used in the antipoverty programs
of the 1960s. These were applied primarily at the level of the local
neighborhood or community setting level (Thrasher 1926; Cloward
and Ohlin 1960).

Should the policymaker, perchance, turn to criminologists for some fairly sensible and specific answers to questions about the identification of particular aspects of the citywide or national environment that affect crime rates, evasive answers would have to prevail. Is there a limit to the size of the city, beyond which increases in size and density appear to be too high in suffering and budgets related to crime? Not much research attention has been given to the temporal aspects of this question (Ogburn and Duncan 1964, p. 133). How do business cycles and unemployment affect crime? The answer is again uncertain, depending upon the researcher consulted. It is an anomaly that more work was done on this question in the nineteenth century (Bonger 1916; 1967), without modern statistical tools, than in the twentieth. (See Chapter 3 for details.)

Theoretical Emphasis Upon
the Individual

At least part of the explanation for the above is that U.S. criminology (Mills 1959; Jeffery 1972; Reasons 1975) has been consistent with public opinion insofar as it has emphasized the individual as the target unit for understanding. This is essentially the case for theories relating to differential association, neutralization, labeling, socialization, and containment or control. The basis of this assessment is readily evident with a cursory examination of these theories for the object of discussion, which is, repeatedly, the individual. Even Merton's seminal structural analysis, while initially concerned with the prediction of crime rates, for the first few pages, then shifts to the well-known paradigm for individual adaptations, to which most of the essay is devoted. Thus, to this investigator the time seems overly ripe to shift the balance of effort and concern from the social psychological to the development of greater sophistication in macromodel building, to theoretical development at the structural level, and to statistical sophistication attendant upon these.

DISCONTINUITIES IN
PUBLIC OPINION

The inconsistency between the causes of crime and what should be done about the problem is revealed in opinion polls, sampling the U.S. public (U.S. Department of Justice 1975, pp. 176-77, 203-07). Asked the question:

> Which in your opinion is more to blame for crime
> and lawlessness in this society—the individual or
> society?

58 percent in 1970 responded, "society," and 35 percent, "the individual." When answering a question as to the main reason why people become criminal, 59 percent responded with "parents are too lax," 16 percent, "poverty," and 12 percent, "unemployment." Yet the large majority, or 84 percent, thought in 1972 that police should be tougher and 79 percent favored tougher sentences for lawbreakers (U.S. Department of Justice 1975, pp. 176-77; 203-07). The question of accountability, then, represents some notion of causation and appears to give direction to political policies and monies spent for the control of crime. Thus, the research problem being addressed here is thought to have implications for crime control policies, and these will be suggested in the final chapter. Suffice it to say, at this point, that the operating assumption which predominates in institutions and treatment is largely that the attitudes and values of individuals must be changed through counseling procedures before behavior of the individual will change. The fact that such efforts have largely missed their mark has not altered either lay thinking or widespread institutional practice.

    If it can be shown, then, that identified facets of the social structure account for most of the variation in crime rates, then the congruent logical implication for social control of crime is that society must be altered in order to effect changes in crime rates, rather than focusing on the individual will, vice, or attitudes. Brenner (1973), as a result of his investigations on business cycles and mental hospitalization, arrived at a parallel conclusion; that is, that economic downturns within the larger society account for increased psychiatric symptoms, and that this etiology is not dealt with in clinical psychology. Within sociology, the logical transition from structural, or social research facts to interpretations of an individual, psychological nature has been called the reductionist fallacy (Zito 1975, pp. 12-14). Thus, the thesis of this volume, in its action implications, is that there exists a fundamental discontinuity between the social or structural antecedents of fluctuating crime and deviance rates, and the treatment or control postures aimed at individual change paramount in this country.

REFERENCES

Blau, Peter M. 1960. "Structural Effects." American Sociological Review 25: 178-193.

Bonger, William Adrian, 1916, 1967. Criminality and Economic
    Conditions. New York: Agathon Press.

Brenner, Meyer Harvey 1973. Mental Illness and the Economy.
    Cambridge, Mass.: Harvard University Press.

Clark, Kenneth B. 1965. Dark Ghetto. New York: Harper and Row.

Cloward, Richard A. and Lloyd E. Ohlin. 1960. Delinquency and
    Opportunity: A Theory of Delinquent Gangs. Glencoe, Ill.:
    Free Press.

Cohen, Albert K. 1955. Delinquent Boys. Glencoe, Ill.: Free Press.

Erlanger, Howard S. 1974. "The Empirical Status of the Subculture
    of Violence Thesis." Social Problems 22 (December): 280-92.

Gustavson, Carl G. 1955. A Preface to History. New York: McGraw-
    Hill.

Jeffery, Clarence Ray. 1972. "The Historical Development of Criminol-
    ogy." In Pioneers in Criminology, ed. Hermann Mannheim.
    Montclair, N.J.: Patterson Smith.

Merrill, William C. and Karl A. Fox. 1970. Introduction to Economic
    Statistics. New York: Wiley.

Miller, Walter. 1958. "Lower Class Culture as a Generating Milieu
    of Gang Delinquency." Journal of Social Issues 14: 5-19.

Mills, C. Wright. 1959. The Sociological Imagination. New York:
    Oxford University Press.

Nisbet, Robert A. 1965. Emile Durkheim: With Selected Essays.
    Englewood Cliffs, N.J.: Prentice-Hall.

Ogburn, William Fielding and Otis Dudley Duncan. 1964. "City Size
    as a Sociological Variable." In Contributions to Urban
    Sociology, ed. Ernest W. Burgess and Donald J. Bogue.
    Chicago: University of Chicago Press.

Park, Robert E. and Ernest W. Burgess. 1924. Introduction to the
    Science of Sociology. Chicago: University of Chicago Press.

Reasons, Charles E. 1975. "Social Thought and Social Structure."
    Criminology 13 (November): 40-73.

Thrasher, Frederic M. 1926. The Gang. Chicago: University of Chicago Press.

U. S. Department of Justice. 1975. Sourcebook of Criminal Justice Statistics: 1974. Washington, D. C.: Government Printing Office.

Wolfgang, Marvin E. 1967. Studies in Homicide. New York: Harper and Row.

Zito, George V. 1975. Methodology and Meaning: Varieties of Sociological Inquiry. New York: Praeger.

2

THEORETICAL
ORIENTATIONS

But is it by its wealth or by its cohesion that
civilization makes crime recede? By its cohesion
without any doubt. This cohesion of religion, of
science, of all forms of work and power, of
different innovations, mutually confirming one
another, in reality or appearance, is a true
implicit coalition against crime (Bonger 1916;
1967, p. 154).

Three major theoretical traditions on social structure are
specified here as having implications for crime rates and as being
testable, directly or indirectly, with archive data. These comprise
the following: economic; anomie; and deterrence. Little consensus
is possible as to the paramountcy of these factors from accumulated
findings with varying methodological practices from one research
enterprise to the next. (See Chapter 3 for documentation.) The
rationale for the present effort may be considered, in a sense,
an exploration of the feasibility of testing competitive theories with
archive data. At the same time, the longitudinal framework of this
study allows for an examination of the dynamic aspects of change
processes.

It is likely that the complexity of the phenomenon under
examination may appear at first to be effect, and in turn becomes
cause. In the reality of social existence, as opposed to the reality
that science attempts analytically to capture, every factor in a
situation is being influenced by and is influencing every other factor,
with cause and effect interacting in such ways as to preclude the
probability of a single chain of causal influence. What appears, then,

is that crime rates are joint products of numerous causes and simultaneously causes of numerous effects. This is more than a notion of multicausality, however. It is an exploratory attempt to get some notion of weight approximations of factors, of alternations in influence, of the dynamics of time settings and variations in patterns mutually interacting.

The objective of this chapter is to provide the theoretical context necessary to document the nature of the logical transitions to be made here from concepts to operational measurement. Detailed substance, critiques, and contrasts of the theories will be avoided, since these are available in numerous other volumes. Much of the ideational debate results as an aspect, perhaps, of dysfunctional side effects of analytic schemes becoming mental prisons for scientific ideologies. The quest for theoretical primacy can be viewed in two senses: as a factor identified as first in a causal link and thus determining all other social phenomena, or as the efficiency of one determining factor over others (Sorokin 1928; 1964, pp. 528-29). The use in this work tends toward a test of the second.

There has been relatively little attention paid to the delineation of mutually interdependent aspects of structural theories, of common boundaries or "loops" (Klausner 1967, p. 29). The second objective of the chapter is to identify these.

SOCIAL FACTS AND SOCIAL CONTROL

Before undertaking the case outlined above, the close parallels between substance and method championed by Durkheim (1959), with regard to the general import of social control, will be noted. Park (1955, p. 227) regarded social control as the "central fact and the central problem of society":

> Just as psychology may be regarded as an account
> of the manner in which the individual organism, as
> a whole, exercises control over its parts or rather
> of the manner in which the parts co-operate together
> to carry on the corporate existence of the whole,
> so sociology, speaking strictly, is a point of view
> and a method for investigating the processes by
> which individuals are inducted into and induced to
> co-operate in some sort of permanent existence
> which we call society.

Within that context, this research effort may be viewed as a search for the forces that tend to push people outside the bounds of formal social regulation embodied in law.

Durkheim attempted to perform the role for society that Freud succeeded in accomplishing for the individual, but without the latter's far-reaching practical influence on institutional life. Freud called attention to the individual's unconscious processes, thereby helping to make him conscious and capable of choice. The former pointed to the regulating mechanisms of society, even though not consciously recognized by the body politic or by the individual. Social facts, according to Durkheim, are another breed of force, independent of the will of any individual and endowed with "coercive powers":

> They come into each one of us from without and carry us away in spite of ourselves . . . I do not feel the pressure they exert upon me . . . Thus, air is no less heavy because we do not detect its weight. (Durkheim 1959, p. 309)

All innovations (including criminal) must thus come up against the resistance of the force of social facts "the proof thereof being that it asserts itself as soon as I attempt to resist it." Durkheim identified a wide range of constraining social facts, including legal and moral rules, public conscience, religious denominations, political, literary, and occupational associations, internal migrations, and even styles in housing and clothing. These forces await their discovery and are revealed, Durkheim demonstrated, in other social facts, such as rates of suicide, crime, birth, and marriage. Here, then, is the nucleus of the idea that crime rates are to be considered a product of the social body, whose mechanisms await self-conscious examination and social awareness.

ECONOMIC AND CONFLICT THEORIES

> . . . since immemorial time thinkers were aware of the important role played by "economic factors" in human behavior, social organization, social processes, and in the historical destiny of a society. (Sorokin 1928; 1964, p. 514)

Sorokin documented the above statement on the import of economics in social life in the thinking of Confucius and Buddha, the ancient Greeks and Romans, and of numerous writers from the seventeenth to the nineteenth centuries. He viewed Marx and Engels within this long historical context and concluded critically that their "general formulas" are an "exaggeration and generalization" of what other authors had said before them (Sorokin 1964, p. 523). Nevertheless, the works of Marx remain perhaps the primary intellectual referent and context for current thinking in criminology on the impact of economics on crime. To document the nature of this thought for the purposes stated earlier is not intended to imply here that economic paramountcy must have Marxist ideological paramountcy.

Karl Marx: The Primacy of the
Economic Structure

There are at least three facets of Marxian perspectives that contain implications for the subject of economics and crime. Marx's basic premise is that economic relations determine all other manifestations of mankind, including the juridic order, as well as religious, philosophical, artistic, criminal, and so on. In his often-quoted words:

> In the social production of their life men enter into fixed, necessary relationships in production, independent of their will, relationships which correspond to a definite stage in the development of their material powers of production. The sum total of these relationships forms the economic structure of society, the real basis upon which the juristic and political superstructure is erected, and to which definite forms of social consciousness correspond. The form of production of the material life conditions the social, political, and intellectual life-process in general. It is not the consciousness of mankind that determines their being, but their social being that determines their consciousness. (Bonger 1967, p. 128)

Conflict

In recent years, a number of criminologists have developed this idea into what has been called a conflict thought model (Vold 1958; Quinney 1974; Denisoff and McCaghy 1973; Chambliss 1973). Their views incorporate, oversimply, the perspective that the power structure of each society makes the laws, protects the status quo, and penalizes others from challenging either. Crime is a reflection of power struggles (Turk 1966, p. 339). A number of attempts have been made to codify conflict perspectives into testable propositions (Turk 1966; Denisoff and McCaghy 1974; Davis 1975). The research design here is not intended to test the conflict aspect of economic models. However, a series of unanticipated findings may be interpreted within the general purview of this orientation.

The hypothesis here is that a decrease in resources among the rulers will increase conflict (and crime rates). More specifically, population numbers are commonly conceded to be one source of power. With this assumption, the changing effects of numbers, or population ratios of blacks and whites, can be inspected. The history of this central city of the District of Columbia can be viewed as a case of population transformation: from a sizable minority, or one-third black in 1890, to a sizable two-thirds majority black in 1970. Thus, recent years have presented a new numerical minority status to the white population. It is, indeed, found that as the black population increases, rates of personal violence among whites shows some tendency to increase. The opposite case also shows some evidence, but to a lesser degree. These findings will be detailed in later chapters.

Functions of Crime

A second theme of Marx points towards a twofold analysis on the functions of crime in capitalist society:

> Crime takes off the labour market a portion of the
> excess population, diminishes competition among
> workers, and to a certain extent, stops wages from
> falling below the minimum, while the war against
> crime absorbs another part of the same population.
> (Bottomore 1964, p. 159)

These side effects, then, of imprisonment and of the criminal justice force help to maintain the class system by delaying the timing of the inevitable fall of capitalism. The implication is that the effects of the business cycle are to some degree nullified by these factors, just as unemployment insurance and other social benefits cushion the effects of business cycles on crime rates. Business cycle measures are the datum used here for tests of economic perspectives, Marxian or otherwise. Before moving to this subject, the quotation above may also be viewed as part of the basis for an implied doctrine of population which can be drawn out.

Veblen (1919; 1969, p. 429) held that Marxist theory contains the seeds of a doctrine of social growth and population insofar as a growing reserve of unemployed labor is postulated. There is the suggestion that there is possible reliance upon a first principle of population expansion, and that poverty does not check the propagation of the race. The number of laborers, that is, are thought to proceed independently of their miserable state.

Business Cycles and Crime

"Business cycles are a species of fluctuations in the economic activities of organized communities." Further, they are

recurrences of rise and decline in activity, affecting most of the economic processes of communities with well-developed business organization, not divisible into waves of amplitudes nearly equal to their own, and averaging in communities at different stages of economic development from about three to about six or seven years in duration. (Mitchell 1956, p. 468)

There are many types of theories about business cycles and their causations, including physical processes, such as weather and planetary influence; emotional processes, such as moods of optimism and pessimism that affect birth and death rates and thus alternations of prosperity and depression; and institutional processes, such as innovative waves, lacks in equilibrium of producing and consuming, in dispersing and spending incomes, in consuming and investing, and so on (Mitchell 1956, pp. 50-53). Theories on business cycles remain in a state of empirical and thought flux, and here are taken as givens. Marx held that recurrent depressions are an inherent aspect of capitalist society. Unemployment, declining rates of profit, uncertainty, and instability are accompaniments of these cycles. Researchers in the socialist tradition (Bonger 1967) have moved in almost every conceivable direction in drawing up hypotheses as to the effects of business cycles on crime.

The instabilities that Marx predicts can be translated into a vocabulary of recurrent crises, changes, and insecurities (stress), vocabularies that parallel other structural themes. Quetelet, a nineteenth century statistician, was among those noting the influence of change on crime:

It is these sudden changes from one state to another that give birth to crime, especially if those who suffer from them are surrounded by temptations, and are irritated by the continual sight of luxury and an inequality of fortune that makes them desperate. (Bonger 1967, p. 33)

Alienation and Anomie

Marx is credited with coining the concept of alienation. Currently, there is some tendency to reserve this concept for psychological estrangement of the individual. Anomie, which Marx may have intended as correlated with the capitalist system, is reserved to describe the state of a society. Marx contended, of course, that the capitalistic organization of the means of production breeds alienation:

> The work is external to the worker, he does not fulfill himself in his work but denies himself, has a feeling of misery, not of well being, does not develop freely a physical and mental energy, but is physically exhausted and mentally debased. His work is not voluntary but imposed, forced labour. It is not the satisfaction of a need, but only a means for satisfying other needs. The alienated character of work for the worker appears in the fact that it is not his work but work for someone else . . . in work he does not belong to himself but to another person. (Bottomore 1964, p. 169)

The structural shift, then, in this line of thought is from the political nature of the capitalist economic system, to a state of anomie, to a greater likelihood of crime. This skeletal framework has much in common with the later writings of Merton (1938) and others who focused on anomie. Marxian, and more generally, economic analysis contains implications for other structural themes relating to population, to social change, and to anomie.

ANOMIE AND SOCIAL DISORGANIZATION

Theories variously labeled as those of anomie and social disorganization actually have a good deal in common with each other, as well as with the vocabularies referred to earlier within economic purviews. The basis for this statement will be briefly documented.

Anomie

Durkheim (1951) defined anomy as "deregulation, social chaos resulting from the absence of needed restraints upon the passions of men." De Grazia (1948, p. xii) later defined anomie as "the disintegrated state of society that possesses no body of common values

or morals which effectively govern conduct. " Widespread breakdown
in morality and values is expected to correspond to higher pro-
clivities of societies towards criminal actions. What, then, are the
social sources that lead to disintegration of the social conscience?
Clearly, according to Durkheim, these emanate from collective
trends. He attributed these, in his writings, to structural changes
such as industrialization, division of labor, heterogeneity, and
sudden economic fluctuations. These, he thought, contributed to social
isolation, "collective sadness," and the loss of "collective conscience,"
or common beliefs and practices. He clearly linked moral conscience
to religion and both, in turn, to man's ability to achieve his "place
among things. " Our very language, our inventive instruments, our
rights, our knowledge, our morality—all find their source outside
of ourselves. These, in turn, depend upon external causes located
in, and influenced by, society and the structural changes that affect
its nature. (See Bellah 1973, p. 174.) Merton's treatment of anomie
is consistent with these thoughts, emphasizing the impact of social
surroundings upon the intimate nature of social interaction:

> Above all else, they [the rules] are deprived of
> legitimacy. They do not comprise a social order
> in which one can confidently put their trust. For
> there is no longer a widely shared sense within the
> social system . . . of what goes and what does not
> . . . or what may be legitimately expected of people
> in the discourse of social interaction . . . a social
> condition admirably suited for producing insecure
> relations with others. (Clinard 1964, pp. 226-27)

Faris (1955, p. 39), Clinard (1964, p. 5) and Tarde (Bonger 1967,
p. 157) are among others who linked abruptness of change to breakdown in controls, morality, and crime. These symptoms of anomie,
long discussed by sociologists, sound much like today's public
opinion poll results.

Social Disorganization

Thomas and Znaniecki (Traub and Little 1975, p. 35)
defined social disorganization as "the decrease of influence of
existing social rules of behavior upon individual members of the
group," a definition remarkably close to the meaning of anomie.
Faris (1955, p. 81) defined social disorganization as "the weakening
or destruction of the relationships which hold together a social
organization. " Both authors are quick to clarify that disorganization

context applies primarily to institutions and only secondarily to individuals. Park (Park, Burgess, and McKenzie 1967, pp. 105-10) is among those identifying the nature of the social changes leading to disorganization. Interestingly, he stated that the "automobile bandit" is the "most demoralizing single instrumentality of present-day civilization." Communications media, movements of population, and the very idea of progress in (in common with Durkheim) contain the seeds of anomie and breakup of the social order.

From this brief documentation, distilled for reasons of space limitations here, it can be seen that theories of anomie, of social disorganization, and of economics contain interweaving vocabularies which, in action, have a number of common boundaries. All are concerned with change and the impact of change, whether stemming from economic fluctuations, economic and political developments, population change and mixes, migrations, technical inventions, and/or changes in attitudes and morality that appear to spring from these, and thence lead to crime, directly and/or indirectly. The primacy of any one factor has remained an area for intellectual conviction, in much the same way as the old chicken-egg controversy.

The theories identified above, economic and anomic, are structural in essence. A lesser structural case can be made for the general direction of deterrence theories, but one delineated aspect is relevant for this research effort.

DETERRENCE

The assumption of most deterrence (and some economic) theories is that of rational decision-making processes on the part of the individual. Zimring and Hawkins (1973, p. 7) correlate deterrence with declarations of harm, loss, or pain that will follow noncompliance; that is, some form of threat is involved. The rationale of punishment is preventive, deterrent in the sense that it allows the individual to make decisions about possible risks, harms, and benefits from a criminal act (Grupp 1971, p. 373; Sullivan 1973). This rationale does not concern us here, since it is not primarily a structural concern, but rather an individual decision-making process.

Jerome Hall (Grupp 1971, p. 398) suggests, however, a systemic function of the criminal justice system:

> In immediate relation to the criminal law, responsi-
> bility is associated with punishment. But in the wide
> realm of freedom protected by the criminal law,
> responsibility connotes a way of life to be sought,
> maintained and enlarged. To be a responsible person

in this sense is to be a mature participant in social
life, sensitive to other persons' needs and poten-
tialities as well as to one's own development. In
this context, the principal purpose of a system of
criminal justice is to preserve and improve the moral
fabric of interpersonal relations upon which social
life, freedom, and individual creativity depend . . .
those who have harmed their fellow man . . . helped
to participate in this value-cosmos.

Thus, Hall's reasoning is not unlike that of Durkheim: the function of
punishment is to refurbish, reembellish, remind the conforming
populance of what they stand for.

It is possible that a highly visible arm of justice, the police
force, has a mass impact of numbers, communicated en masse by
the relative visibility of a detterent threat to masses of citizens.
Thus, changing deployment of police forces would simulate this
logic and potentially alter the opportunity* of committing crimes with
a lesser or greater degree of deterrence probable. This aspect of
meaning may be operationally translated, Chapter 4 will detail the
translation of the meanings suggested in this chapter of concepts
to indexes available from archive sources, as well as describe
methodological strategies and limitations.

REFERENCES

Bellah, Robert N., ed. 1973. Emile Durkheim: On Morality and
    Society. Chicago: University of Chicago Press.

Bonger, William Adrian. 1916; 1967. Criminality and Economic
    Conditions. New York: Agathon Press.

Bottomore, T. B., ed. and translator. 1964. Karl Marx: Selected
    Writings in Sociology and Social Philosophy. New York:
    McGraw-Hill.

Chambliss, William J. 1973. Sociological Readings in the Conflict
    Perspective. Reading, Mass.: Addison-Wesley.

---

*The relationship between opportunities, social disorganiza-
tion, and subcultural response is the subject, of course, of the
widely circulated volume by Cloward and Ohlin (1960).

Cloward, Richard A. and Lloyd E. Ohlin. 1960. Delinquency and
    Opportunity: A Theory of Delinquent Gangs. Glencoe, Ill.:
    Free Press.

Clinard, Marshall, ed. 1964. Anomie and Deviant Behavior. New
    York: Free Press.

Davis, Nanette J. 1975. Sociological Constructions of Deviance:
    Perspectives and Issues in the Field. Dubuque, Iowa:
    Brown.

DeGrazia, Sebastian 1948. Anomie. Chicago: University of Chicago
    Press.

Denisoff, R. Serge, and Charles H. McCaghy. 1973. Deviance,
    Conflict, and Criminality. Chicago: Rand McNally.

Durkheim, Emile. 1959. "The Rules of Sociological Method."
    In The Making of Society, ed. Robert Bierstedt. New York:
    Random House.

_____. 1951. Suicide. Translated by John A. Spaulding and
    and Goerge Simpson. Glencoe, Ill.: Free Press.

Faris, Robert E. L. 1955. Social Disorganization. New York:
    Ronald Press.

Grupp, Stanley E. 1971. Theories of Punishment. Bloomington, Ind.:
    University of Indiana Press.

Klausner, Samuel Z. 1967. The Study of Total Societies. Garden City,
    New York: Doubleday.

Merton, Robert K. 1938. "Social Structure and Anomie." American
    Sociological Review 3 (October): 672-82.

Mitchell, Wesley C. 1956. Business Cycles. New York: National
    Bureau of Economic Research.

Park, Robert E., Ernest W. Burgess, and Roderick D. McKenzie.
    1955. Society. Glencoe, Ill.: Free Press.

_____. 1967. The City. Chicago: University of Chicago Press.

Quinney, Richard. 1974. Criminal Justice in America. Boston:
    Little, Brown.

Sorokin, Pitirim A. 1928, 1964. Contemporary Sociological Theories. New York: Harper and Row.

_____. 1937. Social and Cultural Dynamics. Vol. 2: Fluctuations of Systems of Truth, Ethics, and Law. New York: American Book.

Sullivan, Richard F. 1973. "The Economics of Crime: An Introduction to the Literature." Crime and Delinquency 19 (April): 138-49.

Thomas, W. I., and Florian Znaniecki. 1920. The Polish Peasant in Europe and America. Boston, Mass.: Gorham Press.

Traub, Stuart H., and Craig B. Little. 1975. Theories of Deviance. Itasca, Ill.: Peacock.

Turk, Austin T. 1966. "Conflict and Criminality." American Sociological Review 31 (June): 338-52.

Veblen, Thorstein. 1919, 1969. On Marx, Race, Science, and Economics. New York: Capricorn Books.

Vold, Goerge B. 1958. Theoretical Criminology. New York: Oxford University Press.

Zimring, Franklin E., and Gordon J. Hawkins. 1973. Deterrence. Chicago: University of Chicago Press.

ERRATA

Page 11, line 7   For Bonger 1916 read Gabriel Tarde, in Bonger 1916

Page 37, line 22   The sentence, "The result was an inverse correlation of -.36." should be deleted.

Page 107, figure   For title read Percent Variance by Macrostructural Factors, Class I Violent Crimes and Suicide, for Three Time Periods
For B: Economic read E: Economic

Page 120, line 12   For aggravating effects on whites read aggravating effects on nonwhites

Page 128, table   Column 2, entry 9: For -.60 read -.06

Page 139, table   Column 6, entry 1: For .62 read -.62
Column 8, entry 8: For -.26 read .26
Column 8, entry 9: For .26 read -.26

Page 161, line 16   For -.59 read -.57

Page 162, line 25   For effective-emotional read affective-emotional
line 26   For considered a nonviolent variables read considered a nonviolent crime. Etiological variables suggest

Page 168, line 30   For factors are more truly read other factors are more truly

Page 174, table   Column 4, entry 2: For .12 read .14
Column 6, entry 1: For .10 read -.10

Page 180, line 20   For Merton and Nisbet read those of Merton and Nisbet

Page 183, figure   Left-hand heading of outer ring: For Ecological Stability-Instability read Economic Stability-Instability
Wavy line should intersect outermost ring
Third ring from outside, bottom head: For Educations Systems read Educational Systems

Page 199, line 3   For Niobet read Nisbet

Gloria Count-van Manen, Crime and Suicide in the Nation's Capital: Toward Macro-Historical Perspectives (New York: Praeger Publishers, 1977)

3

PREVIOUS RESEARCH: METHODOLOGICAL INCONSISTENCIES AND CUMULATIVE UNCERTAINTY

An assessment of the state of cumulative knowledge on structural research is peculiarly important as the setting for the findings to be reported here. Ultimately, the strength of a case history must rest upon replication. In this instance, comparisons should be made with findings from case histories of other cities. Unfortunately, the multivariate longitudinal design used here, with measures of independent and dependent variables, is not replicated in other publications. Cumulative results of findings from studies with a number of other research designs (multivariate cross-sectional; univariate longitudinal; and multivariate longitudinal, without measurement of independent variables) are plagued by an apparent lack of marked results and by inconsistencies from one work to the next. Assessments of the state of the literature seem to belie the biases of the particular writer. Bonger (1916; 1967, p. 669) for example, after an exhaustive survey of a massive number of studies on economic conditions and crime of the nineteenth and early twentieth centuries, concluded that "upon the basis of what has gone before, we have a right to say that the part played by economic conditions in criminality is preponderant, even decisive."

Just a decade later, Thomas (1926, p. 37), after a literature review including Bonger's important work, suggested:

> The criminologists . . . have made no real attempt
> to measure the relative influence of economic influences
> upon crime. They use and abuse statistics outrageously,
> presenting short series, frequently of less than ten
> years, and claiming general causality from such
> comparisons. . . . A review of the literature on the

subject suggests that discussions of the relations of
crime and economic conditions are still in the realm
of metaphysics.

Serious studies of business cycles by sociologists remain few in
number (an exception is the study of Henry and Short 1954; 1964),
and Thomas could well make a similar statement today, forty years
later. It is not uncommon for widely circulating criminology textbooks to leave the reader in doubt that economic factors have an
impact upon crime. A not atypical conclusion reads:

> . . . the more than 140 years of research on the impact
> of business cycles upon crime rates have produced
> the unsatisfactory "finding" that crime may increase
> with BOTH good times and bad. It therefore seems
> logical to conclude that NEITHER the poverty nor the
> wealth of nations is a major determinant of the level
> of criminal conduct . . . . (Nettler 1974, p. 119)

The above quotation represents a measurement and theoretical
nonsequitur. At the same time, it does illustrate both a fairly typical
conclusion and the kind of confusion that still is extant in the literature.
There is often a failure to link explicit facets of a theory to specific
measures used and to enunciate the nature of the transition being made
from theoretical concept to operational procedures. In this instance,
the relative wealth of an aggregate social entity, as measured by
median income, is being compared implicitly with business cycles,
which are often measured by a price index. There is no reason to
think that the results of the two measures should coincide. The first
poverty or wealth measure relates to an idea of individual need,
while the business cycle measure, although related to need, also
taps the important notion of change. In fact, measures of the former
tend to show findings in the opposite direction expected by researchers—
that is, the more wealth, the more crime. Measures on business
cycles in two centuries have tended toward some significance. Documentation on these points follows shortly.
    The unenviable state of the discipline reported above could
reflect the reality of weak relationships, or inadequate theories.
Alternatively, inconsistencies and low correlations could be due to
variations in measurement techniques and to poorly tuned methodological practices. In spite of the well-known limitations of official crime
data, it is the writer's thesis that widespread and inadequate measurement treatments have contributed heavily to these ambiguous results.
    In what follows, specific issues will be raised. The structural
literature will be reviewed with the aim of providing illustrations of

varying empirical results found with varying measurement practices, and an overall evaluation of the balance of evidence on variables under investigation here. No claim is made of the exhaustion of all resources, but perhaps the studies reviewed can be considered representative. At the same time, this chapter serves as a context for the methodology of this study (discussed in Chapter 4). A few findings from this study will be reported within the context of the topics discussed.

Studies on the relationship of crime to social class and to ecological variations within cities are not discussed. While obviously relevant to structural concerns, the units of study in both instances are not generally comparable. Research on social class typically rests upon samples of individuals, and thus does not qualify as aggregate data. The reason for this practice, no doubt, is that social class measures are not readily derived from criminal justice sources of data, although these can be sometimes obtained with additional time and effort on tabulations. Ecological studies tend to focus on within-city variations (counties or police districts), and have exhibited relatively strong and consistent results. Since the units of analysis differ from those of large aggregate data, the results of these studies should not be considered directly comparable. Both ecological and social class findings, further, are generally described in widely circulated criminology textbooks. Excellent research reviews and reprints are available in a number of other sources. (See, for example, Voss and Petersen 1971, for ecological studies.) On the other hand, structural studies in the traditions followed here can be located only after patient and time-consuming search through scattered sources. (See Count-van Manen 1976, for a recent collection of aggregate crime studies.) Thus, the findings and practices of these structural traditions on large social aggregates are not as widely circulated as other facets of criminology research.

METHODOLOGICAL INCONSISTENCIES

Variations in measurement that contribute to variations in research findings center around the following units of analysis:

1. Method of calculation of dependent variable rates—age-specific versus nonspecific; race-specific versus nonspecific; grouped crime classifications versus nongrouped.

2. Space and time units—cross-sectional versus longitudinal; city, state, or region; synchronous versus lag effects.
On the above points, research practice tends toward the use of nonspecific crime rates, crimes grouped into person and property categories, cross-sectional or one-point-in-time samples, and

synchronous time effects. Variations in procedures on these points can be expected to contribute to variations in findings. A few illustrations of empirically based evidence on variations in results by alternations in measurement practice follow.

Age-Specific Crime Rates

The crime rates of juveniles and adults have been reported to respond differentially to social structural elements. Depressions have been associated with increases in adult crime rates and decreases in juvenile crime rates (Bogen 1944). Wars have been observed to be associated with increases in delinquency and decreases in adult crime rates (Rosenbaum 1940; Wiers 1944; Fleisher 1966).

Glaser and Rice (1959) and Ross (1976) advised that correlations between economic variables and crime rates have been minimized in past research by the failure to utilize age-specific crime rates. Evidence does verify their conclusions for instances in which age-specific rates are used. Significant correlations have tended to result. (See Wiers 1945; Glaser and Rice 1959; Fleisher 1966; Ross 1976; Wellford 1974, in upcoming sections of this chapter.) In the current study, unfortunately, it is not feasible to utilize age-specific rates, since yearly population estimates by age are not available. Further, the age categories established by decennial census reports do not correspond to those utilized by the District of Columbia Police Department in reporting arrests.

Race-Specific Rates

It is hypothesized that structural facets of the social environment will differentially affect blacks and whites, as long as these groups tend to receive differentiated treatment by the social system. Count-van Manen and Josiah (1974) have illustrated this point. They found that, during World Wars I and II, crime rates of whites tended to go down, as hypothesized. Those of nonwhites, however, tended to escalate in the District of Columbia. They interpreted this variation in the impact of war as due to the national policy of excluding blacks from service (Franklin 1967). With the reversal of this practice during recent wars, less differentiated crime reactions from the two groups would be expected. Typically, downswings in crime accompany war periods. This observation has been attributed to the increased cohesion that accompanies most wars and to the absence of the most crime-prone elements of the populations—that is, young males, who are impressed into war activities (see Bonger 1916, 1967; Rosenbaum 1940).

It can be hypothesized that additional structural variables will have differentiated effects (inverse versus direct) upon varied status subgroups within the population, as long as these receive discriminating modalities of treatment within the social system. Again, the net effect will be to reduce correlational size and to nullify comparisons between samples varying both by time and area specifications, if population composition is not held constant. Numerous aspects of the social structure can by hypothesized to differentially affect blacks and whites. In this study, it is found that there are examples, varying by time epochs, of inverse relationships found for one group and direct for the other, and vice versa. This is the case for population composition, population size and change, size of the police force, and business cycle measures. Findings are detailed in Chapters 5, 6, and 7.

The changing population composition of American cities in recent decades has surely contributed much to variations in findings from varying time and geographic area samplings and to minimized size of relationships reported—if population composition is not held constant, and it usually is not. The migration of blacks from southern agricultural regions in recent decades, as rapid mechanization was taking place (Taueber 1958, p. 139), has been compared to rivaling in scope that of the massive emigrations of whites to the United States from foreign shores in earlier periods. The movement of the former peaked in the 1940s and 1950s, thus coninciding with a number of cross-sectional crime studies that utilized 1940, 1950, and 1960 census data.

It is almost incomprehensible, then, that race specific rates are not utilized in U.S. structural crime studies. Moreover, there is not the problem of accessibility to data for such usage, as there is for age-specific rates. Categories of both nonwhite or Negro and white are generally available in both police and Federal Bureau of Investigation reports, as well as in census records.

Most structural studies have inspected the relationship of percent nonwhite to total crime rates. These have shown marked consistency, or relatively high correlations to homicide and assault rates (Ogburn 1935; Schuessler and Slatin 1964; Quinney 1966; Swimmer 1974). The present study utilizes percent white as well as percent nonwhite with race-specific crime rates. There are some interesting same-race and cross-race variations in effects through time. For example, in the earliest time era sampled here, the percent white is associated highly with crime rates (see Chapters 5 and 6).

Only a few studies, in addition to the current one, have controlled for race (Fleisher 1966; Green 1970). In these instances, race tended to cancel out as an explanatory variable.

Crime and Deviance Classifications:
Person and Property

The use of archive data (usually Class I crimes) means that legal crime categories are used, and these are based upon the nature of the criminal act. It is common practice in structural studies utilizing aggregate data to combine classifications of burglary, robbery grand larceny, and auto theft into property crimes. Homicide, aggrevated assault, and rape (but not manslaughter) tend to be combined into person crimes (Thomas 1926; Glaser and Rice 1959; Swimmer 1974; Beasley and Antunes 1974; Wellford 1974). In this study, scrutiny of the relationship of each specific crime category to every other, both with the use of correlations and by visual inspection of graphs, demonstrated that combining legal crime categories is not always empirically justifiable. More specifically, it was found (Count-van Manen and Josiah 1974) that the relationship of assault and rape rates over time was fairly close, but that homicide rates, especially those of the nonwhite population, correlated more closely with burglary and robbery rates than with other person crimes. Homicide, although typically showing inverse relationships to suicide, did not do so in the third and most recent time epoch (1946-70) of this study. Auto theft increasingly over time did not correlate with other property crimes. Swimmer (1974) achieved improved results when he eliminated auto theft from his property crime group in a 1960 study of cities. Hagstad (1975) was disappointed in correlations from a structural study of states in 1970. He recommended that future work utilize specific crimes rather than person and property combinations.

The pioneering work of Thomas (1926) on business cycles in England and Wales, 1895 to 1913, has been widely referred to since Vold's work (1958) as a landmark pointing toward relatively low correlations of business cycles with crime. Thomas is not always quoted accurately, for she did make distinctions between grouped types of crime that are glossed over. She reported that the most frequent type of crime, property without violence, exhibited significant results with business cycles. She grouped, however, types of crime that may in retrospect be suspected of exhibiting varying causal modalities. Her category of offenses against property with violence included not only burglary and robbery, but also sacrilege and extortion. Larceny included fraud and bankruptcy. Murder and assault were grouped with manslaughter and intimidation and molestation. Thus it is likely that at least some of the relatively low range of correlations she recorded could be in part accounted for by the practice of grouping crimes etiologically incomparable.

Longitudinal versus
Cross-sectional Studies

Consistency between longitudinal and cross-sectional studies should not be expected. Real changes in etiology may occur. Controls, as mentioned, are generally not exercised for changes in composition of varying status groups. Further, longitudinal research has tended to utilize time periods of from 20 to 25 years (Thomas 1926; Fleisher 1966; Count-van Manen 1975, 1976). Within these periods, correlations can be reduced by inverse and direct relationships, or cross-current effects of cyclical variations within the larger periods. This point will be illustrated empirically with findings in upcoming chapters of this study.

Time Lags

It is uncommon for criminologists, though accepted practice on the part of econometricians, to examine the effects of delays in time of variables. Logically, it might be expected that at least some kinds of structural change would take some time to produce an impact upon crime rates. The studies of Thomas (1926) and of this writer have utilized synchronous, as well as one, two; and three-year lags. In the case of each of these research efforts, variations in correlational results are evident for the effects of business cycle indexes upon crime rates, most notably upon violent crimes. Thomas, (1926, p. 144) for example, found that a two-year lag raised violent crime correlations from .14 to .40 for the period 1895-1913, and a three-year lag from -.20 to .38 during 1857-74. Ross (1976, pp. 240 and 241) found that unemployment correlated most highly with crimes of violence with a two month lag for ages 16-20, at .54, while no lag yielded a .10 correlation. For ages 20 years and over, crimes of violence correlated at .22 with no lag, and .30 for a two- and a three-month lag. Ross (1976, p. 233) did not expect sex offenders to be influenced by economic conditions as much as theft. This author applied the individual rational gain-loss calculation model to aggregate data on unemployment in Toronto, with age-specific crime rates. He reported being surprised to discover that unemployment affected assault rates. This finding is inconsistent with a theoretical model emphasizing rationality. Swimmer (1974) used a similar model and likewise did not anticipate the effect of economic variables upon violent crime. In the current research effort being reported, it is found that time lags affect violent crimes considerably. For example, correlations of rape with the Consumer Price Index, for the period 1946-70 rose, for nonwhites, from -.20 for synchronous time to

-.88 with a three-year lag. The comparable data for white rates is
-.3 to -.41. Chapters 6 and 7 detail further results from this work
with the use of time lags.

Spatial Units

Doerner (1975) observed that variations in correlational
results are found to depend upon the size of the geographic unit
studied. Quinney (1966) found that there was a good deal of variation
on within-state units—that is, by rural, urban, and standard metropolitan statistical areas, both in the size of the relationships and
sometimes in direction. Hagstad (1975), like Quinney, found relatively low correlational results with state data and recommended
cities as the unit of study. Thus, variations within state borders,
as with other types of units previously discussed, can work to
minimize the size of relationships reported. Wellford (1974)
recommended, in his cross-sectional study of cities for 1970, that
further work of a longitudinal nature is advisable to aid in assessment of the effects of competing structural theories upon crime rates.

PREVIOUS RESEARCH FINDINGS

Substantive results reviewed in what follows should not be
considered as exhausting the literature. The directions of the findings,
however, can probably be considered fairly representative of studies
in their class.

Economic Variables

There are at least four conceptually distinct aspects of
economic theories. In practice, these are not always distinguished and
may overlap in operational measurements. These approaches may be
summarized as variously emphasizing (1) need, arising out of poverty,
or from expectations concerning economic status; (2) alienation
(individual) or anomie (societal), arising from the very nature of the
economic system or from social changes; (3) psychological aggression,
stemming from economic and/or status-frustrations; and (4) rational
decision-making processes calculating pleasure-pain balances, as
recently developed by economists (Fleisher 1966; Becker 1968;
Sullivan 1973).

     The avoidance of ecological fallacies would seem to require
ideally that the first two types of structural theories be tested with

aggregate data, while the avoidance of the reductionist fallacy would seem to require the last two theories to utilize, ideally, data on individuals. Attention is not always given to these transitions between theory and testing. For example, Ross (1976) and Spector (1975) applied the rational individual type model to aggregate data, and Henry and Short (1954; 1964) used an aggression model with aggregate data on business cycles and homicide and suicide. Some measure of aggregate wealth is often implicitly used to get at individual need.

Median Income

Measures used frequently in cross-sectional studies rely upon ready access to census data. These have included median income and, in the 1970 census, a measure of poverty levels. Nineteenth century measures of the wealth of societies did not succeed in attributing crime to poverty, for these tended to show that the wealthier the area, the higher the crime rates (Bonger 1916; 1967). This author was sensitive to the idea of the possible contrast, in relation to crime, between absolute and relative poverty. He made a still pertinent observation:

> The division between rich and poor is many centuries old and does not belong to capitalism alone, although under capitalism the distance between the two has greatly increased and is still increasing. The greater this distance is, the more, other things being equal, cupidity increases. (Bonger 1967, p. 572)

In this century, Wiers (1944), Quinney (1966), Swimmer (1974), and Hagstad (1975) are among those finding that aggregate measures of wealth do not correlate inversely with crime. Swimmer (1974, pp. 309-10) commented:

> . . . median income relates significantly with fewer violent crimes, but not fewer property crimes, apparently contrary to our economic model of crime . . . median income may be a better proxy for social class than distribution. . .

Business Cycle Measures

Among the measures that have been utilized as indicators of business cycles in crime studies are those of production levels, price indexes, levels of taxation, and unemployment. In the nineteenth century, price fluctuations were compared to crime rates with the use of graphs (Bonger 1916; 1967). Bonger, as noted earlier, arrived at generally positive conclusions in his summations of a mass of studies. There are, interestingly, only a handful of major efforts in the twentieth century. Thomas utilized an index combining national measures of British exports, unemployment, prices, production, and bank clearings. She regarded price measures as "the best single representative of the general state of business" (1926, p. 13). More recent landmarks are the relatively careful studies conducted by a few researchers, all of whom report positive findings. Fleisher (1966) utilized unemployment and median income with delinquency rates. Ross (1976) used unemployment and age-specific property and assault rates and reported inverse correlations with property offenses and a positive one with assault. These results are not unlike the work of earlier studies (Bonger 1916; 1967). Henry and Short (1954; 1964) reported positive results using the Ayres national index of business activity, with race-specific rates of homicide and suicide. Burglary and robberies show "strong and consistent tendency to fall in prosperity and rise in depression" (pp. 179-85). Glaser and Rice (1959) utilized age-specific rates, with national unemployment data and city and national crime data and found significant and stable relationships.

What is the range of correlations found on business cycle measures and crime rates? Thomas (1926) did not find any consistent or strong relationship on her "offenses against property without violence," which is primarily the frequent but unstable crime of larceny. On the category "offenses against property with violence," she included burglary, robbery, and extortion, and reported "on the whole, [it] has [not] been greatly affected by changes of law or administration . . . there is a fairly strong inverse correlation with the business cycle." She reported for the British series, 1857-1913, -.44 with synchronous items, with the maximum of -.51 with a lag of one year for 1857-74. For 1875-94, a maximum was obtained with synchronous items, at -.51. She concluded, but is not generally quoted on this point, "The constance of these coefficients, and the fact that they are always high enough to be significant, tends to show evidence of a real relationship between this class of crimes and the business cycle. Burglary, housebreaking and shopbreaking, and robbery, comprising 95-99 percent of this class, show a definite tendency to increase in a business depression and to decrease with prosperity." (Thomas 1926, p. 139). Wiers (1944) used age-specific rates in a delinquency study of court cases for Michigan counties (excluding Wayne) during 1921-43. His correlations reached over .7 or .8, depending upon the measures used, notably retail sales or

income tax returns. In a study of three cities, 1930-56, Glaser
and Rice (1959, p. 683) reported unemployment correlated at from
-.23 for property theft to -.42 for person crime arrests of males age
10 to 17 years; and from .53 to .93 for property and .10 to .79, ages
21-44. These correlations could be underestimated, since use was
made of national unemployment rates and local city arrest rates, as
well as possibly unrelated etiological crime types. Person crimes
included arrests for rape, intended homicide, and assault. Larceny,
burglary, robbery, and auto theft were combined into the property
category. Ross (1976) maximized correlations with a two-month
lag for person and for property crimes, running somewhat over .5,
for Toronto, 1965-72. He, too, combined robbery, burglary, and
larceny into property crimes. Further, assault is considered a
notoriously invalid measure in the United States.

Wellford's (1973) work is peculiarly interesting within the
context of the emphasis of this analysis, insofar as he is the only
author who utilized crime rates refined by age and by race in his
cross-sectional study of 21 of the largest urban centers, in 1960
and 1970. Unfortunately, he combined the crime rates into property
and violent crimes (without specification of crimes included) and did
not report the individual correlations for each socioeconomic variable,
some of which might be indexes of varying theoretical approaches.
Multiple correlations are identified only for the three subsets of
independent variables, namely, demographic, social, and crime
control. Under the second rubric he included male unemployment
(totals and rates), male nonwhite unemployment (totals and rates),
percentage of owner-occupied homes, median family income (total
and nonwhite), median school years completed (total and nonwhite),
percentage of homes overcrowded, and the percentage of women
divorced or separated. Thus, at least the possibility exists of both
inverse and positive correlations being grouped together within the
subsets of independent and dependent variables. Wellford made no
comment on this possibility. His total results showed relatively high
multiple correlations, with the socioeconomic variables accounting
for 59 percent of the variation in total crime rates in 1960 and 55
percent in 1970; 68 percent of the variation in 1960; and 35 percent in
1970 for the refined violent crime rate; and 57 and 56 percent,
respectively, for the refined property crime rates. The multiple
correlations reported for each sub-set of variables ranged from .74
to .83 (Wellford 1974, pp. 200-203).

Given the state of the structural literature, it would seem
that publication of detailed results of correlations for individual
measures of both independent and dependent variables would be
justified until knowledge as to how these should be grouped rests
upon more solid empirical ground. Although regression, or multiple

or partial correlations, may be the major choice of statistical treatment, publication of straight correlation results, as well, would facilitate comparisons with past work.

Among the outstanding historical studies that have examined the effects of business cycles, without quantitative or local measures, is the study of Ferdinand (1967) on Boston. He concluded that the highest rates of robberies in this city, as well as in Chicago and New York, occurred during the years 1931-33. Murder and manslaughter showed little sensitivity to depressions and wars. Rates of rape, on the other hand, declined during depressions and rose during prosperous years, or exhibited an inverse relationship.

The carefully designed studies reported have tended to exhibit positive findings on economic variables in this century, including the current effort. In common, these concentrated upon cities as the unit of study and on longitudinal periods. The work of Thomas (1926) and of Wiers (1944) included studies, as well, of larger geographic units. Time periods varied widely, with the work of Thomas preceding World War I. The results of findings of Glaser and Rice (1959) Fleisher (1966), and Henry and Short (1954; 1964) are fairly comparable in time sampling, covering the spans of the thirties (with Henry and Short going back to 1903-41), through part of the fifties for Fleisher and for Glaser and Rice. Wellford (1974) utilized cross-sectional sampling, for 1960 and for 1970, while the time period of the work of Ross, 1965-72, was both shorter in scope and more recent than that of other writers (Ross 1976).

What about other research that has reported negative evidence on economic variables and crime? Two early studies, those of Simpson (1935) and of Vold (1935) are in this group. Vold's study may, indeed, have influenced his assessment of the literature. In both instances, it should be noted that these authors combined data for youth with those for adults (using admissions to correctional and adult penal institutions). As demonstrated earlier, the practice of combining crime rates of youth and of adults has worked to lower the correlational sizes found, by the averaging of both direct and inverse relationships for the varying age groups. Simpson used an index of employment for the state of Illinois, 1923-31, which he graphically compared with total crime rates during the years of the Great Depression. Vold, like Ferdinand, visually inspected crime trends for Minneapolis, 71 cities, and the United States, 1926-33. For most cities, however, no local measures of economic activity are typically used. Surely local areas can vary from the national tendencies of business cycles. Thus, it would appear that the methodological limitations of these studies may have helped to account for their negative results. More recently, Spector (1975) and Swimmer (1974) reported a lack of positive evidence. Spector examined violent crimes and unemployment rates for 103

standard metropolitan statistical areas in 1970 and Swimmer, 119
cities of over 100,000 population in 1960. Both utilized an unemployment measure and property- and person-grouped crime categories.
Neither utilized age- or race-specific rates, which could be expected
to vary widely by city. Hagstad, in an unpublished (1975) study of
states in 1970 was likewise puzzled by relatively low negative correlations between unemployment and property and person crimes.
His study, as well, utilized neither age- race- nor crime-specific
categories. Powell (1966), in a longitudinal study of Buffalo, New
York, from 1854 to 1956, reported inconsistent results between
crime and economic activity. He, too, utilized generally recognized
national impressions of business depression years, without empirical
measures for the city. Ross (1976, p. 24) has suggested that still
another variable may have to be introduced to help account for some
of the seeming lack of consistent relationships between crime and
economic conditions during depressions. He suggested that the
timing of relief programs must be taken into account and when
this was done, he noted greater consistencies in previous empirical
work. That is, crime troughed during 1936 as relief rose to a peak.

Anomie and Social Disorganization Variables

As explained in Chapter 2 concepts of anomie and of social
disorganization are combined here, since these are held to be
causally related inasmuch as each has a common concern for social
change. The concepts, by definition, contain normative and cultural
dimensions. There is, thus, some problem of tautology insofar as
operationalized measures are related to crime rates, and these are
also normative by definition. Although there has been a good deal of
measurement work on the alienation of individuals (and sometimes this
work is referred to as anomie), there has not been an equal emphasis
on achieving societal measures of anomie. To date, no direct measure
has been obtained. Angell's (1942, p. 575), observation still seems
pertinent:

> There seems to be no satisfactory way of getting at
> questions of community loyalty directly, and very
> few satisfactory indices of community spirit have
> been suggested.

His landmark research was perhaps the most direct aggregate measure
located in the literature using an index of welfare to suggest the degree
to which cities were morally integrated. Most measures, then, can

achieve at most either a prior or later step in the causal theoretical chain posited by theory. Thus, examples of prior links in the chain used to measure anomie have included of mobility, unemployment, population size, population change (in the research being reported), and population composition. Varied subgroups in the population are posited, in the last case, to be associated with cultural conflict and thence disorganization and/or anomie. Examples of the consequences of anomie/social disorganization are, of course, suicide, crime, and other forms of deviance. In factorial studies (such as Schuessler and Slatin 1964) these dependent variables have been confounded with other prior independent variables in anomie verbalizations.

Population Size

Population size, an ecological variable, has been vaguely alluded to in sociology as possibly related to urbanization, social disorganization, and deviance. The overall impression on limited research efforts is one of disparate findings on these fairly straight-forward measures. Among those reporting negative results for city size have been Powell (1966), Schuessler and Slatin (1964), and Berman (1973) in a study of Israel. Wellford reported an r^2 of .9 for demographic variables and property and person crime rates. He included in demographic variables the size of the total population, size of the younger population, and size of the nonwhite population. These groupings make it impossible to evaluate his precise results. Powell presented no data, but observed that "the largest cities do not have the highest crime rates" (Powell 1966, p. 167). Spector (1975) reported a strong positive relationship with city violence.

The work of four researchers suggests the possibility that curvilinear relationships may be working to confuse reported results. Ogburn (1935) found a correlation of .36 for population size and crime rates for small (36,000 to 58,000) nonsouthern cities and inverse correlations in the same range for cities with populations of 100,000 and over. Angell (1942) noted that population size up to 250,000 in 1940 and 1947, for U.S. cities, exhibited a positive correlation to crime, but irregular relationships for cities with larger numbers. Swimmer (1974, p. 310) in a study of U.S. cities over 100,000 in 1960 reported that "as population increases, property and violent crime rates increase at a decreasing rate." In the current longitudinal study being reported, size of the population in the capital city is correlated to crime rates in the earliest period, but not for the two later periods (see Chapters 5 and 6). More systematic longitudinal testing on individual cities would aid in testing the possibility of a curvilinear relationship.

Population Change

With the concept of change central to structural theories, it might be expected that population change, a readily measured variable, would be frequently experimented with by researchers. Such is not the case. A notable example of the discontinuities in structural research efforts is provided, in fact, on this measure. Ogburn (1935) found, in his 1930 study of cities, that there were weak relationships and inconsistent results for a percent change measure on population with crime rates of small (-.09), medium (.27), and large (-.11) cities. When he used a rate of growth measure, however, the correlations increased and became consistent in direction, with results, respectively, of -.53, -.30, and -.46. Ogburn made no heavy theoretical statements in this particular research piece, but explained the relationship of an increasing rate of growth with lower crime rates as attributable to economic opportunities increasing, in common with population growth and therefore less crime. Years later, Schuessler and Slatin (1964) used a percent change measure only, in their cross-sectional study of cities, and reported, again, relatively low correlations (-.13 to murder, .16 to burglary, and .11 to robbery). Pettigrew and Spier (1962) reported -.36 correlation between nonwhite population change and black homicide rates in 26 states between 1940 and 1950. The result was an inverse correlation of -.36. The current study likewise utilizes race-specific percent changes in population and rates of changes, following the Ogburn formulas, with race- and crime-specific rates. In some time periods, race-specific population changes do not seem to have a significant impact upon crime rates, and in other periods they do. More specifically, when population composition is drastically changing, change rates do have a significant effect upon some crimes. For example, the rate of growth of the white population during 1946-70, when the city experienced large losses of whites, is inversely correlated to both nonwhite and white homicide rates, with correlations of over -.70. See Chapters 5 and 6 for further details on these points.

A number of writers have investigated geographic movements, often within the theoretical context of factors associated with urbanization (see Wirth 1938) and deviance, generally with significant empirical findings. Angell (1942) reported that a mobility index (in- and out-city migration) inversely correlated to a moral integration index (-.49) and positively related to a crime rate index (robbery, burglary, and homicide) of 28 cities. Pettigrew and Spier (1962) linked interstate mobility (percent nonwhite from out of state) and the homicidal culture of the South to black homicide rates. Quinney (1966) used the census measure, percent change in residence, as an indicator of social change and found it positively correlated with specific offenses for urban areas: .72 with auto theft; .63, larceny; .62, robbery; .65, forcible rape; and .52, burglary. Correlations for states as a whole were considerably lower and nonsignificant, with the highest at .16 for murder. He interpreted the findings as follows: "offenses thus appear to be a product of change in behavior patterns—or the lessening of social integration" (Quinney 1966, pp. 48-50). Such a logical transition or jump between theoretical concept and measurement is not atypical of the cross-sectional studies in the literature.

The research traditions designated as anomie are, at first perusal, apparently abundantly measured. There exists a review of over 100 anomie studies in Clinard (1964). Most of this work however, represented psychological attitudes of samples of respondents. Anomie— in the sense of collective sentinents intended by Durkheim, utilizing aggregate measures—is relatively rare. Social disorganization research, as linked to a vocabulary of urbanization is, on the other hand, fairly common. It has been dominated, however, by factorial analysis as the favored statistical technique (Abrahamson 1974). So used, the technique is an admission of theoretical inadequacies (Hirschi and Selvin 1967). In practice, measures used may be identical with those labeled as indicative of anomie, but variously linked to urbanism or social disorganization, often with little distinguishing theoretical logic.

Powell (1966) noted that the historical dimension of anomie has been largely ignored since Durkheim. Powell utilized empirical measures of crime, but relied upon historical qualitative data for evaluations of changing trends in anomie over time. He made explicit hypotheses and the logic for these: all types of crime, he suggested, whether against person, property, or public order, will increase in "times of institutional dislocation" and anomie. As to property crimes:

> Property, after all, is the creation of a culture,
> of a belief system. When individuals lose respect for
> the normative order which protects private property
> increases in burglary and larceny are to be expected.
> (Powell 1966, p. 171)

Crimes of violence against persons, he suggested, are due to the fact that "men feel they can no longer rely on established authority for protection." They take the law into their own hands. The similarity between violence in slum areas of the city and frontier violence is noted. Blacks, especially, he documented, have not felt that they have police protection. This point has been more recently affirmed in victim surveys (U.S. Department of Justice 1975).

The empirical work of Angell (1942) represented a pioneering attempt, the seriousness of which has not since, been reaffirmed, in this writer's opinion, to obtain an aggregate measure of anomie. Angell searched for an index of community spirit, or community loyalty, an aggregate phenomenon with an aggregate measure, consistent with Durkheim's original statement of concern with anomie. Angell (p. 575) spells out his conceptual link to the measure used:

> One of the most important questions we can ask about a human aggregate of any kind is whether its members are closely knit together by a common outlook and common aspirations . . . . Perhaps we may regard those cities that shoulder a larger proportion of their local welfare responsibilities, everything else equal, as being better integrated than those that make less effort. There would seem to be a more vital moral order in the former than in the latter.

He proceeded to rank-order 28 cities by their welfare and their crime indexes for the period 1936-40. He found that these orderings were consistent with his hypotheses in 20 of the 28 cities. That is, cities tended to have either a high welfare effort index and a low crime index, or a low welfare effort index and a high crime index. He then made an analysis of the eight cities representing deviant cases. He found that four of these had a good welfare index and a poor crime index, and that all of these were located on geographic boundaries between the North and the South. His interpretation is potentially applicable to the current study:

> . . . the real line of cleavage in the community between Negroes and whites is not . . . affected [by the welfare index] and this is a prime factor in social disorganization. (p. 591)

More recent work, using the factorial approach, is that of Schuessler and Slatin (1964), Boggs (1965), and Abrahamson (1974). Schuessler and Slatin identified one of their factors as anomie, in a cross-sectional study of cities. Included were measures of the percent divorced, property crimes, and suicide. They admitted, "we have not advanced towards a solution of the crime rates in terms of a social factor which is not entangled with the specific effects it is adduced to explain" (p. 144).

Boggs (1965) utilized an urbanization index as an indirect measure of anomie. Her index included a fertility ratio, the proportion of single family dwelling units, and the proportion of women in

the labor force. The assumptions of Wirth's (1938) classic essay
on city life was interpreted as consistent with Boggs' rationale that
"highly urbanized neighborhoods permit only a limited development
of informal shared norms for regulating conduct" (p. 905). Spector
(1975, p. 399) commented on census tract studies (Boggs utilized
census tracts for St. Louis) negatively, and suggested that these
studies have confounded neighborhood demographic characteristics
with socioeconomic variables of interest. This procedure is a
"serious flaw in previous research." Abrahamson (1974) investigated
social dimensions of urbanism and included deviance and crime in
these, but did not mention anomie. He utilized a number of demographic, social, and economic variables in a factorial study of
standard metropolitan areas, presumably for 1970. He included
factors named size-density and disorganization-deviance. Among
his findings was the conclusion that the form of urbanism is not
dominated by variables of any one type (for example, demographic).
Nevertheless, the later identified size-density as one of the most
important factors. He noted regional variations in factors that were
still consistent with structural positions. He questioned, however,
the idea that urbanism "has a recurrent form regardless of historical
or cultural differences" (pp. 381-82). Factors named isolation and
subgroup vitality were less explanatory than size-density.

A very recent study, as yet unpublished, of Dunham and
Kiyak (1975) focused on homicide, and utilized national public opinion
polls as an anomie indicator, with a specific rationale for hypotheses:

> Every society rests upon some fundamental belief
> structure which must have a wide and broad consensus
> among its people . . . . Once such a belief structure
> ceases to have broad consensus, its power as a form
> of a social control diminishes. It is our contention
> that something like this has been happening in our
> society. (Dunham and Kiyak 1975, p. 6)

The authors suggest that the beliefs measured by the Roper public
opinion polls coincide with trends in homicide in 13 cities of the
United States, for the period 1940-73. The high points in disaffection
are in 1964 and 1965, coinciding with high levels of homicide rates.
Correlations of the two measures were in the very high range of
.85 for San Francisco, .93 for Washington, D.C., and .95 for Boston.
Graphs of homicide rates for nonwhites and white and of public opinion
poll responses appear to closely coincide in oscillations. The authors
cite additional evidence for their thesis of widespread anomie in the
last decade: the decline in beliefs coinciding with participation in the
unpopular war in Vietnam; the increased use of drugs among youth;

the university-student confrontations; the deterioration of cities; the increased use of bombs, political kidnapping, and airplane hijacking; the establishment of communes; and the rise of new types of psychiatric therapy.

Deterrence and the Police

The police are one of the most visible aspects of the criminal justice system and are "by far the most expensive aspect of law enforcement" (Zimring and Hawkins 1973, p. 53), along with prisons. A good deal of work has been done on the effect of punishment, and this has been reviewed in a number of sources, including that of Zimring and Hawkins. Less work has been done on the police. How effective are increased resources of police forces in reducing crime rates? How does this aspect of formal control compare to other facets of the social environment in regulating crime rates? Conrad (1968) wrote that the connection between economic, political, and social conditions had not been illuminated by data or correlations. Five years later, Zimring and Hawkins (1973, p. 23) noted that so little evaluative research had been accomplished, that there was little pressure to rethink the unitary positions of official weapons, that is, the primary use of threat and punishment in the war against crime.

The omnibus Crime Control and Safe Street Act was enacted in 1968, and the Law Enforcement Assistance Administration was created. Its work afforded an opportunity for a massive evaluation of the impact of a program largely dedicated to strengthening the police. Eight years later, the Washington Post (May 10, 1976, p. A-4) was to report that 4 billion dollars had been awarded by LEAA in grants to local communities to help fight crime. The Mitre Corporation was awarded 2.4 million by LEAA to evaluate the eight-city, high-impact, $160 million program to reduce stranger-to-stranger crime. Still another private evaluation agency was reported by the Post to have recommended the abolishment of LEAA, since crime rates in the cities continued to climb, and the high-impact program was irresponsible, and ill-conceived. The LEAA's defense, as reported the next day (May 11, 1976) in the Post was that crime would have been even worse if the target cities had not benefited from the LEAA funded programs.

A central problem in all evaluation research is, of course, the basis on which such a judgment can and should be made. Zimring and Hawkins (1973, pp. 26-27) suggested:

Detailed study of historical trends in the crime rate, or comparisons with untreated areas [are

> necessary]. . . . Providing a baseline, so that
> reliable determinations can be made about the degree
> of crime reduction attributable to particular counter-
> measures, is an absolute necessity in any but the
> most wasteful of crime control policies.

On these same points, and underscoring them, Count-van Manen
(see Viano 1975, p. 116) had suggested the feasibility of establishing
longitudinal data banks for major American cities. These should
contain basic data on socioeconomic and criminal justice measures,
ongoing over time, that would provide a continuing backdrop for
evaluation studies of costly crime control (and other) programs.
Only by the collection of such before-and-after data is it feasible
to assess the effects of a particular change program or policy
against the background of alternative explanations of change and
within the context of long-term time trends and short-term cycles.
    As previously noted, the size of the police force and/or
amounts spent for police expenditures have not been utilized until
fairly recently as measures of the certainty of apprehension in order
to evaluate the impact of formal control efforts. What do the correlations tend to show? Except for one study utilizing a unique
statistical treatment, the few studies extant tend to report perverse
results and relatively small effects on crime rates. There are,
however, some variations in the nature of the findings and, once
again, facts appear to vary with variations in methodological practices.
Until more standardized research procedures are adopted by inves-
tigators, it is difficult to be sure of cumulative interpretations.
    Wellford (1974) first forced socioeconomic variables into
his multiple correlation equations in a 21-city study for 1960 and
1970. He omitted demographic variables since, by themselves, these
explained over 90 percent of the variance. His conclusion was that
associations are generally in the directions of inverse relations
hypothesized. That is, the greater the expenditures for police and
the greater the size of the force, the less crime, but the deterrent
effect of apprehension discernible is moderate that is, correlations
range from -.07 to -.45. For total crime rates correlated with per
capita police budget, he reported correlations of -.14 for 1960 and
-.36 for 1970. Six percent of the variation in 1960 was accounted
for and 8 percent in 1970. The correlations reported for police effort
and violent crime were -.21 and -.21 and for total police, -.20 and
-.21 for these years. Wellford (1974, p. 204) cited two related
research efforts that arrived at similar estimates of police effects.
He reported that Phillips and Votey (1972) found that 98 percent of
the variation in property arrest rates of 18- and 19-year-olds
between 1952 and 1966 are explained by changes in economic

opportunities, and police levels explain little of the variation. Kobrin is cited by Wellford in an unpublished study as finding that socio-economic characteristics accounted for 50 percent of the variation in crime rates, while police measures accounted for another 23 percent in California counties of more than 500,000 population. Wellford concluded that the police make minimal contributions to variations in recorded crime. Hagstad (1975) in unpublished research arrived at a similar conclusion for a 1970 study of states. Using unrefined property and violent crime categories also, he reported that a partial correlation treatment, after holding constant demographic and socioeconomic factors, appears to affect crime rates perversely; that is, the more police, the higher the homicide and other violent crime rates. The correlation was .39 (.01 significance) with violent crime including homicide and .16 (nonsignificant) with homicide only. The results found were in the expected inverse direction for property crime, but of negligible size (.06) and nonsignificant. Police expenditure measures yielded the inverse correlation, -.30 (significant at .05) with violent crimes, but nonsignificant results for both property and homicide rates.

Some of the current research findings being reported are congruent with the perverse of positive findings context. There are, however, considerable variations incorrelational size from one time epoch to the next, from one racial group to the next, and from one specific type of crime to the next. Correlations of the earliest time period, for which there is no basis for comparison with other studies, tend to be considerably higher than those for later epochs. (See Chapters 5 and 6.)

There is one research effort that appears partially to challenge the results of earlier research, that of Swimmer (1974). His research procedures utilize a two-stage least-squares process in a study of cities over 100,000 population in 1960. His theoretical rationale is that

> [t]he decision to commit crime is based upon gains from successful crime, the losses if apprehended and convicted, the likelihood of being convicted, and sociological or psychologically determined tastes for crime . . . the smaller the gain, the greater the probability of conviction, and the harsher the punishment, the less crime there would be. (Swimmer 1974, p. 294)

Thus, the rational individualistic hedonistic model is again being tested with aggregate data. Swimmer found, however, that lower crime rates with greater police implementation were not verified and, again, there were perverse effects. He explained these as attributable to the possibility that increased crime rates lead to increased size of the police force. The research results of Jones (1974) appear to directly contradict this assumption. Jones inspected year-to-year changes in crime rates within each of 155 U.S. cities, 1950-68, and showed that "there tends to be a constant increment in police protection expenditures regardless of changes in crime incidence" (Jones 1974, p. 520). One-, two-, and three-year lags for nonspecific, personal, composite, and murder crime rates were used. Correlations ranged from .07 to .19, with the highest of these reported for murder. Inspection of scatter diagrams, Jones reported, tends to confirm linear relationships. The author's conclusion is that U.S. cities are not relying on past crime incidence experience to make present decisions on police expenditures.

Swimmer's work, then, is at odds with previous research and with the upcoming research to be reported in Chapters 5 and 6 insofar as, when socioeconomic variables were held constant, he found that increased police expenditures significantly reduced crime. Chapter 4 describes the methodology of this study in greater detail.

REFERENCES

Abrahamson, Mark. 1974. "The Social Dimensions of Urbanism." Social Forces 52, no. 3 (March): 376-83.

Angell, Robert C. 1942. "The Social Integration of Selected American Cities." American Journal of Sociology 47: 575-92.

Beasley, Ronald W. and George Antunes. 1974. "The Etiology of Urban Crime: An Ecological Analysis." Criminology 2: (February): 439-61.

Becker, Gary S. 1968. "Crime and Punishment: An Economic Approach." Journal of Political Economy 76 (March-April): 169-217.

Berman, Yitzchak. 1973. "Size of Population and Juvenile Delinquency in Cities in Israel." Criminology 11 (May) 105-14.

Bonger, William Adrian. 1916, 1967. Criminality and Economic Conditions. New York: Agathon Press.

Bogen, David. 1944. "Juvenile Delinquency and Economic Trend." American Sociological Review 9: (April) 178-84.

Boggs, Sarah L. 1965. "Urban Crime Patterns." American Socio-
    logical Review 30 (December): 899-908.

Clinard, Marshall, ed. 1964. Anomie and Deviant Behavior. New
    York: Free Press.

Count-van Manen, Gloria. 1975. "Macrostructural Sources of
    Variation in Homicide Victim Rates in the Capital City."
    In Victims and Society, ed. Emilio Viano. Washington,
    D.C.: Visage Press.

_____. ed. 1976. Social Systems, Crime, Delinquency, and
    Deviance: A Reader in Structurally-Oriented Studies.
    Washington, D.C.: University Press of America.

Count-van Manen, Gloria and Cecil Josiah. 1974. "Person and Pro-
    perty Crimes as Etiological Types: Some Empirical Evidence
    for the District of Columbia, 1890-1970." Unpublished paper.
    delivered at the Annual Meetings of the International
    Sociological Society, 1974, Toronto, Canada.

Doerner, William G. 1975. "A Regional Analysis of Homicide Rates
    in the United States." Criminology 13 (May): 90-101.

Dunham, H. Warren and Asuman Kiyak. 1975. "Cultural Change and
    Homicide: An Interrelationship." Unpublished paper.

Ferdinand, Theodore N. 1967. "The Criminal Patterns of Boston
    Since 1849." American Journal of Sociology 73 (July):
    84-99.

Fleisher, Belton M. 1966. The Economics of Delinquency. Chicago:
    University of Chicago Press.

Franklin, John Hope. 1967. Slavery to Freedom. New York: Knopf.

Glaser, Daniel and Kent Rice. 1959. "Crime, Age, and Employment."
    American Sociological Review 24 (October): 679-86.

Green, Edward. 1970. "Race, Social Status, and Criminal Arrest."
    American Sociological Review 35 (June): 476-90.

Hagstad, Michael A. 1975. "A Macro-Sociological Approach to
    Crime and Social Control." Washington, D.C.: American
    University, Center for Criminal Justice.

Henry, Andrew F. and James F. Short, Jr. 1954, 1964. Suicide and Homicide. New York: Free Press.

Hirschi, Travis and Hanan C. Selvin. 1967. Delinquency Research: An Appraisal of Analytic Methods. New York: Free Press.

Jones, E. Terrence. 1974. "The Impact of Crime Rate Changes on Police Protection Expenditures in American Cities." Criminology 11 (February): 516-24.

Nettler, Gwynn. 1974. Explaining Crime. New York: McGraw-Hill.

Ogburn, William. 1935. "Factors in Variation of Crime Among Cities." Journal of American Statistical Association 30 (March): 12-20.

Pettigrew, Thomas F. and Rosalind Barclay Spier. 1962. "The Ecological Structure of Negro Homicide." American Journal of Sociology 67 (May): 621-30.

Phillips, L. and H. Votey. 1972. "An Economic Analysis of the Deterrent Effect of Law Enforcement on Criminal Activity." Journal of Criminal Law, Criminology, and Police Science 63 (September): 330-43.

Powell, Elwin H. 1966. "Crime as a Function of Anomie." Journal of Criminal Law, Criminology, and Police Science 57 (June): 161-71.

Quinney, Richard. 1966. "Structural Characteristics, Population Areas, and Crime Rates in the United States." Journal of Criminal Law, Criminology, and Police Science 57 (March): 45-51.

Rosenbaum, Betty B. 1940. "The Relationship Between War and Crime in the United States." Journal of American Institute of Criminal Law and Criminology 40: 723-42.

Ross, Marvin. 1976. "Economic Conditions and Crime in Metropolitan Toronto, 1965-1972." In Social Systems, Crime, Delinquency, and Deviance, ed. Gloria Count-van Manen. Washington, D.C.: University Press of America.

Schuessler, Karl and Gerald Slatin. 1964. "Sources of Variation in U.S. City Crime, 1950 and 1960." Journal of Research in Crime and Delinquency 1 (July): 127-48.

Simpson, Ray Mars. 1935. "Postwar Trends in Employment, Crime, Insanity and Heart Disease." Journal of Social Psychology 6 (February): 125-29.

Spector, Paul E. 1975. "Population Density and Unemployment." Criminology 12 (February): 399-401.

Sullivan, Richard F. 1973. "The Economics of Crime: An Introduction to the Literature." Crime and Delinquency 19 (April): 138-49.

Swimmer, Gene. 1974. "The Relationship of Police and Crime: Some Methodological and Empricial Results." Criminology 12 (November): 293-314.

Taueber, Irene. 1958. Population Bulletin 14, no. 7 (November), Population Reference Bureau pp. 125-51.

Thomas, Dorothy Swaine. 1926. Social Aspects of the Business Cycle. New York: Gordon and Breach.

U.S. Department of Justice. 1975. Sourcebook of Criminal Justice Statistics: 1974. Washington, D.C. Government Printing Office.

Viano, Emilio ed. 1975. Criminal Justice Research. Lexington, Mass.: Lexington Books.

Vold, George B. 1958. Theoretical Criminology. New York: Oxford University Press.

_____. 1935. "The Amount and Nature of Crime." American Journal of Sociology 40 (May): 796-803.

Voss, Harwin L. and David M. Petersen. 1971. Ecology, Crime, and Delinquency. New York: Appleton-Century-Crofts.

Wellford, Charles F. 1974. "Crime and the Police." Criminology 12 (August): 290-305.

_____. 1973. "Age Composition and the Increase in Recorded Crime." Criminology 11 (May): 61-70.

Wiers, Paul. 1945. "Wartime Increases in Michigan Delinquency." American Sociological Review 10 (August): 515-23.

_____. 1944. Economic Factors in Michigan Delinquency. New York: Columbia University Press.

Wirth, Louis. 1938. "Urbanism as a Way of Life." Journal of Sociology 44 (July): 6-15.

Wolfgang, Marvin E., ed. 1968. Crime and Culture. New York: Wiley.

Zimring, Franklin E., and Gordon J. Hawkins. Deterrence. Chicago: University of Chicago Press.

The historical method attempts to explain behavior in
particular time epochs rather than for all time. Use is made of
both qualitative and quantitative data. Previous historical studies
of crime (Powell 1966; Erikson 1966; Ferdinand 1967; Tobias 1972)
have tended to emphasize qualitative or event data as independent
variables, while utilizing counts of crimes as dependent variables.
The uniqueness of the current study within criminology research
(that is, longitudinal measurement of numerous independent variables)
means that a number of elementary questions must be raised and
experimented with before moving on the refinements of statistical
treatments and possibly further successive analyses. These include
explorations of such questions as: What types of crime should be
combined? Should indexes be constructed? What time period lengths
should be used? What measures can serve as the most valid and
reliable indicators of both independent and dependent variables for
particular locales? What types of statistical treatments should be
applied to multivariate analysis of time series data?

More generally, the historical method does not require
precise measurement of functional relations or the preliminary
setting up of complete theoretical models. Inferences and interpretations are made only after examinations of the available evidence and
the application of a variety of statistical techniques. Cyclical variations
should be placed within the context of the dynamic forces of relatively
long time periods (Kondratieff 1963).

Each research strategy and each statistical technique,
including those used here, yield some advantages and some limitations.
Further, it is unlikely that any completely unchallenged and undisputed
operational measurements will be achieved in the foreseeable future for

the theoretical concepts under study here. The constancy of these predicaments for structural studies means that the subject will remain one of benign neglect unless further experimentations with archive time series are undertaken (Count-van Manen 1975).

The pressing problems of the discipline of criminology to which this study addresses itself are seen as (1) the need for tests of competing structural theories of levels of crime generated in society, and (2) knowledge of the effects of time sampling upon the dynamics of change affecting crime rates. With these ambitious goals in mind, one overriding pragmatic questions guided the initial data-gathering effort of this study: What existing archive sources yield aggregate time series data on the District of Columbia that may serve as potential, direct or indirect, indicators of the structural concepts under test? The empirical findings to be reported in the ensuing chapters, then, constitute a case history of one city. The threads of theoretical and empirical continuities and discontinuities previously documented should be brought to bear on these. Chapter 4 relates the specifics of methodological strategy, measurement, statistical treatment, and limitations of the study.

INVESTIGATIVE AIMS

The specific investigative aims that relate directly to decision making on the methodology pursued are summarized below:

1. Identify and collect time series data from existing archive sources for testing central theoretical concepts on social structure and crime;

2. Inspect the configurational patterns of social structure, with time as the setting for major individual events (notably wars and depressions);

3. Establish the groundwork for the development of theoretical and structural equation models for the explanation of levels of crime rates;

4. Obtain rough estimations of the weight of the contribution of each structural factor in explaining the variance of crime rates.

Fox (1968, p. 2) discussed some of the assumptions of model building in his volume on econometrics. Those applicable here are (1) that the behavior of variables is determined by the joint and simultaneous operation of a number of economic and ecological variables; (2) that a model, although representing a simplification of complex realities, will delineate the crucial aspects of the sector of the system studied; and (3) that from an understanding of the model of the system will eventuate predictions of future movements of the system and the possibility of control of movements for the improvement of human welfare.

It would seem evident in the complex factors at work in this investigation, that what may be an effect at one point in time may become a cause at the next, and that both cause and effect can work jointly. Further, as Mitchell (1956, p. 471) well stated: almost every effect dealt with here can be the "joint product of numerous causes," and "one among several causes of numerous effects." In light of these complications, it is perhaps wise to view this problem in terms of relationships among a number of complex policy-related variables.

Statistically, the eventual goal—for which it is hoped this research constitutes a preliminary step—would be the building of structural equations or nonexperimental models.* These should be based not only upon regression equations, but also upon the results of qualitative analysis eventuating from collections of case histories of cities in varied stages of economic and social development, and with varying social structures and cultures. The development of such equations is premature at this point, until additional case histories of cities are accumulated and collated and until further statistical work explores possible refinement of multiple regression equations, and/or other multivariate statistical treatments with time series.

In attempting to measure the effects of the three theoretically based factors identified in this research, then, interest is not in correlations to the nth degree, but rather a search for gross indications of change that may have implications for policies aimed at the social control of crime in cities. At the same time, the behavior of variables that may exhibit relatively small statistical effects will not be omitted. There is the possibility that these cases may be important in interaction with other variables, and/or may change over time, or may be crucial for theory development. Finally, it may well be that this exploration in multivariate analysis of time series—the first prototype in criminology of which the author is aware—will produce unexpected findings. Existing theories do not always point toward specificity of hypotheses. Further, existing structural empirical work has been dominated by sample, rather than aggregate studies (as for social class), and most of the work on aggregate data has not examined race-specific crime rates. Unexpected findings did indeed occur, and these require post hoc hypotheses.

---

*It is planned that further experimentation with statistical techniques on problems associated with the use of time series, multiple regression, and other multivariate statistical methods will be carried out with Dr. Lien-fu Huang, Department of Economics, Howard University. This work will proceed toward the building of structural equation models.

RESEARCH STRATEGY

City Studies

It has been shown that states have been found to be too large as units of study for testing theoretically based hypotheses. At the same time, this writer believes that—while the neighborhood focus that has dominated the thinking of ecological studies has been fully justified—there is also an important rationale for inspecting spatial perspectives at larger points of political policy decision making which filters down, in turn, to the smaller units. Willbach (1938) argued that the city is the optimum unit for an analysis of trends of crime. An advantage of the city is its existence as a political and accounting unit. Perhaps its major weakness is that it does not take into account the development of suburban areas. When such concerns are raised, the most deep-rooted problem of cutoff points in human and nonhuman existence are posed, problems occupying the interest of many for centuries. Where are the inter-action boundaries to be drawn? Poets and philosophers have long answered that there are no really legitimate points at which life does not interact. The scientist, however, is obligated to work with somewhat arbitrary boundaries in order to examine his boxlike concepts. Further, social scientists in this field have not had large research funds available, so there has not been the luxury of studying "the world." Thus, through oversimplifications of realities, the aspiration is that, as suggested earlier, the essential dimensions of the macrocosm that is society will be represented in the microcosm sampled.

Time

There are numerous reasons to begin to inspect more closely the effect of time settings upon crime rates. Perhaps the most cogent here is that the pursuit of history inevitably brings into play the testing of divergent interpretations (Gottman et al., 1969; Count van-Manen, 1976). Heirich (1964) built a case for time as yielding strong evidence for or against postulated relationships. Gottman, McFall, and Barnett (1969, p. 299) have noted that time series data constitute a "method to eliminate major sources of rival hypotheses." Hirschi and Selvin (1967, p. 151) and Wellford (1974) have suggested the use of historical time series as a means of alleviating problems of ambiguous causal ordering.

Much earlier, our sociological elders counseled for the principle of the use of social histories. Marx (Bottomore 1964, p. 23)

stressed the importance of historically oriented sociology for the
identification of a set of categories for analyzing social systems, and
for taking into account the constancy of systemic processes of change.
Durkheim (Nisbet 1965) ennunciated the classic brief that understanding of the present and of the future is only possible by study of
the past. Simmel (1950, p. 16) urged the study of historical changes
in sociological forms. The anthropologist Nadel (1958, p. 146)
detailed numerous limitations of one-point-in-time studies. (See
Count-van Manen 1976, for summary details.) Time, then, can
function as the setting for events, as a measure of quantitative and
qualitative relationships, as a tag for sequential change processes,
and as a base for eventual prediction.

Time Series

Time series represent continuous records of fluctuations
in variables. Statistical measures are collected and recorded at
successive intervals of time (Anderson 1971). Intuitive notions of
time suggest that it proceeds progressively in one direction. Although
these notions of time have been challenged by physicists and mystics
alike (LeShan 1975), the exploration here will be within this every-
day notion. There is a tendency to assume that events close together
in time should be relatively highly related, and that those further
apart should be less strongly related (Anderson 1971, p. 3). Short-
term lags of one, two, or three years begin to suggest, however,
that further experimentation should be done on lagging procedures
for identifying possibilities of cumulative effects from greater time
distances. Some work with short-term lags are reported here, but
the major focus is upon simultaneous relationships between structural
factors and crime rates. Trends refer to a general course, or
direction, or bent (Henry and Short 1954, pp. 142-46). Cycles,
usually considered under the topic of business cycles, are of shorter
duration. There has been little explicit consideration of the length
of trends and cycles within the field of criminology, to the best of
the writer's knowledge. In business cycle research, minor cycles
have been identified as in the order of magnitude of three or three-
and-a-half years duration, with fundamental movement or trends
at seven-, eight-, or even ten-year intervals, and long waves of
50 years or so (Thomas 1926, p. 13; Kitchin 1963; Mitchell 1956,
p. 453). Criminologists Henry and Short (1954) worked with time
periods of 20- and 21-year periods; Thomas (1926), with 22-, 34-,
and 36-year periods; Glaser and Rice (1959), with 18-, and 26-year
periods; and Brenner in his study of mental illness (1973), with
41- and 52-year periods. In this study, the total 81-year period,

1890-1970, is divided into three epochs of 29, 27, and 25 years: from 1890 through 1918, 1919 through 1945, and 1946 through 1970. Varying time lengths were experimented with, with one eye to historical events (World War I and II), and the other to sample size capable of significance tests. Thus, the periods identified here are not inconsistent with previous research practices. Further, it is found that there is considerable variation in the size and even the directions of correlations for smaller, cyclical time periods of five or ten years. Some of the more striking of these findings will be reported within the context of the larger periods.

The benchmarks of 1890-1970 were determined, in turn, by the availability of relatively adequate police data from a series of annual reports of the District of Columbia, covering this period. Statistical accounting must be regularly submitted by the various components of the District government to the federal government, with Congress overseeing local district government matters through the years. Further, the city is treated as a state in state counts by the U. S. Census Bureau and other sources. Thus, it is possible that some data collected for the District may not be as readily available for other cities. On the other hand, the measures utilized, on the whole, would be expected to be kept by other city jurisdictions as well.

MEASURES OF DEPENDENT VARIABLES:
CRIME AND SUICIDE

Police arrest data for Class I crimes—homicide, aggravated assault, rape, grand larceny, burglary, robbery, and auto theft— and for totals of Class I crimes and for all crimes are utilized as dependent variables. In addition, deaths due to homicide and to suicide are obtained from mortality series. Thus, there are two independent sources for homicide measures. Yearly total, nonwhite, and white population estimates are supplied by the Demographic Unit of the District of Columbia government, making it feasible to calculate annual crime rates per 100,000 population. Count-van Manen (1975, p. 114) noted that census takers have been estimated to miss between 12 to 20 percent of young, nonwhite males, thus inflating crime rates of blacks used in this and other studies. Nonwhite, of course, is a census category with little scientific base, but fraught with much social implication.

VALIDITY AND RELIABILITY OF OFFICIAL CRIME DATA

The limitations of police data have been well detailed elsewhere (Sellin 1936; Wolfgang 1970; Seidman and Couzens 1974). The

questions raised include, in summary, concern of bias in police
processing; changes in reporting practices; changes in definitions of
crime; changes in community attitudes; changes in the efficiency of
reporting; and political pressures that affect reliability and validity.
Further, victim research findings (Ennis 1967; U. S. Department of
Justice 1975) have suggested that the validity and reliability of
specific Class I crimes are highly variable. Homicide and auto theft
tend to be regarded as among the most widely and consistently reported
crimes, while rape and grand larceny are thought to be vastly underreported and to fluctuate widely in reporting practices and enforcement over time. Even auto theft has some limitations, as an indicator
of crime (Count-van Manen 1975, p. 119). Notably, it includes joy-
riding, or temporary "borrowing" and returning of cars. Further, the
youth and amateur components of this classification are thought to
be increasing over time. These aspects of auto theft have meant (as
documented in Chapter 3) that auto theft has behaved differentially
from other crimes under social structural changes, such as wars
and depressions. Some argue, however, that the taking of cars, even
for temporary use, is justifiably considered as a criminal act.
Stricter requirements of car insurance and usage of insurance policies
(Bauer 1966) have probably increased reporting over the years.

Homicide, in instances of both police and mortician reports,
has intent in common. The police counts, however, do not include
justifiable homicide by the police themselves, whereas the mortality
series do. Also included in the latter are executions, but not in
the former. More reliance will be placed in the analyses here upon
the mortality series than upon the police series, since the latter
exhibit discontinuities in definitions of homicide over time. Robert
Armstrong, Chief of the Mortality Statistics Branch of the National
Center for Health Statistics, stated to the writer that changes over
time in classifying homicide by medical examiners are not likely to
be great. Although Vold (1952) has argued that both series of homicide are comparable, this does not prove to be the case for the
District of Columbia. It is virtually impossible to disentangle negligent
(frequently auto fatalities) from nonnegligent homicide arrests through
the years until 1968. Perforce, the two are combined here. Obviously,
coroners' reports constitute a body count and police measures have
been characterized as indicative of police activity. One arrest, of
course, may be made for numerous homicides and, conversely, there
may be numerous arrests for one homicide. There has been a marked
tendency for victims of murder to be murdered by members of their
own race (Henry and Short 1964, p. 186).

Auto theft appears to be formally consistent in definition
through time, but it is not reported before 1913. Previous years are
treated here statistically as missing data in correlational computa-
tions. Grand larceny, rape, and assault are generally considered

suspicious measures, and definitions of grand larceny and of assault fluctuated considerably within the District. Robbery and burglary are consistently defined, except in the case of robbery before 1900, when the term highway robbery is used without clear definition. These crimes suffer from inconsistent reporting practices, especially during periods of political pressures to decrease crime, as was the case during the Nixon administration. Downgrading of Class I to Class II crimes has been documented during this period for the District of Columbia by Seidman and Couzens (1974).

Arrest Bias

The question of social class bias in arrest processes is little debated, while the question of racial bias has drawn varying conclusions. The presidential task force report (1967, pp. 178-189) is among those that have concluded in the affirmative, while Black and Reiss (1970) are among those who have made the opposite finding. From the labeling perspective, and from the point of view of those caught in the arrest process, perhaps the distinction between being poor and being black is rather academic. Official tagging processes and their implications for recidivism are fairly clear. Perhaps the question should be framed in terms of the consistency of bias through time, instead of total counts.

This study of the question provides data on the number of policemen per 100,000 population and arrest rates of whites and blacks. An examination of such data for selected crimes (see Table 1 in the Appendix for data on homicide and robbery) exhibits a number of interesting points bearing on the question. These data can be examined from the perspective of how the ratio of increases and decreases in the police force to population affects arrest rates of whites and blacks. It is evident that changes in the police ratio show a higher correlation to changes in black than white arrest rates. For the more valid indexes of crime, homicide, and auto theft, as well as grand larceny the size of correlations favors an interpretation of discrimination against blacks. On the other hand, for the business-centered violent crime of robbery, there seems to be a greater discretionary process apparently favoring whites, and a slight tendency in this direction for burglary. A negative relationship is found between the police force size and arrests of nonwhites for rape and assault. This finding is congruent with previous research suggesting a lack of police enforcement of crimes thought to be normal for the black community (Kephart 1957; Newman 1966). Over time, arrests of blacks for homicide and for robbery appear to be more sensitive to changes in the police force size than do those for whites. Thus, if these evidences are valid, there would seem to be bias favoring black arrests, in most Class I crimes, with the exceptions of assault and rape.

MEASURES OF INDEPENDENT VARIABLES: POPULATION, POPULATION CHANGE, THE ECONOMY, AND THE POLICE

Population and Population Change

Decennial population estimates by race were collected, of course, from 1890 to 1970, by the U. S. Census Bureau. The category nonwhite constitutes, for practical purposes, negro or the black population composition, ranging from 94 percent of the nonwhite population in 1890 to 98.3 percent in 1970. Yearly population estimates between the decade years were obtained from the Demographic Unit of the District of Columbia government, for the period 1900 to 1970. The method this office utilized is one developed at the University of Chicago in the 1950s known as the composite method. It takes into account data on age, sex, race, death and birth rates, school enrollments, and migration. Interestingly, the only available yearly population estimates for the period 1891-99 are from the Metropolitan Police Department Annual Reports, made on the basis of police censuses from precinct-by-precinct counts, during 1894 and 1895. Straight extrapolations from the decennial census are used for the remaining five years of that decade.

Population change is measured in two ways, following the practice of Ogburn (1935): changes in the total percent population change and the percent change in blacks and in whites per 100,000 population; and changes in the rate of growth, or the difference in the percent change of each year from the preceding year. It may be recalled that population size and population change are viewed here as indirect measures of anomie, on the basis of the theoretical concern earlier documented (Chapter 2) relating to social change.

The State of the Economy

The more intensively we work, the more we realize that this term is a synthetic product of the imagination— a product whose history is characteristic of our ways of learning. (Mitchell 1956)

Late in his volume, Mitchell gives a tentative working definition of business cycles as

> . . . recurrences of rise and decline in activity,
> affecting most of the economic processes of com-
> munities with well-developed business organiza-
> tion, not divisible into waves of amplitudes nearly
> equal to their own, and averaging in communities
> at different stages of economic development from
> about three to about six or seven years in duration.
> (Mitchell 1956, p. 468)

Previous studies, when examing the effect of economic cycles upon
crime and deviance (see Chapter 3) have tended to utilize national
measurements to tap local economic well-being (U.S. Department
of Commerce 1975). It is obvious that the economic base of the
capital city varies from that of the nation and from many other U.S.
cities, since the former has a relatively large white-collar bureau-
cracy and a relatively small labor force in industry. In principle,
area-specific business cycle measures should be related as independent variables to corresponding local area measures of dependent
variables, such as crime or mental illness (Brenner 1973). With
recent repetitions of recession-depressions, there has of course
been a resurgence of academic interest in the subject. The last
few years are further testimony to the accuracy of Mitchell's
(1956) perspective that the subject is most complex, and it remains
today in a state of empirical and theoretical flux. For such reasons,
the collection of data on economic conditions for the District of
Columbia began with relatively naive assumptions for data gathering,
while an attempt was made to locate city measures with some correspondence to dimensions used for national measures. Some measures secured (such as electrical consumption) were discarded,
since insignificant fluctuations were exhibited, while other series
were incomplete. Four measures are used. The first of these, the
consumer price index, for the period 1913-70, was obtained from
the U.S. Department of Labor, Bureau of Labor Statistics (BLS), for
the District of Columbia and the Maryland and Virginia suburbs. It
was thought that price fluctuations between the areas would not vary
greatly. The base year for the index is 1967 (100). Thomas (1926)
regarded prices as the preferable business cycle measure, and it
has been used frequently in past research, including that of the
nineteenth century. The consumer price index (CPI) is

> a weighted average of price changes for a sample
> of priced items, expressed as a relative of average
> prices in a reference base as 100 . . . The CPI
> represents the average movement of prices for
> urban wage earners and clerical workers as a

> broad group . . . it measures only time-to-time
> price change . . . (U. S. Department of Labor 1974,
> pp. 88, 92, 93)

Motor vehicle registration was suggested as a measure of affluence by Wilkins (1965, p. 53), and such data are obtained for the District for the years 1926 through 1970. Two additional tax measures are used as possible indicators: taxes on land valuation and land improvement for the entire period, and taxes on public service corporations and banks' gross earnings, from 1900 to 1970. The rate of real estate tax has fluctuated through the 81 years under study, ranging from $1.50 per $100 of assessed valuation to the current rate of $2.50. Taxes on building associations have fluctuated from a rate of 2 percent to 4 percent of gross earnings over the years. Beginning in 1902, national banks were taxed at the rate of 6 percent of gross earnings. In 1949, this was reduced to 4 percent. The rationale for these fluctuations, including possible political manipulation, would constitute a study in itself. Here, these changing rate bases are taken as cautionary statements on reporting practices, which could become important for analyses which follow.

Measures explored but discarded as not feasible for use include the following: electricity consumption, which showed only consistent increases in usage; employment, figures for which could be secured only for the District and the suburban areas; alcohol taxes, data on which were not available for a long enough time period.

Throughout, as in the case of the price index, taxes on banks and corporations, and auto registrations, the early missing years of data are treated as such by the computer program option.

Police

The rationale for utilizing the size of the police force as the one major measure to represent deterrence theory has already been presented. It may be recalled that the police can be considered the most readily observable branch of the criminal justice system, and the most immediate threat of identification. The actual size of the police force, plus the numbers of police per 100,000 total population are calculated. It is known that the total police force is not an optimum measure, inasmuch as the number of those detailed to clerical or nonenforcement work varies over time. It did not prove feasible to pin down this limitation empirically, and so the measure remains a gross indicator of one facet of deterrence theory. The District police report that the ratio of clerks to arresting officers decreased considerably over time, while crime reporting and police efficiency are believed to have increased.

INTERRELATEDNESS OF CRIME TYPES

An examination of the relationship of each type of crime to every other one has been made on the basis of inspection of graphs and of Pearsonian correlations (Count-van Manen and Josiah 1974). On the basis of theory and findings of past research, a number of hypotheses were erected and tested. In the context of the larger study, this scrutiny was made in order to decide which types of crimes should be grouped together, and which should be treated separately. Much of past research practice (as documented in Chapter 3) grouped, for example, person and property crimes. On the basis of the findings in this study over the three time periods, the decision was reached to treat each crime separately. Generally, changes are taking place in the relationship of one type of crime to some others, and crime rates of blacks and of whites—while showing some parallels—also exhibit some differences. A summary of specific findings accounting for this decision are as follows: (see Tables A. 2, A. 3, A. 4, and A. 5 for correlation matrices)

1. The inverse relationship between homicide and suicide found in much previous research is not fully verified here. The overall correlations for the entire period are positive and strongest for nonwhite. The positive correlations are largest for Period I, but these grow weaker with time, with the gap betweeen the racial groups in size of correlations narrowing considerably by Period III. Parallel movements are at least equally as common as inverse relationships for homicide and suicide throughout the time span. This may only point, however, to the abnormal but constant social dislocations that took place during much of the 81-year period, such as wars and depressions.

2. The hypothesis of the etiological relatedness of homicide and assault is not verified by the data for either race. The general weakness of the assault measure, however, interferes with firm conclusions implied by this finding.

3. Homicide and rape, as hypothesized, do not show close relationships to each other for either racial group.

4. Rape and assault are hypothesized to be uncorrelated. This finding tends to be verified for Periods I and II, but not for Period III. During the last period, the curves of the two rates are smiliar.

5. Homicide and property crimes exhibit a greater correspondence than anticipated. The correlations are strongest, however, for both racial groups during Period I, and are nonsignificant for whites by Period III. The size of the relationship decreases over time for nonwhites, but remains at relatively high and significant levels for blacks for the "bellwether" of violent crime, robbery. This finding holds, however, only with the use of the arrest series

on homicide, and these are interpreted to be a less valid indicator than the mortality series.

6. The strong linkage suggested by theory and past research among property crimes as a general category is verified here with relatively high and significant correlations for Periods I and II. During Period III, however, the patterning of these crimes in relation to each other shows some indication of change taking place. Gould's (1969) reasoning that changes in the composition of some property crimes—from professional to amateur—is an interpretation that appears to be warranted in recent developments for Washington D.C., as well. Thus the changing composition of subclasses of offenders within the property crime categories may be affecting the nature of their relationship to each other and to the impact of structural changes since the forties. Other researchers have found, for example, that auto theft rates do not correlate with robbery and burglary rates during times of war (Rosenbaum 1940). An inspection of graphs for the capital city show movements in accord with such previous findings. That is, there are differential reactions to structural changes involved with wars by property crime type.

This phase of the research suggests the hypothesis that— as social stress increases due to increased social disolocations— rates of crime by legal classification types show a more diffuse and random character, with less apparent specialization in the form that deviance takes. The patterns of human violence against other humans appear to become more generalized, with fewer of the rules of relationships of types of crime to each other followed in earlier time epochs.

INTERRELATEDNESS OF INDEPENDENT VARIABLES

As can be seen by an inspection of Tables A.6, A.7, and A.8, a number of the independent variables are, generally, highly related to each other and raise problems of multicollinearity. The two tax measures relate to each other most highly, at .97 correlation for the entire period. The auto registration data relates to other economic measures in the range of .68 to .77, or somewhat lower. Correlations of the price index with other economic measures over the entire period are above .84. Nevertheless, the measures are kept separate from each other at this stage of the research, since it can be observed from correlational sizes within the smaller time periods, that relationships fluctuate over time. The size of the police force relates highly, as well, to economic measures, ranging from .86 to .91, for the total time period. Correlations for population size, economic, and police measures, range from .69 to .91 for the total period. Population change rates, both percent and rate of change, however, show relatively small correlations with other independent variables.

Within the three time periods, there are some variations in these findings. The most noticable is the shift in the second period of the relationship of population size to two of the economic measures, those of price index and of auto registrations. It is likely that the artificial restraints that operated during World War II, limiting prices and auto consumption artificially through controls, help to explain the inconsistency. At the same time, the relationship between the price index and other business cycle measures is less consistent, most notably between the price index and taxes on banks and corporations.

During Periods I and II, population size remains relatively highly correlated with economic measures and with police size, as can be seen in Tables A.6 and A.7. The second most decided shift occurs in the third time period, in which total population size becomes negatively correlated to the other factors—that is, the police size and business cycle measures. This inconsistency may well be due to the fact that it is during this period that the population shift to the suburbs increased so startlingly, and thus the population size, tied to the central city political and administrative boundaries, fails to reflect the interdependence of the swelled suburban populations.

Throughout, as might be expected, the population change rates for the total nonwhite and white population segments, show moderate correspondence between the rate of change and the percent change, but these measures—on the whole—are not highly correlated to other independent variable measures.

Thus, the problem of collinearity, or interdependence of the independent variables, is a major statistical problem, since relatively high relationships are observable in most of the three time eras between the three major theoretical focuses here: that of social disorganization and anomie, as measured by population and population change measures; that of deterrence theory, as indicated by police size measures; and that of economic theory, as indicated by measures on economic conditions. While the multiple regression may not be the ultimate solution to dealing with these difficulties statistically, the regression programs do give some insight into the problem by holding constant the variables in order of their entry for those following for their contribution to the explanation of the variance.

The weaknesses in operation of the multiple regression program, which will be demonstrated in what follows, are that statistical priority is given to the one highest correlation explaining the most variance for the first step in the operation. This arbitrary statistical operation may or may not be prior in the real time sequence.

Second, inverse correlations of statistical nonsignificance can arbitrarily enter early in the operation and exaggerate statistical effects in explaining variance.

STATISTICAL METHODS

At various stages of the research, varied statistical procedures were utilized, including moving averages; partial correlations; graphic comparisons between independent and dependent variables, and between independent and independent and dependent and dependent variables; nonparametric and parametric correlations; scrutiny of scatter diagrams; and changes in rates of crimes. After preliminary explorations of these, primary emphasis is being placed here upon parametric correlations, for purposes of making available comparisons with previously published work. Second, given the primary emphasis of the research aims, the decision was made to use multiple regression. It is a treatment with many problems in application to time series, but, quite simply, there appears to be no better technique to get at explorations of the matters of major concern here. Research of the future may explore in further detail any of the above avenues and others. The author would be glad to make the data available for such purposes.

An inspection of scatterdiagrams does reveal changes in linear functions by time periods. The strongest case for linearity is posed with the dependent variable category, total crimes (including Class I and other crimes). The unwieldiness of the sheer number of independent (17) and dependent (22) variables in this study for three time periods makes for close inspection of these, as well as of the interesting results of partial correlations, foreclosed for reasons of space and time limits at this stage of the research process.

Perhaps it may not be overly presumptive to reiterate here a statement of one of the deans of econometric methods. Fox (1968), in noting the limitations of statistical treatments, pointed to the gross approximation of derived models of reality, with the availability of data determining the units of time. In a statement on the use of statistical methods he remarked that marginal improvements of statistical inference might improve model building attempts by five or ten percent, with an argument for greater increments to be arrived at only by further emphasis upon theoretical developments (Ezekiel and Fox 1961).

Multiple Regression

The classic problem to which multivariate techniques are applied is the assessment of the relative importance and types of

influence of varying factors, all assumed to be in operation simultaneously (Sonquist 1970, p. 6). Multiple regression is the preferred
method utilized by econometrics, whose goals are similar to those
of this research. Obviously that field, in general, has problems and,
more specifically, there are numerous problems worked on for some
decades, associated with the application of multiple regression to
time series. It is likely that much work will continue to be done on
the subject in future decades. Further, on most points there remains
disagreement in scholarly work on particular issues. Some of these
will be summarized in what follows. Both stepwise and nonstep computer programs were initially used, with results of the former
reported here.

> The stepwise multiple regression program is . . .
> a powerful variation of multiple regression which
> provides a means of choosing independent variables
> which will provide the best prediction possible with
> the fewest independent variables . . . . The method
> recursively constructs a prediction equation one
> independent variable at a time. The first step is to
> choose the single variable which is the best pre-
> dictor. The second independent variable to be added
> to the regression equation is that which provides the
> best prediction in conjunction with the first variable.
> (Nie, Bent, and Hull 1970, p. 180)

Sonquist (1970, p. 11) suggested that multiple regression has
the main advantage of "estimating the separate effects of intercorrelated predictors." Multiple regression deals with the problem of
many variables and one of its charms is the directional signals given
to the location of tautological elements (Gordon 1968, p. 614). Its
aspiration, of course, is prediction. Further, multiple regression
is "even the most adequate method presently used for dealing with
interaction effects." (Sonquist 1970, p. 13). At the same time, there
are "downwardly biased correlations." The concept of "main effect
is meaningless." (Sonquist 1970, p. 7).

Limitations of Multiple Regression

Perhaps the most serious limitation to the use of the technique
here is the problem of multicollinearity, or the close relationship in
a series of independent variables to each other, with resultant defi-
ciencies in the standard errors of the regression coefficients. Multicollinearity creates the problem of precision in the estimation only

of regression coefficients. There are differences of opinion on this point. Darlington (1968, p. 166) writes that there is no requirement in multiple regression that predictor variables be uncorrelated, and thus the method has a substantial element of flexibility lacking for analysis of variance. Gordon (1968, p. 596) has made the useful distinction of redundance, referring to a high correlation between two or more independent variables regardless of the exact number of variables, and repetitiveness for the number of redundant independent variable measures. He noted that small variations among the correlations of a highly related set can create large variations among regression coefficients (p. 596). He suggested that the sharp internal competition "is between one variable of one subset against a losing variable from some other similarly competitive subset." This problem makes it difficult accurately to express the relative importance of variables. The eventual use of indexes or the elimination of at least some of the intercorrelated measures would help to obviate this problem. On the other hand, interrelatedness will probably always remain a theoretical and real fact of existence. Population changes, for example, affect business cycles, and business cycles can be postulated, in turn, to affect population changes. Where one formula begins and ends may be impossible of solution. The essence of a dilemma, or a necessary choice between equally undesirable alternatives, remains one constant in this field.

Another assumption for any basically least-squares regression analysis is the independence of samples. Time sampling, of course, is likely to be dependent. For example, if temperatures are being sampled, it is necessary for a lower temperature to pass through all intermediate levels. The argument has been made that the usual error formulas do not apply to aggregate time series while, at the same time, tests for autoregression have been constructed (Ezekiel and Fox 1961, pp. 333–47).

A further serious limitation of these analyses is the question of how much of the resulting variances are explained by increased values attributable to time trends. Some writers, depending upon the purpose of the research, maintained that time trends should not be inserted into the regression equations, but should be allowed to influence the regression coefficients (Frisch and Waugh 1933). In this research, indeed, interest is in the changing nature of long-run trends, as well as cycles. Methods to deal with the former question need further experimentation (Mitchell 1956). Finally, it can be argued that time, in this instance, is influencing both sides of the regression equation and thus may cancel out. It is hoped that this problem will be dealt with more specifically in the future. Thomas (1926) has summarized the methods of dealing with this problem, including moving averages of the dependent variable, fitting lines or parabolas, fitting logarithmic curves, (Ezekiel and Fox 1961), and so on. A few illustrative graphs utilizing three-year moving averages are included in Chapter 5.

The problem of measurement of errors in the data is generall as well as here, handled as Sonquist (1970, p. 12) has suggested by not rejecting hypotheses too easily and by utilizing some judgment in assessing the relative importance of the various factors, while simultaneously keeping in mind the accuracy with which the variables are thought to have been measured. As specified earlier, these accuracies vary with particular measures under consideration. Tests of significance are not normally appropriate (Darlington 1968, p. 178).

The logic of multiple regression analysis assumes "holding constant all independent variables except the one chosen for study" (Sonquist 1970, p. 67). The assumption that such results can then be added together is not totally warranted, and raises, then, still, another basic limitation to the method, but one which has been estimate to give a downward bias (Sonquist 1970, p. 75) to the results.

Having noted some of the serious limitations raised by the use of time series and multivariate analysis, perhaps it is justifiable to note the optimistic conclusion of Ezekiel and Fox (1961, p. 347) the subject, namely, "our position is that the special difficulties and uncertainties associated with time series analysis have frequently been exaggerated . . . ."

This study, then, emphasizes actual magnitudes of the Pearsonian correlations for theoretically based concepts, a step that can be examined for continuities and discontinuities with previous findings. The joint effects of theoretically related measures to the variance explanation will also be noted. Grappling statistically with some of the problems raised here, and with the erection of structural theorems, is planned in future work.

REFERENCES

Anderson, T. W. 1971. The Statistical Analysis of Time Series. New York: Wiley.

Bauer, Raymond A., ed. 1966. Albert D. Biderman: Social Indicators. Cambridge, Mass.: MIT Press.

Black, Donald J. and Albert J. Reiss, Jr. 1970. "The Police Control of Juveniles." American Sociological Review 35 (February): 63-77.

Bottomore, T. B., ed. and translator. 1964. Karl Marx: Selected Writings in Sociology and Social Philosophy. New York: McGraw-Hill.

Brenner, Meyer Harvey. 1973. Mental Illness and the Economy. Cambridge, Mass.: Harvard University Press.

Brown, T.M. 1952. "Habit Persistence and Lags in Consumer Behavior." Econometrics 20 (July): 207-23.

Clark, John J. and Morris Cohen, eds. 1963. Business Fluctuations, Growth, and Economic Stabilization: A Reader. New York: Random House.

Count-van Manen, Gloria, ed. 1976. "The Need for Historical Empiricism in Criminology." In Social Systems, Crime, Delinquency and Deviance: A Reader in Structurally-Oriented Studies. Washington, D.C.: University Press of America.

_____. 1975. "Use of Official Data in the Evaluation of Crime Control Policies and Programs. In Criminal Justice Research, ed. Emilio Viano. Lexington, Mass.: Lexington Books.

Count-van Manen, Gloria and Cecil Josiah. 1974. "Person and Property Crimes as Etiological Types: Some Empirical Evidence for the District of Columbia, 1890-1970." Unpublished paper delivered at the Annual Meetings of the International Sociological Society, 1974, Toronto, Canada.

Darlington, Richard B. 1968. "Multiple Regression in Psychological Research and Practice." Psychological Bulletin 69 (May): 161-82.

Ennis, Philip H. 1967. "Criminal Victimization in the United States." In the Task Force Report: The Police. President's Commission on Law Enforcement and Administration of Justice. Washington, D.C.: Government Printing Office.

Erikson, Kai T. 1966. Wayward Puritans: A Study in the Sociology of Deviance. New York: Wiley.

Ezekiel, Mordecai and Karl A. Fox 1961. Methods of Correlation and Regression Analysis. New York: Wiley.

Ferdinand, Theodore N. 1967. "The Criminal Patterns of Boston Since 1849." American Journal of Sociology 73 (July): 84-99.

Fox, Karl A. 1968. Intermediate Economic Statistics. New York: Wiley.

Frisch, Ragnar and Frederick V. Waugh. 1933. "Partial Time Regressions as Compared with Individual Trends." Econometrica 1 (October): 387-401.

Glaser, Daniel and Kent Rice. 1959. "Crime, Age, and Employment." American Sociological Review 24 (October): 679-86.

Gordon, Robert A. 1968. "Issues in Multiple Regression." American Journal of Sociology 73 (March): 592-616.

Gottman, John M., Richard M. McFall, and Jean T. Barnett. 1969. "Design and Analysis of Research Using Time Series." Psychological Bulletin 72: (October): 299-306.

Gould, Leroy C. 1969. "The Changing Structure of Property Crime in an Affluent Society." Social Forces 48 (September): 1-10.

Heirich, Max. 1964. "The Use of Time in the Study of Social Change." American Sociological Review 29 (June): 386-97.

Henry, Andrew F. and James F. Short, Jr. 1954, 1964. Suicide and Homicide. New York: Free Press.

Hirschi, Travis and Hanan C. Selvin. 1967. Delinquency Research: An Appraisal of Analytical Methods. New York: Free Press.

Kephart, William M. 1957. Racial Factors and Urban Law Enforcement. Philadelphia: University of Pennsylvania Press.

Kitchin, Joseph. 1963. "Cycles and Trends in Economic Factors." In Business Fluctuations, Growth, and Economic Stabilization.: A Reader, ed. J. J. Clark and M. Cohen. New York: Random House.

Kondratieff, Nikolai. 1963. "The Long Waves in Economic Life." In Business Fluctuations, Growth, and Economic Stabilization: A Reader ed. John J. Clark and Morris Cohen. New York: Random House.

Le Shan, Lawrence. 1975. The Medium, the Mystic, and the Physicis Toward A General Theory of the Paranormal. New York: Random House.

Mitchell, Wesley C. 1956. Business Cycles. New York: National Bureau of Economic Research.

Nadel, S.F. The Theory of Social Structure. 1958. Glencoe, Ill.: Free Press.

Newman, Donald J. 1966. Conviction: The Determination of Guilt or Innocence Without Trial. Boston: Little, Brown.

Nie, Norman H., Dale H. Bent and C. Hadlai Hull. 1970. Statistical Package for the Social Sciences. New York: McGraw-Hill.

Nisbet, Robert A. 1965. Emile Durkheim: With Selected Essays. Englewood Cliffs, N.J.: Prentice-Hall.

Ogburn, William. 1935. "Factors in Variation of Crime Among Cities." Journal of American Statistical Association 30 (March): 12-20.

Powell, Elwin H. 1966. "Crime as a Function of Anomie." Journal of Criminal Law, Criminology, and Police Science 57 (June): 161-71.

President's Commission on Law Enforcement and Administration of Justice. 1967. The Task Force Report: The Police. Washington, D.C.: Government Printing Office.

Rosenbaum, Betty B. 1940. "The Relationship Between War and Crime in the United States." Journal of American Institute of Criminal Law and Criminology 40: 723-42.

Seidman, David and Michael Couzens. 1974. "Getting the Crime Rate Down: Political Pressure and Crime Reporting." Law and Society Review 8, no. 3 (Spring): 457-93.

Sellin, Thorsten. 1936. "The Basis of a Crime Index." Journal of Criminal Law, Criminology, and Police Science 22 (September): 335-56.

Simmel, Georg. The Sociology of Georg Simmel. 1950. Translated by Kurt H. Wolf, Glencoe, Ill.: Free Press.

Sonquist, John A. 1970. Multivariate Model Building. Ann Arbor, Mich.: Institute for Social Research, University of Michigan.

Thomas, Dorothy Swaine. 1926. Social Aspects of the Business Cycle. New York: Gordon and Breach.

Tobias, J.J. 1972. Urban Crime in Victorian England. New York: Schocken Books.

U.S. Department of Commerce. 1975. Business Conditions Digest (February).

U.S. Department of Justice. 1975. Sourcebook of Criminal Justice Statistics: 1974. Washington, D.C. Government Printing Office.

Vold, George B. 1952. "The Extent and Trend of Capital Crimes in the United States." Annals of the American Academy of Political and Social Science 284 (November): 1-7.

Wellford, Charles F. 1974. "Crime and the Police." Criminology 12 (August): 290-305.

Wilkins, Leslie T. 1965. Social Deviance: Social Policy, Action, and Research. Englewood Cliffs, N.J.: Prentice-Hall.

Willbach, A. 1966. "The Trend of Crime in New York City." Cited
     in Elwin H. Powell, "Crime as a Function of Anomie,"
     Journal of Criminal Law, Criminology, and Police Science 57
     (June): 161-71.

Wirth, Louis. 1938. "Urbanism as a Way of Life." Journal of
     Sociology 44 (July): 6-15.

Wolfgang, Marvin E. , Leonard Savitz, and Norman Johnson. 1970.
     The Sociology of Crime and Delinquency. New York: Wiley.

5

A PROFILE OF
CRIMINOGENIC FORCES
OF THE CAPITAL

A frequent criticism of macrostructural research (as developed notably by econometricians) is that such studies may miss their predictive objective by failing to take into account developments in and anticipation of crucial variables for which time series data are not available. The first objective of this chapter is to fill out the dimensions of the variables under study with decennial data (where annual data are not possible), with qualitative facts, and with reasoned hypotheses. The second objective is to indicate actual magnitudes of key variables for which time series data are available and which are examined in their relational aspects in upcoming chapters. An attempt is made to profile the balance of forces within the District of Columbia that are thought to affect levels of crime and suicide. The data here, then, are descriptive, while those of ensuing chapters are correlational and predictive in long-run goals. Descriptive studies consider the relationships among many possibly relevant factors, whereas predictive studies focus on key variables, treating the latter systematically with statistical tools. The entire study represents, then, an attempt to explore the possibilities of merging both avenues of approach. Analyses in Chapters 6 and 7 sometimes rely upon the content of Chapter 5 as an added tool for interpretation.

The filters applied to the selection of interdisciplinary facts to be presented stem from directions suggested by central sociological and psychological themes, empirical findings of research (including those of the present study), and reasoned hypotheses for areas in which little empirical work has been done. In the last instance, there are at least two notable gaps: the relationship between politics and crime, and historical fluctuations in levels of group anomie.

POLITICS AND CRIME IN THE DISTRICT

Sociology has been characterized, since its beginnings, by emphasis upon the importance of values in the analysis of society, in general, and of crime and deviance, in particular. A number of authors (such as Durkheim, Merton, Bell, and so on) have theorized that unlimited goals are conducive to a permanent state of anomie and high levels of deviance, if equal emphasis is not placed by society upon opening up the means for their achievement. The necessity of the conversion of U.S. society to goals of limited ends and consumption is now increasingly being recognized by ecologists and others as essential for both national and global survival, in a world of rising expectations and limited resources. Such a value transformation, then, is hypothesized to not only aid in effecting such obvious aims, but also to constitute a central aspect of reducing the deviant bent resulting from the motto, "any means justifies the ends" that has characterized our society. Such a transformation, however, runs against the grain of the direction of the development and history of the country, including today mass advertising stimuli, constantly bombarding all to consume more.

The presidential leadership manner is hypothesized to constitute a collective style, or model for social interaction, that can help to modify the value structure of Washington, D.C., and more generally of U.S. society. It represents a true group synthesis focused in leadership and widely circulated by mass media. Psychoanalysts have documented a number of cases of the symbolic significance of leadership for the identification processes of a nation. The psychoanalyst Jung (Odajnyk 1976) has verbalized a number of concepts and ideas consistent with this viewpoint. He held that there is a "collective consciousness" that exists before the entrance of any one individual onto the scene. Jung's definition is not unlike Durkheim's concept of collective conscience. The former is defined as "the accepted beliefs, biases, attitudes, and principles of a given society or group" (Odajnyk 1976, pp. 13-15). Jung also delineated a "collective unconscious," defined as the "inherited patterns of apprehension and feeling." The contemporary cultural layer" eventually passes into an inherited collective unconscious. His concept of "collective shadow" is defined as "the unrecognized, incompatible, and inferior side of a race, group, or nation. . . usually repressed" (p. 70). Jung, then, discussed the inclination of a society to find a live hero who embodies the charismatic power of the yearnings of its people, and who can both affect the content of the conscious, as well as readjust the relation of the conscious to the unconscious collectivity.

It is reasoned here, then, that what takes place in the collective leadership style of the president in Washington, D.C., intimately affects the patterns of interpersonal interactions within the city, including crime and deviance levels. The empirical testing of such a hypothesis over time would be difficult and constitutes an avenue for possible future research. It is the personal impression of the writer, who has witnessed the area for some thirty years (consistently within the last ten years) that the interpersonal mode of the city varies with interpersonal cues of the presidential collective leadership style. The motto verbalized in word and in action during the Nixon era was "let everyone take care of himself." This included the rejection of demands for changed policies from those on "walks" to Washington—veterans on crutches, the aged, and the unemployed. The important thing was to remember to win. This style seemed to create a penetrating aura of interpersonal rule in the environment of the city. The quality of interaction between people in parking lots, on the road, in department stores, in short, in secondary and primary groups—seems, already in the first month (January 1977) of the new highly publicized style of President Jimmy Carter, to be changing from a model characterized by "he who gets there first wins" to one of increased consideration and civility to others.

Modeling behavior, whether conscious imitation or unconscious identification,[*] tends to proceed from the powerful to the less powerful. Gabriel Tarde (Clark 1969, pp. 60-61, 230) was interested in the "laws of imitation" which guide the acceptance or rejection of beliefs and ideas. He commented upon the role of the capital city in this process. His speculation was that the contagion of criminal acts is more to be feared than that of "virtuous acts." Further, the more "distant the source of communication, the less strong is its influence." He suggested, thus, that the influence of the capital of France, Paris, was weak on outlying sectors of the country. At the same time, he emphasized the importance of newspapers in influencing communication to distant regions. Were he alive today, certainly he would witness the penetration of television into homes throughout the country, as well as newspaper and radio media, and alter this hypothesis.

---

[*]For a summary of socialization processes and verbiage used in psychological and psychoanalytic notions of socialization, including the similarity between more and less powerful as illustrated with parents and children, see Count-van Manen (1973).

Washington, D. C. :
Collective Leadership in Norms and Values

A shift to close the gap in credulity of the U.S. value system
is necessary, the writer believes, to minimize deviance. Presidential
leadership sets a crucial model and tone for such an objective, both
within the capital and in the rest of the nation. Our new president,
Jimmy Carter, appears to be cognizant of this objective. In his first
months in office, he and his staff have displayed a consistent pattern
of symbolic enactment that appears to be geared toward a change in
style. These actions were reported in detail by the news, radio, and
television media. For example, there was widespread comment upon
the following pattern of manners and actions: the attendance of Amy
at a public school; the wearing of an old dress by Mrs. Carter to the
inauguration parties; the dismissal of limousine service for the
presidential executive staff; the opening of the locked doors of the
U.S. Department of Justice; the rehiring of a convicted murderess
as a nurse for Amy; and so on. One local newspaper,[*] both in
editorials and in banner headlines, carried captions such as: "Carter
as Egalitarian," "The Spirit of '77"; "The Carter Style," "Presidential
Receptions: Homespun," "The Mondale Expedition: Mission Austerity,"
"Of the People, for the People," "Symbols Mark Carter Administration." In his manner and attitude of interpersonal style he is portrayed
as a model of loving care and informality, moving toward a reduction
in conspicuous consumption. This model is in marked contrast to the
style of previous presidents. It is hypothesized that—if carried into
the political policy arena—such changes could be crucial in helping
to build up a modified value system in action, in increasing local and
national cohesion, and in lessening the effects of inequality upon the
incentives for crime. Over the long run, then, such a difficult
transformation should increase cohesion and decrease crime levels.
        Policies and events, of course, may facilitate or hinder such
multipronged efforts to change the interpersonal social structure of
the capital and the nation. For example, the record cold spell of the
winter of 1977 may prove to be catastrophic to the economy, to employment, to gross national product, and to the effects of planned
tax cuts. At the same time, it may be the best thing that could happen,
in the long run, to a people who, although gifted with foresight, do
not seem to be using it for energy conservation. Jung might comment

---

[*]Washington Post, January 20, 1977, entire issue; January
21, 1977, p. A23; January 22, 1977, p.E1; January 29, 1977, p.E1;
January 30, 1977, p.A2.

today that the people of the United States, a product of the industrial
revolution and urban living, have lost their instinct to survive. At
any rate, perhaps only repeated crises may succeed in reducing the
circus of lights and increased energy consumption that still is
characteristic in the city and the country. The conversion to a 60-
degree level in factories, stores and homes, to a four-day week, and
so on, are events and trends that may help to shock people into a
more reality-based pattern, assuming world resources are limited.

Such a complex of changing mode of activity and of concern
in interpersonal style, then, seems appropriate to this writer for
the difficult changes that are required to transform the city and,
more generally, the United States into value orientations of limited
goals which would work to decrease crime, as well as to ensure
world survival.

Politics and Crime Data

Crime and politics interact in the city insofar as there is
a national investment in keeping the streets of the city safe for the
conduct of government, for the national leaders based here, and
for visitors to the nation's capital. Thus, crime readily becomes
a political issue. The Nixon campaign, for example, promised a
decrease in crime in Washington, D. C. President Nixon issued an
edict that crime must go down. It did. The then Chief of Police
threatened that there would be dismissal of policemen[*] unless crime
went down. Such political pressures, of course, affect the stuff of
this study.

Self-Government and Crime Levels

Congressional committees have closely supervised the internal
affairs of the city for 160 years. It can be hypothesized that the lack
of self-government in Washington, D. C. has contributed to an increase in municipal apathy. Recent movement toward District
self-government in a city council, along with the election of black
officials in a predominantly black population, should play a visible
symbolic role that contributes to cohesion and a decrease in crime

---

[*]The author interviewed about 200 student policemen of the
city during this era, in classes in criminology. Respondent police
officers stated that it was easy to shift crime categories from Class
I (the crime index base) to Class II, thus lowering the crime rate.
This tendency has been documented more fully in Seidman and Couzens,
(1974).

and deviance levels. The testing of such a hypothesis—a rationale for democracy—would require further research as the transformation continues.

ECONOMICS AND CRIME

Economic Stability

The city has been and remains dominated by civil service, with national agencies as the major employers. While thus less subject to the effects of national business cycles, the politics of cutting back government bureaucracies makes for something of a political seasonality in the labor force of the city. For example, after World War II, government employees who had been appointed during the war, regardless of qualification and performance, were released with the coming of the Eisenhower administration. It would be interesting to examine systematically the possible empirical link of short, sharp cuts and expansions in federal government employment to changes in presidential election years.

The economic backbone of the city, then, tends to provide a stable labor force, with relatively low unemployment rates and relatively high income, as compared to other cities (Council on Municipal Performance 1974).[*] These factors should work to minimize crime. On the other hand, as pointed out previously, findings from two centuries find no necessary accord between median income measures and crime. Gordon (1968) has cautioned that this economic relationship must be sought by checking the frequency of the very lowest economic income brackets against crime rates.

Extremes of Inequality

Conditions of extreme poverty and conspicuous wealth in close proximity have long been observed to encourage crime. The luxurious style of life of the many powerful national and international envoys concentrated in the capital, such as politicians; foreign embassies; lobbyists; and so on, are readily visible. Further, their actions are not infrequently the topic of news reports to local citizens. In recent months, for example, there were complaints about the idling of

---

[*] See S. M. Miller and Martin Rein for definition of poverty and on "Poverty, Inequality, and Policy," in Social Problems, (ed.) Howard S. Becker (New York: John Wiley & Sons, 1966), pp. 426-516. These authors argue that with an upswing of the business cycle, inequalities of income increase, and that downswings are accompanied by reduced inequalities (pp. 480, 497).

limousines, awaiting their occupants, on the streets. An issue was
made of this practice by readers of a local newspaper, and instructions
were given to them as to the proper authority to report the license
plate numbers to in order to bring a halt to this particular wasteful
practice.

Washington, D. C. was found to be the very highest in rank
among 31 cities studied for extremes of inequality (Council on
Municipal Performance 1974). To illustrate, one census tract in
1970 exhibited a mean income of $34,918, while 1.7 percent of the
families in poverty levels in the tract showed a mean income of $1,095
per year (U.S. Census Bureau, pp. 153-65). Other tracts showed over
60 percent of the families below poverty level, as defined by the
Census Bureau. These findings are utilized as evidence contributing
to an interpretation of the relative deprivation hypothesis for findings
on the relationship of economic conditions to property crime levels in
upcoming chapters.

A Postindustrial City

The capital varies from many other U.S. cities in its non-
industrial economic base. As such, it may be viewed as in a post-
industrial stage of development, although it must be cautioned that
it did not pass through an industrial phase. Census categories for
industrial and occupational categories have changed over time, making
historical comparisons difficult. Nevertheless, it is clear that even
in 1880, Washington was dominated by professional and service
positions, with relatively few in the labor force engaged in agriculture
and industry. In 1880 only 2.7 percent of the labor force were engaged
in agriculture and 9.4 in manufacturing (Kuznets 1960). By 1970[*]
these figures had dropped to .3 and 4.2, respectively. The largest
labor force employment categories have been trade, finance, and
so forth, with 13.1 percent in 1880 and 21.4 percent in 1950; and
services and public administration, with 49.7 percent in 1880 and
56.5 percent in 1950. The proportion in private household duties
exhibited a decided decline, from 22.5 percent in 1880 to 4.9 percent
in 1950. In 1970, 24.3 percent were employed in public administration
and another 20.1 percent in professional and related services. The
81,802 in public administration showed an almost equal representation

---

[*]Data for 1970 are from the Census of Population, District of
Columbia, General Social and Economic Characteristics. Series No.
PC (1) Co. Table 47, Volume I, Part 10 (Washington, D.C.: U.S.
Government Printing Office).

of black and white racial groups. There were an additional 67,672 in 1970 employed in professional services, representing a rise in number from 1960, but a drop in percentage. Of these latter, 17.2 percent were classified as negro and 26.7 percent as white.

The construction industry has been one of the major blue-collar forces in the area, employing 14.6 percent of the labor force in 1880, 6.2 percent in 1950, and 4.1 percent in 1970. Seasonality is generally a characteristic of this industry in the nation and in this city.

A CASE HISTORY OF RACIAL SUCCESSION

Simmel (1950) and Wirth (1938) are among those theorists who speculated about the impact of numbers and ghetto life upon social processes. Wirth maintained that the "quantitative aspect of life is transformed directly into qualitative aspects of character." He and others of the Chicago school were concerned, as well, with the impact of population concentration and urbanization upon the loss of primary controls and higher crime rates.

Like many other northern cities, the capital has gained a black majority population in the last few decades. Unlike many other cities, located at the borders of North and South, Washington, D.C. had a substantial minority of blacks in 1890—one-third. By 1970, blacks constituted a 70 percent majority. This case history of racial succession and transformation is thought to have profound implications for the nature of interactions between and within the two groups that might relate to the changing profile of crime. This is not the central focus of the study. Nevertheless, a set of unanticipated findings will be referred back to this facet of the city's historical change in upcoming analyses.

A summary of the race and sex composition of the city from 1890 to 1970 is presented in Table 5.1 below. The capital, in terms of its total numbers, has been considered a small town by its large eastern neighboring entities. Only recently has it achieved big-city status. Population of the central city rose from 230,392 in 1890 to a peak of 802,178 in 1950, and thereafter declined to 756,510. Of this last number, 71.5 percent were classified as negro, 27.7 percent as white, and 1.3 percent as other. If the Standard Metropolitan Area is taken into account, population reached 2,861,123 in 1970. Over two million were outside the central city. Outside of the central District enclave, the neighboring suburban areas of Maryland and Virginia were constituted of overwhelmingly white, or 91 percent, with 7.9 percent negro and 1.2 percent other.

TABLE 5.1

Population by Racial and Sex Groupings,
District of Columbia
1890-1970

Year	Total Population	White	Nonwhite	Male	Female
1890	230,392	154,695	75,697	109,584	120,808
1900	278,718	191,532	87,186	132,004	146,714
1910	331,069	236,128	94,941	158,050	173,019
1920	437,571	326,860	110,711	203,543	234,028
1930	486,896	353,981	132,888	231,883	254,986
1940	663,091	474,326	188,765	317,522	345,569
1950	802,178	517,865	284,343	377,918	424,260
1960	763,956	345,263	418,693	358,171	405,785
1970	756,510	210,878	545,632	351,606	404,904

Source: U.S. Census of Population, 1890-1970.

AGE STRUCTURE

The age structure of the city favors high black crime rates
and high white suicide rates. Within the city, the age distribution of
the black population is decidedly younger than that of the white, with
the median age for the former group 25.1 and for the latter, 41.0
(U.S. Census Bureau 1971, pp.22-26). In 1970, there were some
199,168 nonwhite youths under 18, and 24,938 white. In contrast, the
population of nonwhite over 21 years was 316,592 and for white,
169,495.

Latest national reports[*] indicate that 42 percent of black teen-
agers in 1976 were unemployed. In so-called poverty areas, the figure
reaches an intolerable 53 percent. This situation has been referred
to, for some years now, as social dynamite.

Previous national and local efforts at youth employment programs
have not generated sufficient numbers of jobs to employ more than a
small number of those youths out of school, out of work, and applying
for positions. Age is not a primary focus of this study, however. A
good deal of documentation on the subject has already been accomplished
(see Chapter 3).

[*]Washington Post, August 3, 1976, p. A2.

SEX COMPOSITION

This study does not inspect differences in crime rates by sex or the possible impact of sex composition of the city upon crime rates. Plans are under way to examine the effects of macrostructural variables upon male and female crime rates in the future. Nevertheless, it may be noted (see Table 5.1) that females in the population of Washington, D.C. have consistently outnumbered males. The balance in numbers of those in differing social categories may be expected to affect patterns of social interaction. In this instance, the sex imbalance of the city could affect crime and deviance profiles.

In the view of the relations between the sexes that uses the vocabulary of battle, the numerical superiority of females could be hypothesized to at least make feasible gains in secondary relationships, such as are being emphasized today in the aspiration for economic and political equality emphasized by women's liberation groups. In primary group relationships between women and men, however, the numerical dominance of women can be considered as part of a phenomenon of human oversupply, possibly working to minimize the value of women in intimate relationships. Also, the possible substitutions of one woman for another in primary relationships in the city heightens competition among women for men. The effect could be to undermine cohesion of women as a group in trying to reach objectives for equal treatment in secondary relationships. This effect should be considered in analyses of crime rates for women. As regards crime, more generally, it can be hypothesized that the increasing sexual availability of women in such a situation, influenced at the same time by changing technology of birth control and changing sexual mores, would lead, all other factors being equal, to a decrease in rape rates. This proposition, however, is difficult to test in the research design used here, for at least two reasons. First, it is found that, in fact, macrostructural factors do not remain constant over time. Second, the validity and reliability of rape arrests over time are highly suspect. The hypothesis might be better tested on cross-sectional crime rates for numerous cities, with correlations calculated for the sex ratios of cities and victim-reported rape rates.

MIGRATION

There is every reason to believe that the history of mass movements of peoples, both in immigration and migration, represent important crystallizations of forces that, in turn, are important for understanding fluctuations in crime and deviance levels over time. The role of immigration in explaining high rates of crime of white ethnic

groups who once lived in inner-city areas has been prominent in the
discipline, affecting both theory and empiricism. Classic emphasis
on the theme is an essential element of theories of urbanization,
social disorganization, and culture conflict. White immigrants, themselves, in inner-city areas were found to be largely conforming, while
their children of the second generation exhibited high rates of delinquency (Haskell and Yablonsky 1974, p. 22). Further, it has been
demonstrated that census tracts in inner cities with long-established
black residents tent to exhibit relatively low crime and delinquency
rates (Shaw 1971).

In some contrast, elementary facts on the timing of black
migrations from areas of the South to the Northern cities—rivaling in
scope massive movements of Europeans to America—have not played
a dominant part in explanations of black crime rates today. This
oversight tends to be present not only in the discipline, but also as
a facet of public opinion on the causes of crime. The writer, for
example, has interviewed hundreds of both black and white college
students in sociology groups that should be sensitive to the question.
They are generally ignorant of the timing of the great pushes of black
migrants from the rural areas of the south into cities of the north.

Migration, then, must be considered an essential component
of population change. Time series on the latter will be correlated
with crime rates in upcoming chapters. The general outlines of
migratory and immigration movements that were to transform the
social structure of many cities, including Washington, D. C., is
discernible in Table 5.2. It presents decennial net migration estimates
for the District, from 1870 through 1970, for negros, native whites,
and foreign-born whites.

Nonwhites

It should be recalled that the census classifications, nonwhite
or negro or black—as these names have evolved through the years in
usage—are not scientific physical entities.[*] Nevertheless, the categories have had numerous well-documented social repercussions in
biased beliefs and racist practice throughout the years. Further,
census reports on numbers of the nonwhite population tend to under-
estimate the black segment. The effect is to inflate rates of crime for
the black population (Count-van Manen 1975). So much mixture has
taken place between the races that Sutherland and Cressey (1974) estimated that 50 percent of the blacks arrested as criminals are, in fact,
mostly white.

---

[*]Bogue (1959) has shown that there is little scientific evidence
for census assessments of and reports on racial categories.

TABLE 5.2

Estimated Net Intercensal Migration for Total, Native White,
Foreign-Born White, and Negro Population,
Washington, D.C.,
1870-1970
(in thousands)

	Components Method[a]			Survival Rate Method[b]								
	1960-70	1950-60	1940-50	1950-60	1940-50	1930-40	1920-30	1910-20	1900-10	1890-1900	1880-90	1870-80
Total white and negro	-100	-160	49	-115.1	78.5	157.8	27.3	97.0	41.0	34.3	36.1	18.1
Native white	-137	-213	-14	-165.4	6.7	101.2	5.5	69.3	22.2	20.1	18.1	8.6
Foreign-born white				-0.9	10.7	9.1	5.8	9.3	9.1	5.5	4.7	3.3
Negro	36	51	61	51.3	61.2	47.5	16.0	18.3	9.8	8.7	13.4	6.2

Source: Migration: Internal Migration (Series C1-88) from Historical Statistics of the U.S. Department of Commerce, Bureau of Census, pp. 93-95.

[a]Component of change method of net migration is obtained by subtracting the national increase for the intercensal period (births minus deaths) from the difference between the census count at the beginning and the end of the period.

[b]Survival rate method is obtained by a residual method, using survival ratios derived from census data. The loss through mortality during an intercensal period was estimated on the basis of the ratios of appropriate age groups as enumerated in successive decennial censuses. The difference between the enumerated population at the end of the dicennial period and the estimated survivors from the beginning to the end of the period was assumed to be net migration. . . For the native population, the figures show the estimated amount of net internal migration. For the foreign born, the figures represent the estimated net change attributable to direct movement into the State from abroad and the net gain or loss in the exchange of foreign-born residents with other States," p. 87.

The timing of the massive migration of blacks (negros) to Washington, D.C., can be seen in Table 5.2 to have peaked in recent decades. That is, the highest points of net migration were reached between 1940 and 1950. The process was well under way during the decade 1930 to 1940, and continued to swell in 1950-60. By 1970, the zenith is considered to have been reached in the the third period examined in this study. These movements were followed by great losses in the white population, notable during the decade 1950 to 1960. Of import is the implication that second generations of recent black migrants can be expected to continue to effect a tendency toward the expansion of crime rates in the city, through 1980, while in future epochs, as the effects of recent migrations to the District become spent, this factor should lessen its effects on black crime rates.

At the commencement of the first period for which the decennial data are available, as can be seen from Table 5.2, net migrations of both native whites and of blacks had more than doubled by 1890 over the previous decade, 1870-80. These upheavals, in turn, were consequent to the events of the Civil War, events that were to manifest themselves in swollen crime rates. Thus, as the period under study opened, great changes had taken place. For both groups, migration can be seen to be relatively stable thereafter, with some losses by blacks and some increases by whites. The large jumps in net migration by both groups from 1910 to 1920 are associated with World War I. Whites continued to lead blacks, with more than a tripling of net migration for the former, and almost a doubling for the latter. Then a sharp leveling-off took place of native white migration in the decade from 1920 to 1930, with a lesser decline for blacks. The decade 1930-40, however, encompassed here in Period II, showed a sharp jump in net migration for both groups, from 5.5 to 101.2 per 100,000 for native whites and from 16.0 to 47.5 for blacks. A not unfamiliar pattern then occurred, from 1950 to 1960, with a great loss of the native white population to the suburbs. These changed from a small loss or a small increase (depending upon the method used of computation) for 1940-50 to major net losses of -165.4 per 100,000 population by the survival method of computation (see notes of Table 5.2) and -213 by the components method, for 1950-60. Peak gains for blacks between 1940 and 1950 reached 61.2, leveling to 51.3 per 100,000 in the decade 1950-60. Then there was a decline to 36.0 for the last decade, 1960-70, Period III in this study. Thus, historically the pattern of the total period began with relatively modest black losses and ended with relatively great black gains in the central city area. These data bear witness to the centrality of the transformation of the city in terms of a balance of whites and blacks.

Unlike other eastern cities, Washington was not a historic entry point for foreign white immigrants. The greatest change in the foreign-born white component took place between the first and second decades of this study, when net migration rose from 5.5 in the decade 1890 to 1900, to 9.1 per 100,000 in 1900 to 1910. Before and after this decade, there were relatively minor changes, with another small peak movement during World War II, between 1940 and 1950, with 10.7 net migration. The next decade, between 1940 and 1950, followed with a net loss of -.9, and there is no further evidence of change through 1970.

These aspects of change over time in social structure, then, such as age distributions, economic and other power inequalities, collective presidential leadership, political pressure on the judicial system, and migration are not readily measured with annual time series data. Nor are changes in microstructures, such as family and peer relationships, included in the multivariate analyses of Chapters 6 and 7. All of these factors may contribute something to fluctuations in crime levels. Most of the statistical variance, however, tends to be explained by the dimensions of the factors that are tapped with time series data, as will be demonstrated in upcoming chapters.

The brief sketches that follow aim to highlight substantively the time periods of greater and of lesser structural change. Space does not allow detailed consideration of the rich historical facts. Nor can there be a full exploitation of time series here for their potential methodological development in the treatment of change sequences.

AN OVERVIEW OF SOCIAL STRUCTURE

Change is characteristic of all three time periods under examination, and yet there are differences in degree and kind. The constants in each period include cycles of depression and of prosperity, of war and of peace, of consensus and of dissensus, of changing moods of hope, followed by anomie among the black population. Segregation was constant.* Yet change was more moderate for the first period (1890-1918) than in later periods for all three dimensions measured here—economic conditions, population, and the judicial system. The second period (1919-45) was permeated by extreme contradictions of change, with both heights of prosperity in the late twenties and depths of the depression of the thirties. There was, as well, the beginning of the great population upheaval, from a white to a black majority. Period III foresaw the zenith of this succession, as well as a unparalleled term of affluence, accompanied by long and divisive

---

*Green (1967) is utilized as a source for historical facts that bear on the nature of intergroup relations.

Far-Eastern wars. In the earlier world wars, young blacks were
underrepresented in the armed forces, while in the wars of the last
period, they were overrepresented.

A Synopsis of Long-Term Trends

How do the increases in the independent variable measures
compare with those of crime rates over the total period? In summary,
almost everything expanded, but some variables more than others.
Increases in both inflation and in police force size far outstripped
increases in the more valid of crime indicators. The price index and
the police ratio more than quadrupled, while the homicide rate almost
tripled and auto theft more than doubled. Total Class I crime arrests,
however, kept pace with other inflations, shooting up by more than
four times numerically, but from 66.2 per 100,000 population in 1890
to 138.4 in 1970. Other less reliable crime indicators increased over
the total period, especially burglary; while assault moved downward
by about three times; and robbery moved up astronomically, from
1.6 per 100,000 population in 1890 to 275.0, in 1970. The tax measure
on land assessments and land investments, a measure uncontrolled
by changing dollar content went up over 75 times, or from more than
$137 million in 1890 to almost $8 billion in 1970. The land area of
the central city remained constant, at 69 square miles for the central
city throughout the period.

Population

The capital is a borderline city, influenced by currents from
both the South and the North. It is unlike many northern cities,
insofar as it contained a substantial minority of black, native Amer-
icans early in its history. Many had come from the nearby southern
states of Maryland and Virginia, as well as from North and South
Carolina. In 1840, there were 1,700 slaves registered in the city,
4,800 negros (presumably free), and 16,800 whites (Green 1967).
The ratio of blacks to whiltes was to stay fairly stable for many
decades. By 1890, a few decades following the Civil War, the total
population swelled to 230,392. Of this number, the census classified
154,675 as white and 75,697 as nonwhite, or 32.8 percent. Of the
one-third nonwhite, 94 percent were counted as colored.

With the opening of the period under study, the first phase
showed relatively moderate population increase and rates of increase,
as compared to changes of later decades. Population almost doubled
in Period I, reaching 417,502 by 1918, the end of World War I and

the first period considered here. Within the context of current world annual growth at 2 percent per year (Nam and Gustavis 1968)—with a strain on world resources—growth in the District was great, but by comparison with its growth in later epochs, moderate. The greatest initial upheaval, still perhaps under the influence of the Civil War, was in the first five years of the 1890s, with annual increases of between 3.0 and 4.7 percent. The years following, in the first decade of 1900, showed more modest increases, hovering between 1 and over 2 percent per year, with as much as nearly 4 percent in 1911. Wars affect population upheaval in the capital city. World War I brought sizable gains, typically over 5 percent per year, and as much as 8.4 percent in 1918.

The numerical balance between the races during the first period exhibited increases for whites and modest losses for blacks, unlike the changing balance of later decades. Gains of whites were especially great during World War I, while losses of nonwhites reached as high as -3.7 in 1918.

Population again almost doubled in the second period, from 445,164 in 1919 to 875,000 in 1945. Population increases remained high after World War I, at 6.6 percent for 1919. Then lowered increases continued through the early nineteen twenties. During the depression years, overall gains climbed from 3.6 percent in 1931 to over 7 percent in the next few years. By 1940, a decrease had taken place, but 1941 brought a sharp rise of 15.2 percent. These increases remained large during World War II, at 11.4 percent in 1942 and 5.8 in 1943. Then small losses occurred.

Dramatic changes in population composition took place in the last two periods. Within the larger U.S. scene—and as a part of the upheaval taking place in the District population—were the effects of large-scale mechanization of the cotton and tobacco farms of the south, with subsequent displacement of black labor (Growh 1972). In the 1940s and 1950s, the great historic migrations of blacks to the "promised lands" of northern cities peaked. The movement neared its end by the late 1950s (Taueber 1958).

During Period III, the total population of the city was fairly constant, even showing small declines in the central city, with great gains in the suburbs. Washington, D.C. population peaked in 1946, at 899,000, and then declined to 756,000, in 1970. During the period the total number of the white population decreased in the central city to 210,878 in 1970, from 517,865; the black population increased from 188,765 in 1940 to 545,632 in 1970.

Yearly total losses reached as high as -5.4 percent in 1948. Gains took place from 1961 until 1964, during the Far-Eastern wars. Then yearly losses resumed. Nonwhite percent gains continued throughout the period, except for the last year. Between 1947 and

1950 these hovered around 5 percent, with peaks of 7.9 in 1956 and 8.3 in 1969, two years after the assassination of Dr. Martin Luther King and the civil riots. Losses of 3.3 percent occurred among blacks in 1970. White losses peaked at -11.9 percent in 1947 and -18.5 in 1969, turning to a gain in 1970. Typical of the third period were white losses of between 2 and 6 percent per year.

Thus, Period I can be regarded as showing relatively moderate change, with some black losses and white gains; Period II, with the forties, began the great transition in population change and continued the rate of overall population gains; while Period III saw the stabilized transformation of the city to a black majority and a fairly stable central city population size. Continued expansions were then directed to neighboring Maryland and Virginia areas.

Economic Conditions

Economic changes are tied to changes in population, and vice versa. In economic, as well as population stability, Period I showed moderate fluctuations as compared to later periods. Period II showed perhaps the most marked contrasts, with a number of counteracting cycles within it. It contained both extremes of prosperity of the late twenties and the crash of the thirties. Period III evokes the label of a relatively stable period of affluence, one that some mistakenly perceived as a permanent state, demonstrating that control over business cycles was achieved. This wishful thinking was to come to a close in the seventies. Wars throughout the three periods tended to be associated with relative prosperity in the District: World War I in Period I; World War II in Period II; and the Far-Eastern wars of Period III (the Korean in the early fifties, and the prolonged Vietnam War of the sixties).

Economic indicators for the District tend to be in general accord with national indicators, but with some exceptions, tending toward a lesser degree of recession in the city. For example, national indicators (U.S. Department of Commerce 1975, p. 37) suggest small recessions from 1920-21, 1949-51, 1957-59, and 1960-61, while local measures do not. The average consumer price index (Table A.10) began in 1915 at 31.3 for the Washington metropolitan area and rose to 117.6 by 1970. While the price index tends to coincide in directional oscillations with national business cycle measures, it is occasionally inconsistent with other economic measures used in Period II. A one or two-point increase per year in the price index is not uncommon. Jumps of as much as eight points per year can be seen after World War I (1918) and during World War II (1947); of 6 points after the Far-Eastern wars (in 1969 and 1970).

As can be seen, prices were fairly stable after an initial loss of a few points in 1932 through 1940. Almost no losses took place in the third period.

Annual data on unemployment are not available for the District, nor is there a major economic output measure for the city. The federal government, of course, is the major industry. Inconsistencies in federal employment recording practices, however, preclude the use of these data in upcoming regression analyses.

A good deal of the economic stability of the city can be attributed to the overall rise in civilian employment in the federal government located in the city. It multiplied (see Table A.11) roughly 11 times during the entire period, or from a total of 20,834 in 1891 to 327,369 in 1970. Data are missing for 1890 and for the depression years of 1894 and 1897. With minor setbacks, rises tended to be continuous. During World War I, the number almost tripled, and there were substantial gains in later wars. Following both world wars, some cutbacks occur. A low of 65,506 was reached in 1928, but steady increases took place until 1931, when a drop then occurred. From 1933 until 1936 gains continued in spite of—or perhaps at least partially because of—the national depression. Moderate increases then took place from 1938 until a jump occurred again, from 190,588 in 1941 to a high of 284,665 in 1943, during World War II. Drops followed frequently from 1952 through 1958, with the Eisenhower administration. Then increases steadily resumed.

The tax measures also tend to reflect changes congruent, on the whole, with national business cycles. (See Tables A.10, A.12, A.13, and A.14.) There was some decline, for example, in the depression years of 1896 and 1897, and again in 1900. Upward movements coincided with a tendency toward national prosperity from 1906 to 1912 in the first period. Then drops were registered in the depression years from 1934 through 1936, with an upward trend thereafter. No local evidence is suggested, however, of recessions in the third period, with especially large dollar increments evident for three years: 1960, 1967, and 1970. By 1970, the total sums collected approached $8 billion.

Overall, then, this cursory inspection suggests that economic conditions in Washington are not drastically affected by national downswings in cycles and tend rather to be at least somewhat cushioned by the relatively stable growth of federal employment, even during severe depressions.

The Police

From 1890 to 1970, the total population of the District multiplied over three fold, while the number of police increased by about fourteen times, or from 320 in 1890 to 4,436 in 1970. The police ratio (see Table A.1) rose from 138.9 per 100,000 population in 1890 to 586.4 in 1970. Thus the more than quadrupling of the police coincided with the multiplication of arrests for total Class I crimes. It is said that (measures are not obtainable) the ratio of clerks to arresting officer officers decreased considerably and that the efficiency increased, which should result in increases in deterrence efforts.

In rather similar change patterns to those of previous variables, the increases in police ratio tended to be gradual for the first period, with the exception of the prosperous years 1898 and 1899, for which jumps of 10 and 15 points occurred. During wars, there tended to be some drops in the ratio, with increases—as if to catch up—in one of the postwar years (in 1916 and in 1947). In the last case, the increase was up a hefty 87 points. Great increases were characteristic of the third period, following the civil riots in 1968 and in 1969. The police ratio then escalated in 1970 by well over 100 points. It would be interesting to see how the strike forces of other police units based in the area—such as the park police, the presidential executive forces, the Federal Bureau of Investigation, the Justice Department forces, and so on—swelled the numbers in the area over time. It can be surmised that the totals make the capital the most policed city of the nation.

Crime and Suicide

The number of arrests for Class I crimes, the subject of this study, are a very small fraction of total arrests. That is, Class II crimes, considered misdemeanors, accounted for from 89.8 percent of all arrests (24,372) in 1890 to 98.6 percent of all arrests in 1970. The numbers of misdemeanor arrests over time have increased much more than arrests for felonies. Tables 5.3 and 5.4 show the total numbers of arrests for each Class I person and property crime the total per 100,000 population; and the percent each constitutes of Class I crimes, decenially, 1890 through 1970.

The number of arrests for homicide, the most valid and reliable indicator of personal violence, increased from 21 in 1890 to 225 in 1970. The rate increased from 9.0 per 100,000 population in 1890 to 30.0 in 1970. It should be recalled that negligent manslaughter, which consists most frequently of fatalities from automobile accidents, were included in the series up until the last few years. Since, however,

TABLE 5.3

Number, Rate, and Percent of
Total Class I Arrests
for Person Crimes,
1890–1970

Year	Total Class I Arrests	Homicide			Aggravated Assault			Rape		
		No.	Rate per 100,000 Population	Percent of Total Class I Arrests	No.	Rate per 100,000 Population	Percent of Total Class I Arrests	No.	Rate per 100,000 Population	Percent of Total Class I Arrests
1890	2,453	21	9.0	.85	2,117	920.0	86.0	12	5.29	.49
1900	1,550	18	9.6	1.16	1,149	425.5	74.1	20	7.4	1.2
1910	578	13	4.0	2.2	78	23.6	13.4	4	1.2	.6
1920	1,718	61	14.1	3.5	228	53.0	13.2	7	1.6	.4
1930	2,294	54	11.2	2.3	358	74.5	15.6	8	1.6	.3
1940	2,973	59	8.9	1.9	496	75.1	16.6	19	2.8	.6
1950	8,448	75	9.3	.8	3,091	386.3	36.5	159	19.8	1.8
1960	7,029	96	12.6	1.3	2,566	33.7	36.5	132	17.3	1.8
1970	8,975	225	30.0	2.5	1,954	260.5	21.7	82	10.9	.9

Source: Annual Reports, District of Columbia Police Force.

these must have been few if any before 1900, and since these are excluded in 1970 counts, it is safe to conclude that this extreme form of violence has increased over time by over three times. The share of homicide in Class I crime arrests has increased, as well.

Some rather striking changes in crime arrests over time, as these constitute a greater or lesser part of total Class I crimes, may be noted. The greatest change is for assault, which is notoriously a poor indicator. It exhibited extreme importance in the first two decades, or in 1890 and 1900, accounting for 86 and 74 percent of the Class I arrests, respectively. It would be interesting to follow this lead with further historical research to see whether the period was one of violent upheaval or whether the emphasis on assault was instead a manifestation of changes in police enforcement policies or in reporting practices. The high rate of assault in these early years, at 425.5, was not again approached until 1950, when it reached a height of 386.3. The year 1900 did not register high rates for other violent crimes, such as homicide and robbery, but the rape rate was fairly high. By 1970, assault remained by far the most frequent form of personal crimes of violence.

Burglary was the most frequent type of crime arrest in the District, accounting for over 25 percent of Class I crimes in 1960, a peak of 46.1 percent in 1940, and almost 30 percent in 1970. The lowest rate of burglary occurred in 1910, and the highest in the decennial year 1970, 355.8 per 100,000 population. Even higher annual rates, however, were recorded for the Great Depression of the thirties (see Figures 5.1 and 5.2).

The importance of robbery, sometimes considered the "bellwether" of violence, has increased with time, accounting for a low of .16 percent of Class I crimes in 1890, 13.04 in 1920, and a high of almost 23 percent in 1970. The number of robbery arrests increased from only 4 in 1890 to 2,063 in 1970, or a rate of 275.0 per 100,000 population.

Auto theft accounted for 16.5 percent of Class I arrests in 1920, only 9.4 percent in 1960, and 11.5 percent in 1970. The number of arrests tended to increase almost steadily for each decade, except for a decline in the forties, when auto registrations also dropped (see Table A.12). In 1970, the number of arrests was 1,038, with a rate of 138.4.

Grand larceny is considered one of the most invalid crime measures. Its definition has changed frequently in the District. Further, the data are among the more readily manipulated in police reporting practices for Class I crimes. It was the third highest of Class I categories in 1920, or over 28 percent. It was suspiciously low, or only 4.3 percent, during the Nixon administration of 1970. Juggling such data is an avenue for "reducing" crime.

TABLE 5.4

Number, Rate, and Percent of
Total Class I Arrests
for Property Crimes,
1890–1970

	Burglary			Robbery			Auto Theft			Larceny		
Year	No.	Rate per 100,000 Population	Percent of Total Class I Arrests	No.	Rate per 100,000 Population	Percent of Total Class I Arrests	No.	Rate per 100,000 Population	Percent of Total Class I Arrests	No.	Rate per 100,000 Population	Percent of Total Class I Arrests
1890	153	66.5	6.2	4	1.6	.16	—	—	—	135	58.6	5.5
1900	165	66.1	10.6	20	7.4	1.2	—	—	—	162	60.0	10.4
1910	246	33.5	42.5	93	28.1	16.09	—	—	—	133	40.3	23.0
1920	681	158.1	39.6	224	52.0	13.04	285	66.2	16.5	491	114.1	28.5
1930	1,023	213.1	44.5	236	49.1	10.2	483	112.2	21.0	593	123.5	25.8
1940	1,371	207.6	46.1	551	81.9	18.5	310	46.9	10.4	442	66.9	14.8
1950	2,251	281.2	26.6	1,063	132.8	12.5	644	80.5	7.6	1,048	131.0	12.4
1960	1,818	239.2	25.8	1,066	140.2	15.1	664	87.3	9.4	509	66.9	7.2
1970	2,669	355.8	29.7	2,063	275.0	22.9	1,038	138.4	11.5	393	52.4	4.3

Note: Total Class I arrests are as follows: 1890—2,453; 1900—1,550; 1910—578; 1920—1,718; 1930—2,294; 1940—2,973; 1950—8,448; 1960—7,029; 1970—8,975.

Source: Annual Reports, District of Columbia Police Force.

Table 5.5 below presents the means and standard deviations for each Class I crime for the total 81-year period. Among property

TABLE 5.5

Mean and Standard Deviation of Nonwhite
and White Class I Crime Rates and
Suicide, District of Columbia
1890-1970

| | Nonwhite | | White | | |
	Mean	Standard Deviation	Mean	Standard Deviation	YEARS*
Burglary	372.5	198.0	73.3	42.1	81
Larceny	138.2	71.2	42.8	18.1	81
Robbery	156.8	100.7	23.9	16.2	81
Auto theft	106.3	90.3	37.3	29.1	57
Assault	273.0	256.6	28.9	29.4	81
Rape	13.9	12.4	1.8	1.5	81
Homicide (arrest)	21.6	10.4	4.5	2.4	81
Homicide (mortality)	20.4	14.1	3.4	2.6	64
Suicide	6.7	3.2	21.1	6.7	81

*Indicates total number of years for which data were available during reporting period 1890-1970.

Sources: Annual Reports, District of Columbia Police Force; and U.S. Office of Vital Statistics.

crimes the highest mean was for nonwhite burglary, at 372.5, and for white at 73.3. For person crimes, the highest mean was for assault for both nonwhites and for whites. The indicator of homicide mortality showed a mean of 20.4 for nonwhite and 3.4 for white. Suicide reverses the racial pattern, and the mean registered 6.7 for nonwhite and 21.1 for white. Auto theft showed a mean for nonwhite of 106.3 and for white of 37.3, while robbery was 156.8 and 23.9, respectively.

What years showed peaks and what years lows in crime and suicide rates through time? Figures 5.1, 5.2, 5.3, 5.4, 5.5 which follow present three-year averages for nonwhite and white crime and suicide rates. The first three figures are for personal violent crimes; the second two for property crimes. Peak all-time high rates were frequent in the thirties for the more valid indicators.

FIGURE 5.1

Three-Year Averages of Rape, Rates per 100,000 Nonwhite and White Population, 1890–1970

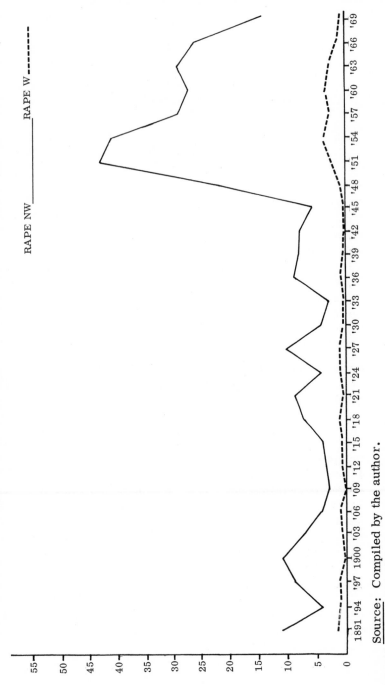

RAPE NW _____   RAPE W -------

Source: Compiled by the author.

FIGURE 5.2

Three-Year Averages of Aggravated Assault Rates per 100,000
Nonwhite and White Population, 1890–1970

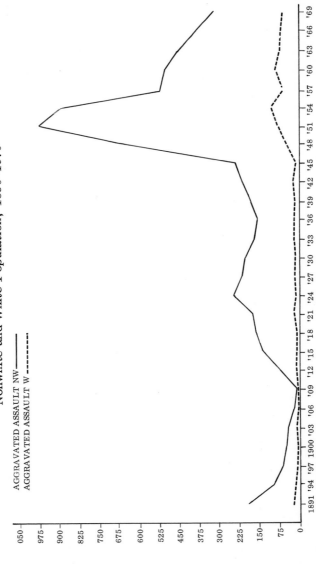

Source: Compiled by the author.

FIGURE 5.3

Three-Year Averages of Homicide and Suicide Rates per 100,000
Nonwhite and White Population, 1890–1970

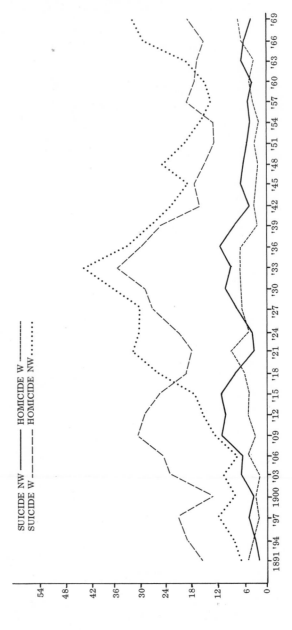

Source: Compiled by the author.

FIGURE 5.4

Three-Year Averages of Larceny and Auto Theft Rates per 100,000
Nonwhite and White Population, 1890-1970

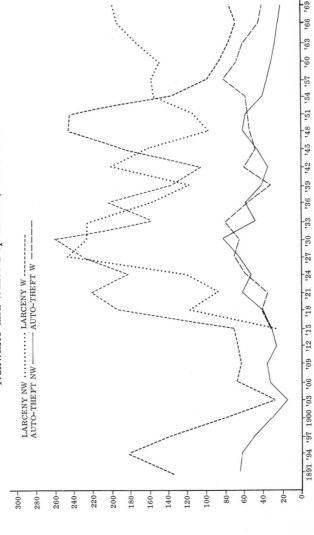

Source: Compiled by the author.

FIGURE 5.5

Three-Year Averages of Burglary and Robbery Rates per 100,000 Nonwhite and White Population, 1890–1970

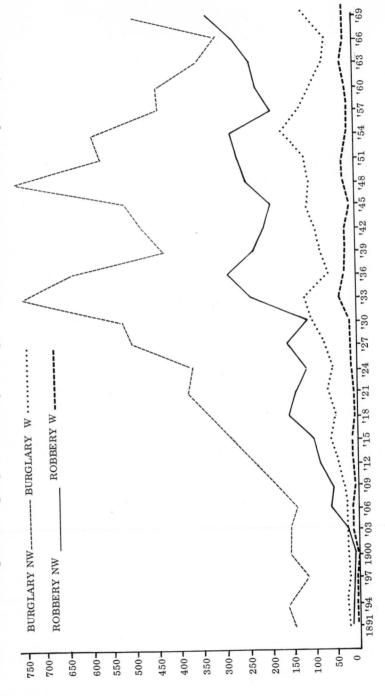

Source: Compiled by the author.

Homicide and Suicide

The variant reactions in extreme aggression by the two racial groups were notable in the peaks of black homicide and white suicide for the years of the Great Depression (see Figure 5.3). In 1934, the second period, the all-time high for nonwhite homicide was reached, with a rate of 44.4, with the lowest point in 1905, the first period, at 5.42. White homicide showed peaks in the second and third periods, or in the early twenties, and again in the last years of the series, with lows in 1902 and again in 1948.

Suicide rates of nonwhites were lowest during the earliest years, at 1.3 in 1890, and showed all-time peaks during the prosperity of 1909 (15.87), through the years of World War I. White suicide rates reached all-time lows during the earliest period and in 1901, at 13.2, just after a recession. An all-time high was registered during the depression of 1933, with a rate of 40.98. These data suggest that World War I provided a cohesive effect on the white population, but not on the black.

Assault and Rape

Rates for rape and assault are regarded as low in validity and reliability. These curves do not exhibit similarities to the curves of other person and property crimes, but do show fairly similar oscillations to each other. Large increases in arrests followed World War II for both racial groups, fitting with notions that war tends to increase the frequency of violent crime. Extreme peaks were reached in the early fifties.

Auto Theft, Burglary, and Robbery

In a number of instances the variant behavior of white and black crime rates suggests the differential impact of social structure upon the two groups. An example of this point can be seen for the curves of auto theft. Also, the auto theft rate—with its highly youthful constituency—sometimes exhibits tendencies that vary from other property curves. All-time lows were reached during the beginning of the series, showing 13.1 for nonwhite and 24.5 for white auto theft. (A slightly lower point was reached in Period II, 1939, for the white group). The highest peaks for nonwhite rates were in Periods II and III during the prosperity of the twenties, with lower peaks during World War II and again in the prosperity of the sixties. White auto theft showed some variance from this pattern, with peaks in the Great Depression years and in the late fifties and early sixties, with the Far East wars.

For burglary the all-time low was reached for non-whites in 1899 at 106.2, two years after that depression period, and for whites in 1890 at 17.5. The highest rates of this frequent Class I crime for nonwhites were reached during Period II in the Depression, peaking at 925.9 in 1934. The peak year for whites followed the Korean War in 1954, at a rate of 190.7. Robbery exhibited similar timings for highs and lows. The lowest robbery rates for nonwhites in the first period were at 3.3 in 1897 and for whites in 1890 at .6. Highest rates for the entire period occurred again during the Great Depression years, at 364.7 in 1936 for nonwhites, and at 57.2 for whites in 1934.

This cursory overview of changes in magnitudes, then, of the independent and dependent variable measures for the three periods showed a consistency. The first period of relatively moderate changes in social structure tended to exhibit the lowest rates of crime and suicide. The last two periods, with years of greatest upheaval in economic and population structure, showed typically larger gains in crime and suicide rates. The very highest peaks, however, occurred in Period II, with the onset of the Great Depression. It is obvious, as well, that similar historical crystallizations of events, as in wars and in riots, represented aspects of the social structure that did not affect all population segments equally, notably those of race and of age. These differences in the effects of social structure were reflected in disparate manifestations on crime and suicide rates through time for the majority and minority groups.

Much more experimentation on the timing, sequences, and degree of changes needs to be undertaken. Technical problems associated with the use of time series have not yet been given much empirical attention within the discipline of criminology. It would seem that this must be done if empirical advances on crucial sociological concepts of social structure and social change are to take place.

REFERENCES

Bell, Daniel. 1953. "Crime as an American Way of Life." Antioch Review 13: 131-154.

Bogue, Donald, J. 1959. "Color-Nativity-Race Composition." In Population of the United States. New York: Free Press.

Clark, Terry N. 1974. The Wealth of Cities, Municipal Performance Report. New York: Vol. 1, No. 3 (April): 10-20.

Count-van Manen, Gloria. 1976. "Macrostructural Sources of Variation in Homicide Victim Rates in the Capital City." In Victims and Society. ed. Emilio Viano. Washington, D.C.: Visage Press.

_____. 1975. "Uses of Official Data in the Evaluation of Crime Control Policies and Programs." In Criminal Justice Research, ed. Emilio Viano. Lexington, Mass.: D. C. Heath.

_____. 1973. "The Validity of Parent-Child Socialization Measures." Genetic Psychology Monographs 88, pp. 201-27.

Count-van Manen, Gloria and Cecil Josiah. 1974. "Person and Property Crimes as Etiological Types: Some Empirical Evidence for the District of Columbia, 1890-1970." Paper delivered at the Annual Meetings of the International Sociological Society, Toronto, Canada.

Dunham, H. Warren and Asuman Kiyak. 1975. "Cultural Change and Homicide: An Interrelationship." Unpublished paper.

Ferdinand, Theodore N. 1967. "The Criminal Patterns of Boston Since 1849." American Journal of Sociology 73: 84-99.

Gordon, Robert. 1968. "Issues in Multiple Regression." American Journal of Sociology 73 (March): 592-616.

Green, Constance McLaughlin. 1967. The Secret City: A History of Race Relations in the Nation's Capital. Princeton, N.J.: Princeton University Press.

Growh, George W. 1972. The Journey to Urban America. New York: Weybright and Talley.

Haskell, Martin R. and Lewis Yablonsky. 1974. Juvenile Delinquency. Chicago: Rand McNally.

Kuznets, Simon; Ann Ratner Miller; and Richard A Easterlin. 1960. Population Redistribution and Economic Growth, United States, 1870-1950. Philadelphia: American Philosophical Society.

Marshall, T. H. 1970. Social Policy in the Twentieth Century. London: Hutchinson and Co.

Merton, Robert K. 1938. "Social Structure and Anomie." American Sociological Review 3 (October): 672-82.

Miller, S. M. and Martin Rein. 1966. "Poverty, Inequality and Policy." In Social Problems—A Modern Approach, ed. Howard Becker. New York: Wiley, pp. 426-516.

Nam, Charles B. and Susan O. Gustavis. 1968. Population: The Dynamics of Demographic Change. Boston: Houghton-Mifflin.

Odajnyk, Volodymyr Walter. 1976. Jung and Politics: The Political and Social Ideas of C. G. Jung. New York: Harper & Row.

Seidman, David and Michael Couzens. 1974. "Getting the Crime Rate Down: Political Pressure and Crime Reporting." Law and Society Review 8 (Spring): 457-93.

Shaw, Clifford. 1971. "Juvenile Delinquency and Urban Areas." In Ecology, Crime, and Delinquency, ed. H. L. Voss and D. M. Petersen. New York: Appleton-Century-Crofts.

Simmel, Georg. 1950. The Sociology of Georg Simmel. Translated by Kurt H. Wolf. Glencoe, Ill.: Free Press.

Sorokin, Pitirim A. 1937. Social and Cultural Dynamics. Vol. 2: Fluctuations of Systems of Truth, Ethics and Law. New York: American Book.

Sutherland, Edwin H. and Donald R. Cressey. 1974. Criminology. Philadelphia: Lippincott.

Taueber, Irene. 1958. Population Bulletin 14, no. 7 (November), Washington, D.C.: Population Reference Bureau, pp. 125-51.

Thrall, Charles A. and Jerold M. Starr, eds. 1971, 1974. Technology, Power and Social Change. Carbondale, Ill.: Southern Illinois University Press.

U. S. Census Bureau. 1971. Income Characteristics of the Population: 1970, General Population Characteristics of Washington, D.C. Washington, D.C.: U.S. Government Printing Office.

U.S. Department of Commerce, Social and Economic Statistics Administration. 1975. Business Conditions Digest (February). Washington, D.C.: U.S. Government Printing Office.

Wirth, Louis. 1938. "Urbanism as a Way of Life." Journal of Sociology 44 (July): 6-15.

6

VIOLENT CRIME:
THE EVIDENCE

What insights can facts give to the long and violent political-ideological debates as to the driving forces of human destiny? Are these constituted by an economic, ideological,* or dire population determinism? As these factors may affect levels of crime generated by a society, does one or the other or a combination thereof hold sway? Or, alternatively, does widespread faith in the ability of the

---

*"A philosophy represents in the individual at least a partial transcendence of social circumpressures, his self-liberation from them; an ideology is the reduction of a philosophy by a kind of committee of the generation into a uniform credo . . . When ideas are used as weapons, they are finally evaluated for their fire-power in psychological warfare, not for their truth." See Feuer (1975, p. 190) for a most interesting discussion of the structural determinants of ideology. Feuer does not look kindly on the role of ideology in society. In this work, ideology is viewed more neutrally as related to value systems, as one of the possible cementing links in society. Feuer, however, reported an apparently contradictory view: "where ideologies flourish, the society is disrupted" (p. 193). Ideology is not under direct test here, but one aim of the research is to identify those structural forces which are thought to tear apart the dominating values and beliefs of society, whatever their nature. These can be interpreted, under Feuer's definition, as ideology. On the other hand, the resolution may lie in the plural versus the singular, or ideologies versus ideology. Rapid change brings about disruptions of society which, in turn, contribute to the multiplication of competing ideologies, or rigid views of life, whose effect is to further contribute to the warfare and disorganization of the social groups within it.

criminal justice system to control crime have an empirical base? If these three types of social forces, indeed, can be shown to regulate to a high degree the output of crime in a given society, are there implications for social input policies that can guide an escape from the very determinism implied? In sum, these are the broad substantive questions to which this research is addressed directly and indirectly through a multifaceted historical exploration.

Multiple regression treatments of time series are used to achieve insights into the ensuing questions: (1) the magnitudes and directions of correlations, along with the amounts of variance explained with the statistical controls exerted by the program; (2) the interactions of independent variables, as suggested by controls; and (3) the tested empirical base for the development of a macrostructural theoretical paradigm suggesting interactions between macro- and microelements affecting crime and deviance aggregate levels.

Multiple regression techniques are commonly used for the purpose of arriving at structural equations. This direction is considered premature at this stage of the research, although further explorations are under way toward this goal. Usage (3) above is uncommon, to the best of the writer's knowledge, at least in the discipline of criminology. The procedure taken here is as follows: at each step of the multiple regression, the amount of variance explained with the controls exerted is summed for each independent variable measure and grouped into one of three theoretically-based classifications. Thus, the percent variances explained by the price index, taxes on land and assessments, on banks, and auto registrations are summed and grouped into the economic factor. Likewise, the variances explained for each measure on population size, composition, and change are summed into the ecological factor; and the police force size and ratio, into the deterrence factor. Multiple regression is then applied—not without difficulties—to classic dilemmas of empiricism. Which independent variables (such as economic) are truly antecedent in time to the dependent variable (crime levels)? Which show substantial correlations, but are spurious in causality (such as race)? Which relationships show modest or even relatively low correlations, but may be crucial for understanding the nature of social processes at work (such as intergroup relations)? As far as the writer knows, there are no ideal techniques for resolving these questions. Multiple regression is used here, then, hand in hand with theoretical logic. After the results of these procedures are examined, in this chapter 6 (violent crimes) and in Chapter 7 (property crimes), the correlations are regrouped by those measures regarded as strategic for the development of theory. The results help to establish the basis for a macrostructural theoretical paradigm developed in Chapter 8, Conclusions and Implications.

LIMITATIONS OF PROCEDURES

It should be recalled that there are four measures tapping economic conditions and changes, seven measures of ecological balances and change, and two measures of police force strength. The unevenness of the number of measures for each concept—maintained for methodological insight and determined in turn by accessibility to date—raises some technical limitations. Empirical results for each measure, however, are not always congruent with the hypothesized directions of the technical effects suggested by others and are therefore reported. These points will become apparent in the analyses that follow.

All of the economic series except one, taxes on land and improvements, contain considerable missing data (over half of the years) for the first time period. Thus, correlational results are presented in the upcoming tables in the first period only for taxes on land, and so forth, for the economic measures. This measure generally proved to be closely correlated to the taxes on banks measure, so the substantive loss is not great. More than half of the yearly data are missing, as well, for two key dependent variables for the first period, namely, homicide mortality and auto theft (Chapter 7). For this reason, attention is drawn to Tables 6.1 and 6.2 on murder arrest rates, which are considered a relatively reliable indicator of extreme violence. Findings for the most recent time period (III) will be discussed first, working back to the earliest period (I). Crime indicators generally considered to have the greatest validity and reliability will be discussed first. Thus, homicide and suicide mortality and the murder arrests series are considered first, since rape and assault arrest rates are greatly underestimated and fluctuate over time in definition and prosecution.

The findings and analyses, it is emphasized, should be considered within the long-run purview of ongoing theoretical and research processes, both within the discipline and within the context of the present effort. The last constitutes an exploratory first step, reporting findings on correlations and multiple regression results relating both to theoretical substance and to measurement technique alternatives. Thus, it is hoped that the work can be considered as breaking ground in multivariate tests with time series, an endeavor of new application for criminology. Documentation is sorely needed on the dynamics of change, tests of competing theories, and on time sequences within one research design. This phase of the work moves, then, both backwards and forwards; that is, from tests of competing theoretical orientations to erection of new hypotheses from unanticipated empirical results, to the examination of these within theoretical frameworks, and to further time tests on the relationships.

Each of the four factors (the three independent sets of variables and the dependent measure on each crime and suicide) can be potentially fitted into the notion of indicators or time series that describe crucial facets of the condition of society. In previous assessments of the accuracy of indicators, the consumer price index, carefully built up over the years by the Bureau of Labor Statistics, is given credence, as is the importance of ecological changes. The Federal Bureau of Investigation crime index, however, is rightfully viewed as highly questionable (de Neufville 1975, pp. 111-19). It is this author's view that critics of the crime index, however, have tended to raise a straw-man issue insofar as the context of their discussion is usually the crime index used in its totality. In practice, this procedure is seldom followed by criminologists. As was documented in Chapter 3, Class I crimes are often grouped in person and property categories, and sometimes inspected individually—notably, homicide and suicide. Here, the tactic is to inspect individual crime measures that may or may not be evaluated eventually as reliable indicators of street crime.

The tables in this chapter present a series of measures for each race-specific crime rate for three time periods: correlations, the R^2s (amount of variance explained by each step in the stepwise regression procedure), the added increments of variance explained at each step, and multiple correlations. Total murder and total homicide rates are included so that the reader can make comparisons that testify to the advisability of utilizing race-specific rates.

OVERVIEW ON THEORETICAL PRIORITY

There is statistical priority for the anomie, or ecological factor for Class I violent crimes (see Figure 6.1) overall, with economic priority for those violent crime measures that are considered most valid; that is, in 13 of the 28 tests, the anomie measures contribute most to the variance. In nine cases, priority is won by the economic measures, and in six, by the deterrence factor. Murder arrests exhibit a notable variant: in four of the six tests, there are superiorities for economic measures, and in two for ecological. Further, if homicide mortality rates are summed for the two periods available, there are victories for economic variables in three of four tests, and for the ecological in the remaining one.

FIGURE 6.1

Percent Variance Explained by Macrostructural Factors,
Class I Violent Crimes,
for Three Time Periods

A: Anomie or Ecological
B: Economic
D: Deterrence or Police

CRIME TYPE	TIME PERIOD		
Homicide mortality	I (earliest)	II (middle)	III (latest)
Nonwhite	—	E 59 A 18 D 5 = 82	A 52 E 40 D 0 = 94
White	—	E 40 A 14 D 1 = 55	E 72 A 24 D 2 = 98
Murder			
Nonwhite	E 44 A 27 D 2 = 73	E 42 A 15 D 8 = 64	E 66 A 27 D 0 = 94
White	A 88 E 0 D 1 = 89	A 28 E 12 D 4 = 45	E 75 A 14 D 1 = 89
Assault			
Nonwhite	D 34 A 24 E 0 = 58	A 38 E 23 D 3 = 64	E 73 A 23 D 0 = 96
White	D 63 A 19 E 1 = 84	A 34 E 20 D 9 = 63	A 67 D 11 E 5 = 83
Rape			
Nonwhite	A 24 D 5 E 2 = 32	A 31 E 27 D 5 = 63	A 50 D 24 E 15 = 89
White	A 41 D 18 E 1 = 59	D 24 A 24 E 9 = 57	A 40 E 29 D 1 = 72
Suicide			
Nonwhite	D 53 A 10 E 3 = 71	D 31 A 22 E 18 = 73	A 55 E 8 D 2 = 66
White	D 33 A 16 E 1 = 65	E 51 D 16 A 14 = 83	A 50 D 22 E 13 = 86

Note: Statistical priority is calculated by the procedure described
in the text with the Multiple Regression IBM Program. In cases in
which measures do not add within one or two points to total indicated,
errors are due to rounding.
Source: Compiled by the author.

Results suggest some variation in the impact of structural
elements by racial group; that is, in all three time tests for nonwhite
murder arrest rates, there is a decided balance favoring economic
interpretations of priority, while in two of the tests for white murder
the balance favors the ecological-anomie interpretation. Since the
homicide mortality measure is more inclusive than that of murder,
identical correlations need not be expected. The balance for homicide
mortality of both groups, however, is strong for economic measures
in the two most recent time periods. Thus, for the more valid crime
indicators of extreme personal violence the antecedent link of
economic conditions is stronger than anticipated.

For the other forms of personal violence reported here, namely assault, rape, and suicide, interpretations are less sure. The correlations and their directions for assault (and rape) change over time, probably in some accordance with changing police arrest policies. For assault, tests yield three cases of support for the anomic-ecological interpretation, two for deterrence, and only one for economic (see Figure 6.1). It is possible that the sight of policemen on the streets in large numbers in the first time period did deter street assault (and rape). Alternatively, the changing priorities of police arrests do not tap real assault and rape crime levels or show consistency over time in bias. Escape from this dilemma plaguing the field is made at least tentatively by recalling the question being asked. What are the macrosocial factors affecting that sample of poor caught in the criminal justice process? A bias towards the powerless can be assumed as consistent over time.[*] Rape rates exhibit an even greater priority for anomie-ecological variables, or superiority in five of six tests, with one case for deterrence. If economic measures are lagged in their effects upon violent crime by two or three years, however, the size of the correlations with rape and assault exhibits marked increases. Thus, changing economic conditions through time are found to substantially affect variations in violent crime levels.

The etiological schema (see Figure 6.1) show unexpected directions for suicide, as well; that is, no prediction is made for the effect of the police force upon this form of deviance. Priority in three of six cases is found for the police or deterrence measures, with anomie-ecological showing priority in two time tests and economic in one. This result may have some theoretical validity. Alternatively, it may be an artifact of the program procedures. A number of ex post facto explanations are possible of the finding that the more police, the more suicide. The police, in collaboration with the coroners' offices, participate in procedures for the diagnosis of suicide (as well as homicide) as the cause of death. It is possible that the larger the police force, the more feasible and likely it is that suicide is followed up as a possible cause of death. As far as the writer is aware, there are no extant research findings on the point. The role of the police in the investigative processes of suicide has not been inspected. A second interpretation possible is that the police, along with other components of the social structure (population, prices, and so on), increase with time. This problem has been discussed in the chapter

[*]For an excellent recent review of the evidence and results of the effects of stereotypes upon the judicial process for homicide see Swigert and Farrell (1977, pp. 16-32).

on methods, and is a possible source of concern throughout the research. Still a third interpretation may seem tenuous at this stage, but it is a logical possibility that finds additional evidence in later findings to be reported. That is, increased police saturation, in the context of minority-majority intergroup relations, can be considered as a factor adding to structural strains and increasing crime and suicide, especially among the nonwhite minority of the city. Thus, this last explanation works in the opposite direction (positive, or plus) from correlational predictions evolving from hypotheses built from the deterrence perspective (minus). This should be borne in mind in upcoming analyses of the effect of police levels on other crime rates. The original context of the tests was for deterrence theory. In essence, the findings point to a development that represents the injection and application of an additional possible macrostructural theoretical orientation which begins, in this research process, to be considered as an alternative to deterrence theory in explaining the nonpredicted direction (plus) of findings with regard to the police, namely, those which fit more appropriately into rubrics of conflict and intergroup relations. It may be recalled that the effects of the police in deterring crime are hypothesized to be most strong in the first period, on the basis of the logic that the police would be more evident in a smaller population. It can be seen that the explanatory value of the variable is confirmed as strongest in Period I, for suicide and assault.

The third unanticipated finding is the impact of ecological change on suicide. The general logic of this work, however, is applicable: the more population change and upheaval, the greater the likelihood of structural anomie and increased levels of crime and suicide. The more common theoretical and empirical concern relates to economic change, with its impact upon changing social status, anomie, and suicide. The findings suggest, then, that changes in ecological processes may be important wellsprings of anomie, as well.

Murder rates represent the police arrest process, while homicide rates show the coroners' assessments of the cause of death. These two events represent two aspects of one interaction duality: the murderers and the murdered. Ascertainment of the cause of death can be expected, perhaps, to provide a more neutral setting for the elimination of human bias than that involved in an evaluation of guilt of a living person. While neither event can be expected to be completely free from bias, both are likely to provide random sampling to a greater degree than measures of other violent crime.

HOMICIDE

1946-70

A very high order of variance is explained for both measures—murder rates and homicide rates—with the etiologically screened measures used here: over 94 percent for nonwhite homicide and murder rates, almost 98 percent for white homicide mortality, and 89 percent for white murder arrest rates. (See Tables 6.1 - 6.6.) In the case of both measures, as was noted, economic variables wrest priority from ecological. Deterrence theory does not appear to be applicable to the nonwhite minority of the period. Moreover, the directions of the findings are consistent: the more police, the more homicide, or the opposite of the direction expected for the deterrence hypothesis. As can be seen in Table 6.1, the size of the correlations are considerable. Police force size tends to show high correlations, for example, .77 (significant at .001) for nonwhite murder. However, with controls no additional variance is explained by the measure. The high saturation of the capital with police during this time epoch can be interpreted—along with the drastically changed racial population balance and the black revolution—as a factor exacerbating structural strains affecting crime levels. Attitudinally, this is reflected in greater cynicism of blacks than whites toward the police (U.S. Department of Justice 1975) as reported in public opinion polls. The police are frequently viewed by District residents as an instrument of the national power structure, exercised in the District through Senate and House committees of the Congress.

The taxes on land and assessments measure is entered first. Correlations range from .54 with nonwhite homicide mortality to .80 with nonwhite murder arrests and .84 with white murder arrests (see Tables 6.4, 6.1, and 6.2). The consistency of the findings lends credence to the relative deprivation hypothesis which suggests positive rather than inverse directions for the relationship. Greater macrostructural strains are expected for those not sharing in the general affluence, in a society constantly encouraging all to share in the good things of life, that is, material consumption.

It is suggested here, more generally, as an interpretation of these and upcoming findings, that a high crime rate is one of the prices that must be paid by all for the current emphasis of corporate capitalism, as it is played out in this country through a penetrating socialization process within corporations and without—reaching even the poorest of homes with the aegis of mass television. This tenet is the working assumption that the only way to maximize profit is to sell by the creation of needs, even where these do not exist, and in spite of the inability of some to purchase. Part of corporation profits,

TABLE 6.1

Multiple Regression of Independent Variables
of Population, Business Cycle, and Police Force Measures
with Nonwhite Murder Rates, by Periods

	Simple R	Multiple R	R^2	Increment in R^2
1890–1918				
Taxes on land assessments and improvements	.66	.66	.44	.44
Rate of growth white population	.23	.68	.47	.02
White percent population change	.12	.71	.51	.04
Percent nonwhite population	-.63	.72	.52	.01
Rate of growth total population	.22	.72	.52	.00
Rate of growth nonwhite population	.12	.76	.58	.06
Total population size	.62	.77	.60	.02
Size police force	.57	.78	.60	.01
Police per 100,000 total population	.35	.78	.61	.01
Nonwhite percent population change	-.13	.79	.63	.01
Total percent population change	.07	.85	.73	.10
1919–45				
Average consumer price index	-.56	.56	.32	.32
Percent nonwhite population	.02	.63	.39	.08
Taxes on land assessments and improvements	-.12	.69	.48	.09
Taxes on banks and corporations	-.06	.70	.49	.00
Police per 100,000 total population	.30	.71	.51	.02
White percent population change	.09	.71	.51	.00
Total percent population change	.09	.72	.51	.01
Nonwhite percent population change	.07	.72	.52	.00
Total population size	-.27	.72	.52	.00
Size police force	-.15	.76	.58	.06
Rate of growth nonwhite population	.15	.77	.59	.01
Rate of growth white population	.15	.77	.59	.00
Rate of growth total population	.15	.80	.64	.05
Percent white population	-.02	.80	.64	.00
1946–70				
Taxes on land assessments and improvements	.80	.80	.63	.63
Total population size	-.14	.91	.82	.19
Percent white population	-.58	.93	.87	.04
Total percent population change	-.11	.94	.88	.02
Vehicle registrations per 100,000 population	.59	.94	.89	.01
Nonwhite percent population change	-.51	.95	.91	.02
Rate of growth total population	-.04	.96	.91	.00
Police per 100,000 total population	.73	.96	.92	.00
Percent nonwhite population	.58	.96	.92	.00
White percent population change	.03	.96	.92	.00
Size police force	.77	.96	.93	.00
Rate of growth nonwhite population	-.30	.96	.93	.00
Rate of growth white population	.31	.96	.93	.00
Taxes on banks and corporations	.70	.97	.93	.01
Average consumer price index	.66	.97	.94	.00

Source: Compiled by the author.

TABLE 6.2

Multiple Regression of Independent Variables
of Population, Business Cycle, and Police Force Measures
with White Murder Rates, by Periods

	Simple R	Multiple R	R^2	Increment in R^2
1890-1918				
White percent population change	.54	.54	.29	.29
Rate of growth white population	.09	.69	.47	.19
Total population size	.50	.75	.56	.09
Nonwhite percent population change	.35	.76	.58	.02
Total percent population change	.53	.93	.86	.28
Size police force	.32	.93	.87	.00
Taxes on land assessments and improvements	.41	.93	.87	.00
Police per 100,000 total population	.03	.93	.87	.00
Percent white population	.46	.93	.87	.00
Rate of growth nonwhite population	.06	.93	.87	.00
Rate of growth total population	.10	.94	.88	.01
1919-45				
Average consumer price index	-.28	.28	.08	.08
Percent nonwhite population	-.19	.46	.21	.13
Total population size	-.26	.51	.26	.04
Rate of growth white population	-.04	.53	.28	.02
Size police force	-.26	.55	.30	.02
Police per 100,000 total population	.04	.57	.32	.02
Taxes on banks and corporations	-.22	.58	.34	.02
White percent population change	.14	.62	.38	.05
Taxes on land assessments and improvements	-.28	.63	.40	.02
Rate of growth total population	-.03	.67	.44	.04
Nonwhite percent population change	.12	.67	.45	.00
Rate of growth nonwhite population	.02	.67	.45	.00
Total percent population change	.13	.67	.45	.00
Percent white population	.19	.67	.45	.00
1946-70				
Taxes on land assessments and improvements	.84	.84	.70	.70
Rate of growth total population	.28	.86	.75	.05
Size police force	.71	.87	.75	.01
Vehicle registrations per 100,000 population	.73	.87	.76	.01
Average consumer price index	.80	.89	.79	.03
Total percent population change	.14	.90	.81	.02
Rate of growth nonwhite population	-.07	.90	.81	.01
Nonwhite percent population change	-.25	.92	.84	.02
Percent white population	-.76	.92	.85	.01
Percent nonwhite population	.76	.93	.87	.02
Police per 100,000 total population	.74	.93	.87	.00
Total population size	-.53	.94	.88	.01
Taxes on banks and corporations	.77	.94	.89	.01
Rate of growth white population	.31	.94	.89	.00
White percent population change	-.02	.94	.89	.00

Source: Compiled by the author.

TABLE 6.3

Multiple Regression of Independent Variables
of Population, Business Cycle, and Police Force Measures
with Total Murder Rates, by Periods

	Simple R	Multiple R	R^2	Increment in R^2
1890-1918				
Size police force	.49	.49	.24	.24
Rate of Growth nonwhite population	.27	.54	.29	.05
Nonwhite percent population change	-.08	.58	.33	.04
Taxes on land assessments and improvements	.49	.61	.37	.04
Police per 100,000 total population	.40	.61	.38	.01
Percent white population	.48	.61	.38	.00
Total population size	.45	.62	.38	.00
White percent population change	.05	.62	.38	.00
Total percent population change	.03	.69	.48	.10
Rate of growth total population	.21	.71	.50	.02
Rate of growth white population	.16	.71	.50	.00
1919-45				
Percent nonwhite population	-.21	.21	.04	.04
Police per 100,000 total population	.19	.29	.08	.04
Total population size	-.20	.31	.10	.01
Consumer price index	.01	.36	.13	.03
Nonwhite percent population change	-.10	.38	.15	.02
Taxes on banks and corporations	-.13	.42	.17	.03
Rate of growth white population	.06	.47	.22	.05
Taxes on land assessments and improvements	-.02	.48	.23	.01
Total percent population change	-.06	.49	.24	.01
White percent population change	-.05	.53	.28	.04
Rate of growth total population	.05	.53	.29	.04
Size police force	-.14	.53	.29	.00
Percent white population	.21	.53	.29	.00
Rate of growth nonwhite population	.03	.53	.29	.00
1946-70				
Taxes on land assessments and improvements	.96	.96	.93	.93
Total population size	-.47	.97	.95	.02
Nonwhite percent population change	-.41	.98	.95	.01
Vehicle registrations per 100,000 population	.83	.98	.96	.01
Rate of growth total population	.06	.98	.97	.00
White percent population change	-.05	.98	.97	.00
Average consumer price index	.89	.99	.97	.00
Size police force	.87	.99	.97	.00
Police per 100,000 total population	.87	.99	.97	.00
Taxes on banks and corporations	.90	.99	.97	.00
Percent nonwhite population	.84	.99	.97	.00
Percent white population	-.84	.99	.98	.00
Total percent population change	-.02	.99	.98	.00
Rate of growth nonwhite population	-.27	.99	.98	.00
Rate of growth white population	.32	.99	.98	.00

Source: Compiled by the author.

TABLE 6.4

Multiple Regression of Independent Variables of
Population, Business Cycle, and Police Force
Measures with Nonwhite Homicide (Mortality)
Rates, by Periods

	Simple R	Multiple R	R^2	Increment in R^2
1919–45				
Average consumer price index	−.69	.69	.48	.48
Percent nonwhite population	.05	.75	.57	.09
Taxes on land assessments and improvements	−.13	.82	.67	.10
Police per 100,000 total population	.48	.84	.71	.04
Rate of growth nonwhite population	.09	.86	.74	.02
White percent population change	_.09	.87	.75	.01
Taxes on banks and corporations	.02	.87	.76	.01
Size police force	−.12	.87	.76	.01
Total population size	−.32	.89	.79	.03
Rate of growth white population	.15	.90	.81	.02
Rate of growth total population	.14	.90	.81	.01
Percent white population	−.05	.90	.81	.00
Nonwhite percent population change	.04	.90	.81	.00
Total percent population change	.08	.91	.82	.01
1946–70				
Taxes on land assessments improvements	.54	.54	.29	.29
Percent nonwhite population	.26	.84	.70	.41
Vehicle registrations per 100,000 population	.26	.87	.76	.06
White percent population change	−.04	.91	.83	.06
Rate of growth total population	.11	.92	.85	.02

114

Average consumer price index	.37	.93	.87	.02
Taxes on banks and corporations	.37	.94	.88	.01
Nonwhite percent population change	-.38	.95	.89	.02
Total percent population change	-.12	.95	.90	.01
Rate of growth white population	.23	.95	.91	.00
Rate of growth nonwhite population	-.10	.95	.91	.00
Police per 100,000 total population	.50	.96	.91	.00
Size police force	.53	.96	.92	.00
Total population size	.08	.97	.94	.02
Percent white population	-.26	.97	.94	.00

Source: Compiled by the author.

then, must be reckoned as citizen costs in devastated lives (both for victims and perpetrators) and in taxes for ever-escalating public expenditures made in the name of crime control, that is, the manipulation of the criminal justice system. Efforts of political control so exercised have yet to be documented as succeeding, except temporarily under extreme totalitarian conditions of control in which the elimination of the enemy is complete in aim. Such historical horrors have ranged under the labels of almost all political hues; under German socialism in the case of elimination of millions of Jews in concentration camps; under communism in the elimination of millions of small farmers in Russia; under democracy in the elimination of black males in revolt against their American fate; and under black nationalism in the elimination of thousands of countrymen for the maintenance of power.

The ecological measures show a superior weight (or 52 percent of the variance, as contrasted to 40 percent for economic variables) for nonwhite homicide mortality. The percent nonwhite, increasing in this time epoch, shows the effect of increasing homicide rates, even with controls. The variance contributed is insubstantial for the murder rates, but for nonwhite homicide (see Table 6.4) there is a moderate correlation (.26), with an increment in variance of 41 percent. Thus, the implications of the subcultural hypothesis is not clearly refuted for this time period; that is, the more blacks, the stronger the subculture (assumed), and the higher the violence.

TABLE 6.5

Multiple Regression of Independent Variables
of Population, Business Cycle, and Police Force Measures
with White Homicide (Mortality) Rates, by Periods

	Simple R	Multiple R	R^2	Increment in R^2
1919–45				
Taxes on banks and corporations	-.55	.55	.30	.30
Average consumer price index	-.20	.63	.40	.10
Size police force	-.53	.64	.41	.01
Percent nonwhite population	-.36	.66	.43	.02
Total percent population change	.13	.69	.48	.04
Taxes on land assessments and improvements	-.53	.69	.48	.00
Rate of growth white population	.11	.69	.48	.00
White percent population change	.12	.69	.48	.00
Nonwhite percent population change	.13	.73	.53	.05
Rate of growth nonwhite population	.13	.74	.55	.02
Total population size	-.45	.74	.55	.00
Percent white population	.36	.74	.55	.00
Rate of growth total population	.11	.74	.55	.00
Police per 100,000 total population	-.13	.74	.55	.00
1946–70				
Taxes on land assessments and improvements	.76	.76	.58	.58
White percent population change	-.42	.84	.70	.12
Taxes on banks and corporations	.61	.91	.83	.13
Total percent population change	-.13	.94	.89	.06
Nonwhite percent population change	-.10	.96	.92	.03

Percent white population	-.65	.97	.93	.01
Average consumer price index	.70	.97	.94	.01
Rate of growth nonwhite population	.13	.98	.95	.01
Police per 100,000 total population	.67	.98	.96	.01
Size police force	.64	.99	.98	.01
Total population size	-.46	.99	.98	.00
Percent nonwhite population	.65	.99	.98	.00
Vehicle registrations per 100,000 population	.67	.99	.98	.00
Rate of growth white population	-.01	.99	.98	.00
Rate of growth total population	.15	.99	.98	.00

Source: Compiled by the author.

However, findings are in the opposite direction for other time epochs, as will be discussed. The findings overall suggest that changes taking place in this epoch—of an increasing black majority—work to provide greater cohesion among the black population, rather than greater anomie and stress. For example, it is shown that the greater the nonwhite rate (-.10; -.30) and percent growth (-.38; -.51) in population, the less nonwhite homicide and murder.

There are a number of examples of correlations showing cross-race effects of ecological variables. In each case in this time test, however, while the correlation size may be moderate or even high, controls exerted with economic and ecological variables entered first, negate almost all or all of the additional variance explained by the variable. For example, note that the greater the growth of the white population, the more nonwhite murder (.31 in Table 6.1) and nonwhite homicide (.23 in Table 6.4). On the other hand, in this instance the percent white correlates -.58 with nonwhite murder and -.26 with nonwhite homicide. In all instances, most of the variance is explained away by prior entered economic and population variables. In the opposite case, the larger the percent nonwhite, the greater the white murder (.76, in Table 6.2) and homicide rates (.65, in Table 6.5). Again, little additional variance is added with controls exerted previously by economic and other population variables. The changing balance of majority-minority population ratios, then, shows some face evidence of creating strain on the opposite racial groups as changes in population composition favor one group over another. These findings are tempered by the effects of statistical controls. Should such findings hold up more consistently in other cities, there is the suggestion of interpretation of intergroup conflict theory.

TABLE 6.6

Multiple Regression of Independent Variables
of Population, Business Cycle, and Police Force Measures
with Total Homicide (Mortality) Rates, by Periods

	Simple R	Multiple R	R^2	Increment in R^2
1919-45				
Taxes on banks and corporations	-.43	.43	.18	.18
Taxes on land assessments and improvements	-.20	.53	.28	.09
Police per 100,000 total population	-.08	.61	.37	.09
Average consumer price index	-.07	.66	.44	.07
Nonwhite percent population change	-.10	.68	.46	.02
Rate of growth white population	.06	.73	.54	.08
Rate of growth nonwhite population	.02	.76	.59	.04
Total population size	-.24	.77	.59	.01
Size police force	-.30	.79	.62	.02
Percent nonwhite population	-.20	.80	.64	.02
Total percent population change	-.08	.80	.64	.00
White percent population change	-.07	.80	.64	.01
Rate of growth total population	.05	.80	.65	.00
Percent white population	.20	.80	.65	.00
1946-70				
Taxes on land assessments and improvements	.90	.90	.81	.81
Percent white population	-.74	.93	.86	.06
White percent population change	-.19	.95	.89	.03
Total percent population change	-.08	.95	.91	.01
Police per 100,000 total population	.83	.96	.92	.01
Nonwhite percent population change	-.30	.97	.93	.02

118

Rate of growth white population	.23	.97	.95	.01
Taxes on banks and corporations	.77	.97	.95	.00
Size police force	.82	.98	.96	.01
Total population size	-.43	.98	.96	.01
Average consumer price index	.82	.98	.97	.00
Rate of growth total population	.12	.99	.97	.00
Rate of growth nonwhite population	-.12	.99	.97	.00
Percent nonwhite population	.74	.99	.98	.00
Vehicle registration per 100,000 population	.74	.99	.98	.00

Source: Compiled by the author.

1919-45

The strength of the opposition of shorter, cyclical tendencies within the longer scope of this second and middle period is expected to minimize the strength of the overall associations. Included in Period II are the prosperity of the late twenties, the Great Depression, the prosperity that accompanied World War II, and the population changes that came with war. Total variances explained range from 45 percent for white murder to 64 percent for nonwhite murder. The economic indicators again tend to explain the greatest weight of variance (except for white murder), with the control procedures.

Note the shift in direction of the signs—that is, the better the economic conditions, the less homicide and murder, for both racial groups. Perhaps the era or eras are not to be characterized by rising expectations, giving more weight instead to an absolute model of deprivation weighted by the years of the Great Depression, with inequality lessening during World War II and increasing thereafter (Miller and Rein 1967).

The strongest correlation and the measure entered first for all four tests in the Period is an economic variable, usually the price index. It exhibits a correlation of -.69 with nonwhite homicide mortality and explains 48 percent of the variance. The lowest single correlation for economic measures is for white murder rates, at -.28, explaining 8 percent of the variance. Population changes of the period tend to work towards some maximization of homicide and murder levels of both groups, but the correlations and variance

explained are at relatively low levels. For both groups, the higher
the population size, the less homicide and murder. Correlations, for
example, are -.45 with white homicide, -.26 with white murder, -.32
with black homicide, and -.27 with black murder. Relatively little
is added to the variance. The ratios of the two races, as these move
towards parity in this time epoch, do not significantly affect the crime
rates. In principle, at least, the question can be raised as to what
should be the balance of population in the presence of majority-
minority groups to minimize crime levels.

Police measures tend to show relatively low correlations and
to explain little of the added variance, with controls. However, differences in the effects of the variable tend to be opposite by racial
group, showing aggravating effects on whites. For example, the
number of police per 100,000 population exhibits a correlation of .48
with nonwhite homicide and .30 with nonwhite murder, adding in each
case a few percent to the variance with controls. While the correlations
for white homicide for the police per 100,000 is -.13 and the size of
the police -.26 with white murder, little variance is added. It is
possible, then, that the effects of increased police size affect the
two majority-minority groups differentially in direction. Those with
vested interests in society are, it has been observed, more likely
to be deterred by penalties, along with those for whom change in life
chances are little anticipated. It can be argued that the latter point
was probably at its strongest for blacks in the earliest period.

1890-1918

The summing procedures suggest that ecological changes,
accompanied by white immigration in this period, are the most
important variables in explaining the variance of white murder rates
(88 percent of a total of 89). Throughout, the direction of the relationship is positive: the more growth and rate of growth, the larger
the population size, the higher the murder rates. For black murder,
the land tax measure is correlated at .66 and accounts for 44 percent
of the total 73 percent of the variance explained. Population changes
contribute most of the remainder.

The direction of the relationships to the economic variable is
positive once again, giving support for the relative deprivation
hypothesis for both races. It is likely that these results are explain-
able by even greater class inequalities during the first period than
the third, but no direct test can be made here of this point.

A striking finding, at odds with the possible time biases of
cross-sectional structural studies of the forties and fifties, is the
direction of the findings for the measure, percent nonwhite. That is,

the percent nonwhite is highly correlated, but inversely so, to non-white murder rates (-.63). With controls, the variable adds little (1 percent) to the variance, suggesting once again the spurious nature of the relationship. The same finding, in the opposite direction, is relevant for white murder; that is, the higher the percent white (.46 R), the more white murder. Again, nothing is added to the explanation of the variance, with controls. The effects, then, of race variables (that is, percent nonwhite, percent white) are mediated by other variables associated with them, such as economic. This interpretation is not new in the literature.

Thus, the constellation of factors takes on a varying weight nexus by time epochs, with occasional reversal of directions of impact, for the racial groups by crime types. In summary, a glance at Tables 6.3 and 6.6 with totals (that is, nonspecific by race) for murder (94 percent) and homicide rates (81 percent) shows that the economic variables contribute by far the largest amount to the explanations of the variance in the third and most recent period. Those for total homicide and total murder in the middle period give a lesser edge to the economic, and a proportionately greater to anomie. In the first and earliest period, the pattern for total murder rates alters yet again, with emphasis upon police measures and ecological changes.

ASSAULT AND RAPE

Assault and rape rates show oscillations over time that are similar to each other, but at considerable variation from those of homicide. In the third period the economic factor shows superiority in explaining nonwhite assault rates, or 73 out of a total of 96 percent explained. The direction of the relationship, however, is inverse and contrary to that found for homicide and murder. Ecological variables outweigh others for white assault in the most recent period, with 67 of 83 percent so explained. Population size and white population change tend to minimize or show inverse relationships to white assault.

The theme of cross-race effects again shows some impact, but again typically little is added to the variance with controls; for example, the more whites (see Tables 6.7 and 6.8), the more nonwhite assault, with .65 R in period III, but only 1 percent added in variance; the more blacks in the population, the more white assault, showing .44 R, with 5 percent additional variance explained. In the middle period, non-white percent population change correlates .42 with white assault, and .17 in the earliest period, while percent nonwhite correlates .39 in the middle period and .44 in the earliest. Population changes are generally associated with white assault in the middle period.

TABLE 6.7

Multiple Regression of Independent Variables
of Population, Business Cycle, and Police Force Measures
with Nonwhite Assault Rates, by Periods

	Simple R	Multiple R	R^2	Increment in R^2
1890-1918				
Police per 100,000 total population	-.58	.58	.34	.34
Percent nonwhite population	-.06	.76	.58	.24
1919-45				
Average consumer price index	.39	.39	.15	.15
White percent population change	.10	.45	.20	.05
Police per 100,000 total population	-.04	.47	.22	.02
Taxes on banks and corporations	-.17	.49	.24	.02
Taxes on land assessments and improvements	-.01	.55	.30	.06
Rate of growth white population	.06	.56	.32	.02
Rate of growth total population	.05	.58	.34	.02
Rate of growth nonwhite population	.04	.60	.36	.02
Size police force	-.08	.61	.37	.01
Total population size	-.02	.68	.47	.10
Percent nonwhite population	-.19	.77	.60	.13
Nonwhite percent population change	.08	.77	.60	.00
Total percent population change	.09	.80	.64	.04
Percent white population	.19	.80	.64	.00
1946-70				
Taxes on banks and corporations	-.67	.67	.44	.44
Vehicle registrations per 100,000 population	-.36	.81	.66	.22
Percent nonwhite population	-.65	.91	.82	.16
Taxes on land assessments and improvements	-.62	.94	.89	.07
Total population size	.10	.96	.92	.03
Total percent population change	-.18	.97	.94	.02
Rate of growth white population	-.07	.97	.94	.01
Percent white population	.65	.97	.95	.01
Nonwhite percent population change	.21	.98	.95	.00
Size police force	-.63	.98	.96	.00
Police per 100,000 total population	-.59	.98	.96	.00
White percent population change	.04	.98	.96	.00
Average consumer price index	-.52	.98	.96	.00
Rate of growth nonwhite population	.15	.98	.96	.00
Rate of growth total population	.09	.98	.96	.00

Source: Compiled by the author.

TABLE 6.8

Multiple Regression of Independent Variables
of Population, Business Cycle, and Police Force Measures
with White Assault Rates, by Periods

	Simple R	Multiple R	R^2	Increment in R^2
1890-1918				
Police per 100,000 total population	-.79	.79	.62	.62
Nonwhite percent population change	.17	.80	.64	.01
Rate of growth nonwhite population	-.01	.81	.65	.02
Percent nonwhite population	.44	.81	.66	.00
Total population size	-.49	.85	.72	.06
Size police force	-.69	.86	.73	.01
Rate of growth white population	.08	.86	.73	.00
White percent population change	.06	.86	.74	.00
Total percent population change	.09	.86	.75	.01
Rate of growth total population	.05	.90	.82	.07
Percent white population	-.44	.91	.83	.01
Taxes on land assessments and improvements	-.37	.92	.84	.01
1919-45				
White percent population change	.46	.46	.21	.21
Average consumer price index	-.45	.56	.32	.11
Police per 100,000 total population	-.21	.64	.40	.09
Taxes on banks and corporations	.24	.68	.47	.06
Percent nonwhite population	.39	.71	.50	.03
Rate of growth white population	.09	.73	.53	.03
Nonwhite percent population change	.42	.74	.55	.01
Total percent population change	.45	.75	.57	.02
Taxes on land assessments and improvements	.25	.77	.59	.03
Rate of growth total population	.09	.77	.60	.01
Rate of growth nonwhite population	.09	.78	.61	.01
Size police force	.31	.78	.61	.00
Total population size	.37	.79	.63	.01
Percent white population	-.39	.79	.63	.00
1946-70				
Total population size	-.73	.73	.53	.53
Police per 100,000 total population	.28	.75	.57	.04
Size police force	.20	.77	.60	.03
Rate of growth nonwhite population	.07	.79	.62	.02
White percent population change	-.18	.80	.64	.02
Average consumer price index	.48	.81	.65	.01
Percent nonwhite population	.44	.84	.71	.05
Taxes on banks and corporations	.36	.86	.74	.04
Rate of growth white population	-.00	.88	.78	.04
Rate of growth total population	.15	.89	.80	.02
Percent white population	-.44	.90	.80	.01
Nonwhite percent population change	.10	.90	.81	.00
Total percent population change	-.01	.91	.82	.02
Taxes on land assessments and improvements	.32	.91	.83	.00
Vehicle registrations per 100,000 population	.58	.91	.83	.00

Source: Compiled by the author.

In general, relatively low correlations are found for nonwhite assault in the middle period, with the price index exhibiting the largest relationship, at .39 R.

Rape arrest rates are considered among the least valid of the index crimes and are among the most underreported. Again the question might be raised: Is the bias over time consistent? It seems likely that males of low social class have been more consistently arrested for rape than have those in upper classes. It is of interest to note that there is a decided change over time, however, in the total amount of variance explained by macrostructural variables for black rates. Only 32 percent of the variance is explained by structural measures in the first and earliest time period, with increasing amounts explained through the second, or 62 percent, and finally 89 percent in the third period (see Table 6.9). The same directional tendency may be seen, but less accentuated, for white rape rates (see Table 6.10). No interpretation of this finding is possible, possibly until replication is found in other cities. It may be recalled that the ecological factor obtains a slight majority over others in five of six rape test cases, with the deterrence factor heavier than for murder-murder-homicide. This is the rare case in which there is found an inverse relationship with the size of the police force, or an apparent deterrence effect, notably in the last period for nonwhite rape (and to a lesser degree for white). It is apparent, as well, in the first period for both racial groups. The effect of population and population change shows for individual measures relatively low correlations, but cumulatively adds weight for the total factor, particularly in Period I for the white rape rates.

Correlations for the economic indexes vary in their effects somewhat by time period and by particular violent crimes. During the third and most recent period, a positive correlation is shown, that is, the more prosperity, the more murder and homicide for both racial groups, as well as for white assault. There is a tendency toward an inverse relationship for rape rates of both groups and for black assault. This inverse correlation holds for rape in both periods II and III. Thus, it is at least possible and logically likely that rape shows a variant structural etiology from homicide. The one case of an inverse relationship for homicide occurs in the middle period and may well be due to the varying cycles within the longer period. Further tests in other cities are needed for those indicators that are highly suspicious, but for which ex post facto rationalization in a theoretical vein can be made. It is possible that the more prosperity, the more alcohol consumption and the more murder. On the other hand, extended unemployment and depressed economic status could bring about a psychological state of powerlessness or anomie among large numbers of men affected, a state for which rape may be considered symptomatic relief.

TABLE 6.9

Multiple Regression of Independent Variables
of Population, Business Cycle, and Police Force Measures
with Nonwhite Rape Rates, by Periods

	Simple R	Multiple R	R^2	Increment in R^2
1890-1918				
Total population size	-.23	.23	.05	.05
Rate of growth white population	.14	.29	.08	.03
Nonwhite percent population change	-.12	.34	.11	.03
Rate of growth total population	.14	.37	.13	.02
Size police force	-.21	.40	.16	.02
Police per 100,000 total population	-.12	.43	.18	.02
Taxes on land assessments and improvements	-.20	.45	.20	.02
Rate of growth nonwhite population	.10	.46	.21	.01
Percent white population	-.22	.47	.22	.01
Total percent population change	-.08	.47	.22	.00
White percent population change	-.05	.56	.32	.10
1919-1945				
Rate of growth white population	.25	.25	.06	.06
Rate of growth total population	.23	.31	.10	.04
Size police force	.19	.34	.12	.02
Taxes on land assessments and improvements	-.13	.62	.39	.27
Total percent population change	.08	.72	.51	.13
Total population size	.10	.75	.56	.04
Police per 100,000 total population	.11	.76	.58	.02
Nonwhite percent population change	.10	.76	.58	.00
White percent population change	.07	.78	.61	.03
Rate of growth nonwhite population	.15	.79	.62	.01
Percent nonwhite population	.15	.79	.62	.00
Average consumer price index	-.04	.79	.62	.00
Taxes on banks and corporations	.10	.79	.62	.00
Percent white population	-.15	.79	.62	.00
1946-1970				
Size police force	-.46	.46	.21	.21
Total population size	-.28	.75	.56	.35
Police per 100,000 total population	-.39	.77	.59	.03
Rate of growth total population	.26	.80	.65	.06
Percent nonwhite population	-.23	.83	.70	.05
Taxes on banks and corporations	-.28	.88	.78	.09
Vehicle registrations per 100,000 population	.01	.90	.80	.02
Taxes on land assessments and improvements	-.34	.91	.84	.03
Percent white population	.23	.92	.85	.01
Average consumer price index	-.20	.92	.85	.01
Total percent population change	.01	.94	.87	.02
Rate of growth nonwhite population	.27	.94	.88	.01
Nonwhite percent population change	.34	.94	.88	.00
Rate of growth white population	-.07	.94	.88	.00
White percent population change	-.04	.94	.89	.00

Source: Compiled by the author.

125

TABLE 6.10

Multiple Regression of Independent Variables of
Population, Business Cycle, and Police Force
Measures with White Rape Rates, by Periods

	Simple R	Multiple R	R^2	Increment in R^2
1890-1918				
Police per 100,000 total population	-.42	.42	.18	.18
White percent population change	.26	.46	.22	.04
Total population size	-.32	.51	.26	.05
Percent white population	-.28	.55	.31	.05
Rate of grwoth white population	.07	.60	.35	.05
Nonwhite percent population change	.18	.64	.41	.06
Total percent population change	.25	.68	.47	.06
Rate of growth total population	.09	.71	.51	.04
Rate of growth nonwhite population	.11	.75	.57	.05
Taxes on land assessments and improvements	-.28	.76	.58	.01
Size of police force	-.41	.77	.59	.01
1919-45				
Police per 100,000 total population	.45	.45	.20	.20
Average consumer price index	-.36	.50	.25	.05
Rate of growth white population	-.01	.55	.31	.05
Total percent population change	-.00	.57	.32	.02
Taxes on banks and corporations	.12	.57	.32	.00
Taxes on land assessments and improvements	.03	.60	.36	.04
Percent white population	-.10	.61	.37	.01
Total population size	-.11	.66	.43	.06
White percent population change	-.00	.66	.44	.00
Rate of growth total population	-.01	.69	.48	.04
Rate of growth nonwhite population	-.04	.71	.51	.03
Nonwhite percent population change	-.01	.73	.53	.02
Size police force	.08	.76	.57	.04
Percent nonwhite population	.10	.76	.57	.00
1946-70				
Total population size	-.44	.44	.19	.19
Taxes on land assessments and improvements	-.12	.66	.44	.25
Total percent population change	.05	.69	.47	.03
Vehicle registrations per 100,000 population	.16	.71	.50	.03
Nonwhite percent population change	.16	.72	.52	.02
Average consumer price index	.03	.73	.53	.01
Police per 100,000 total population	-.10	.73	.54	.01
White percent population change	-.02	.75	.56	.02
Rate of growth nonwhite population	.03	.76	.57	.01
Rate of growth white population	.03	.76	.57	.00
Rate of growth total population	.17	.77	.59	.01
Taxes on banks and corporations	-.09	.77	.59	.00
Percent nonwhite population	.05	.77	.59	.00
Percent white population	-.06	.85	.72	.12
Size police force	-.17	.85	.72	.00

Source: Compiled by the author.

SUICIDE

Suicide is the price of civilization (Masaryk 1881; 1970). At
the same time, rates that are too high or too low (Durkheim 1951)
for a particular society are regarded as symptoms of something
gone wrong with the social state. Although Durkheim well recognized
that there could be exceptions to his general rule on the inversion of
the relationship of homicide to that of suicide, research since his
time has tended to verify the emphasis of his thought on oppositional
movements (Henry and Short 1954). Further, Durkheim and others
have suggested that sudden upward or downward changes in fortunes
should result in higher rates.

Suicide rates, then, are among the more dependable indicators
of extreme self-directed personal violence, thought to show etiological
opposition to homicide. Structural research on suicide has concentrated upon the correlation of business cycles, as a precursor of
anomie, to suicide. Less empirical emphasis has been placed upon
ecological changes as precursors of anomie, strain, and suicide. In
six tests (three time periods and two race-specific rates for suicide),
anomie-ecological factors carry the weight in two cases, the economic
in one, and unexpectedly, the police measure in three (See Tables
6.11 and 6.12). For the third period 86 percent of the variance for
white suicide is explained. The ecological variables account for 50
percent (population change positive association; population size,
inverse) of the variance; the police measures (positive association),
22 percent; and the economic measures (positive direction) 13 percent. About 66 percent of the variance of nonwhite suicide is explained,
with 55 percent attributable to the ecological variables, 8 to economic
measures, and two for the police (inverse direction). Thus, the
findings are consistent with what could be expected from the previous
broad outlines of the macrostructural upheavals in the most recent
period, emphasizing heavy population turnover and racial succession
effects more than prosperous economic conditions. Somewhat more
of the variance is explained for white suicide than for black in the
latest and middle periods. This is in contrast to the tendency for
crime rates, where less variance tends to be explained for white
crimes than for nonwhite. It is possible, then, in the last case that
microstructural processes may be more at work.

For nonwhite suicide the three factors are distributed fairly
evenly in the middle period with the largest weight for the police
(positive direction) at 31 percent of the variance, 22 percent for
ecological, and 18 for economic. In line with expectations, the
largest weight for white suicide is for economic measures, with 51
percent of the total 83 percent of variance so explained.

TABLE 6.11

Multiple Regression of Independent Variables of
Population, Business Cycle, and Police Force
Measures with Nonwhite Suicide Rates,
by Periods

	Simple R	Multiple R	R^2	Increment in R^2
1890-1918				
Size police force	.73	.73	.53	.53
Nonwhite percent population change	-.31	.75	.57	.04
Taxes on land assessments and improvements	.69	.77	.59	.03
Rate of growth white population	.14	.78	.61	.02
Rate of growth total population	.09	.79	.62	.01
Total population size	.67	.80	.64	.02
Rate of growth nonwhite population	-.09	.80	.64	.01
Police per 100,000 total population	.60	.80	.64	.00
Total percent population change	-.60	.80	.64	.00
White percent population change	.03	.81	.66	.02
Percent white population	.69	.82	.67	.01
1919-1945				
Police per 100,000 total population	.56	.56	.31	.31
Average Consumer Price index	-.53	.67	.45	.14
Rate of growth white population	-.04	.76	.57	.12
Percent nonwhite population	.32	.77	.59	.02
Total population size	-.11	.78	.61	.02
Total percent population change	-.06	.80	.64	.03
Size police force	.15	.81	.65	.01
Taxes on Banks and Corporations	.30	.82	.68	.03
Nonwhite percent population change	-.05	.83	.69	.01
Taxes on land assessments and improvements	.08	.84	.70	.01
Rate of growth nonwhite population	-.07	.85	.72	.02
Rate of growth total population	-.05	.85	.73	.01
White percent population change	-.07	.86	.73	.00
Percent white population	-.32	.86	.73	.00
1946-1970				
Total population size	.61	.61	.37	.37
White percent population change	.34	.64	.42	.04
Taxes on banks and corporations	-.19	.68	.46	.04
Vehicle registrations per 100,000 population	-.46	.69	.48	.02
Percent nonwhite population	-.33	.71	.50	.02
Percent white population	.33	.73	.54	.04
Taxes on Land assessments and improvements	-.25	.74	.55	.01
Size Police force	-.19	.75	.56	.01
Police per 100,000 total population	-.25	.76	.58	.02
Nonwhite percent population change	-.13	.76	.58	.01
Total percent population change	.25	.78	.62	.03
Average consumer price index	-.36	.79	.63	.01
Rate of growth nonwhite population	-.08	.81	.65	.02
Rate of growth total population	.02	.81	.65	.00
Rate of growth white population	.07	.81	.66	.01

Source: Compiled by the author.

TABLE 6.12

Multiple Regression of Independent Variables of
Population, Business Cycle, and Police Force
Measures with White Suicide Rates,
by Periods

	Simple R	Multiple R	R^2	Increment in R^2
1890-1918				
Size police force	.58	.58	.33	.33
Rate of growth nonwhite population	-.18	.62	.38	.05
Total population size	.46	.64	.40	.02
Police per 100,000 total population	.54	.75	.56	.15
Taxes on land assessments and inprovements	.51	.75	.57	.01
Nonwhite percent population change	-.27	.76	.58	.02
Rate of growth white population	-.03	.77	.60	.01
Rate of growth total population	-.08	.78	.61	.01
Percent white population	.51	.78	.61	.00
Total percent population change	-.17	.78	.61	.00
White percent population change	-.13	.81	.65	.04
1919-45				
Average consumer price index	-.71	.71	.50	.50
Police per 100,000 total population	.61	.82	.67	.16
Nonwhite percent population change	-.14	.87	.75	.08
Percent white population	-.21	.87	.75	.00
Taxes on land assessments and improvements	-.04	.87	.76	.01
Taxes on banks and corporations	.21	.87	.76	.00
Rate of growth white population	.20	.87	.76	.00
Rate of growth nonwhite population	.09	.88	.77	.01
White percent population change	-.13	.88	.78	.00
Total percent population change	-.14	.89	.79	.01
Rate of growth total population	.17	.89	.79	.00
Size police force	-.02	.89	.80	.00
Total population size	-.29	.91	.83	.03
Percent nonwhite population	.21	.91	.83	.00
1946-70				
Rate of growth total population	.51	.51	.26	.26
Police per 100,000 total population	.30	.59	.35	.09
Nonwhite percent population change	.26	.66	.44	.09
Vehicle registrations per 100,000 population	.13	.75	.57	.13
Size police force	.26	.84	.70	.13
Percent nonwhite population	.27	.87	.75	.06
Total percent population change	.31	.90	.81	.05
Percent white population	-.27	.91	.83	.02
Rate of growth nonwhite population	.28	.92	.84	.01
White percent population change	-.03	.92	.85	.01
Taxes on banks and corporations	.15	.92	.85	.00
Total population size	-.26	.93	.86	.00
Taxes on land assessments and improvements	.22	.93	.86	.00
Average consumer price index	.22	.93	.86	.00
Rate of growth white population	.17	.93	.86	.00

Source: Compiled by the author.

For the earliest period, the largest amount of variance for both groups is accounted for in the police factor (positive direction of correlations), which explains 53 percent of the total 71 percent for nonwhite and 33 percent of the total 65 percent for white. Anomie-ecological variables total second in both cases, while economics place third. The weight, then, of ecological changes superseding economic is a finding that suggests further tests for other cities.

The weight of the police force in contributing to suicidal tendencies among the population may be variously interpreted. First, as has been pointed out, the police take part in the interpretive process, along with the coroners' offices, both for homicide and suicide as causes of deaths. It is possible then that the more police, the more likely will be the reporting attention given to suicides. A second possible interpretation is that the presence of the police may be regarded as a foreign source of control by those outside of the power system, in judicial processes that have pretensions to justice and equal treatment but which, in fact, have been shown—and are believed—to be unjust (Swigert and Farrell 1977). The larger the police force, then, the greater are the anomie-alienation processes and suicide rates. This explanation may seem strained, but it makes sense of some other unexpected findings as well. A third interpretation is the weakness of the multiple regression program which arbitrarily enters the police force size in this instance first, since it exhibits the very largest correlation, even though other variables also show relatively sizeable correlations. Yet it is obvious that the size of the population and the economic conditions of the city are more likely to control police size, than police size to control these structural characteristics. Thus, the correlation is interpreted as spurious in its effects.

1946-70

As has been shown, there is relatively little empirical test of the popular and commonplace notion of rapid change. Here "rapid" has the potential of an empirical assessment. In comparison to past actual changes in size, there is an identifiable thread throughout this research: population change does significantly correlate with crime and deviance rates. A notable example, in this instance, is the highest correlation found between rate of growth of the total population and white suicide, or .51, explaining 26 percent of the variance; the faster the rate of change, the more white suicide. This finding is congruent with the hypothesis erected.

A second theme repeated with tests on other forms of violent deviance is found: that is, cross-race population effects that are posited to affect intergroup relations. Note (Tables 6.11 and 6.12) that the measure nonwhite percent population change shows a cross-race effect, or increases in white suicide. The correlation is modest, .26, but explains an additional 9 percent of the variance, with controls. Similarly, the percent nonwhite population shows a cross-race effect on white suicide, or a correlation of .27, explaining an additional 6 percent of the variance. The interpretation favored here of this consistent moderate but unpredicted tendency is that changing population ratios between groups characterized by the complexity of majority-minority relationships—with all of the ramifications that these unfortunately have meant—are sources of macrostructural strains on intragroup relations. Thus, increases in the size of one group is viewed and experienced as a power threat by the other. Realignments associated, then, with changing population ratios are posited as requiring, in both macro- and microstructured worlds, changes accompanied by stress.

Measures of economic conditions tend to show unexpectedly low correlations with white suicide, for example, .13 for the vehicle registration measure. Entered first among the economic measures, it accounts for 13 percent of added variance with controls. The largest correlation is .22, for taxes on land, with nothing added to the variance. Thus, the affluence of the period does not appear to substantially affect levels of white suicide, but does so in a positive direction: the more affluence, the more white suicide.

Correlations, with nonwhite suicide rates, are in the opposite direction, -.46 for vehicle registrations; thus, the greater the prosperity, the less black suicide. This fits with the logic of economists suggesting that the poor gain proportionately more than the affluent in periods of prosperity. Summed, the economic measures add only 8 percent to the variance, less than anticipated.

The strongest correlation (.61) for nonwhite suicide in Period III is for population size, accounting for 37 percent of the variance. It can be inferred that, given the tendency towards second-class status of the District minority in housing, increases in the size of population hold ramifications for increasing density that affect crowded black populations, as hypothesized. Population size of cities has received little empirical attention in a historical context. and the finding deserves tests in additional cities.

A modest cross-race effect can be noted again: the greater the white percent increase in population, the more the nonwhite suicide, with a correlation of .34, explaining an additional 4 percent of the variance. Consistently, the larger the white population, the greater is the nonwhite suicide rate, with a correlation of .33, and 4 percent of the variance explained with controls.

1919-45

The weight of the economic factors is more substantial in the second period. Note that price measures are not consistent in direction for correlations with other measures of economic conditions during this period, both for suicide and crime. The artificial controls exerted on prices during World War II is the likely explanation. Economic prosperity may out balance depression years, with the post-World War I and II years. The price index is entered first, with the largest correlation for white suicide, or -.71, explaining 50 percent of the variance; the more prosperity, the less white suicide. World War II, no doubt, exercised a cohesive effect on the white population. The second largest correlation is for the police size per 100,000 population, with a correlation of .61, explaining an additional 16 percent of the variance. Speculations on the nebulous meaning of this measure for crime levels was discussed earlier, and may again be relevant. Varying directions of the correlations for population change are evident. World War II, it can be recalled, brought about a great deal of migration to the city, and a changing population balance of minority-majority groups. Percent nonwhite shows a cross-race effect, again, of .21 R, but adds nothing to the variance with controls. The population change measures show low-order correlations, but tend to act as expected: the more change, the more white suicide. Individually, little is added by the measures to the variance, but summed, these account for 14 percent.

The more police there are, the more nonwhite suicide, with the police ratio measure entered first, showing a .56 correlation and accounting for 31 percent of the variance. The possible interpretations made earlier apply again. The price index shows almost as high a correlation, and is consistent in direction to the test on white suicide for the period, or -.53, explaining an additional 14 percent of the variance; the more prosperity, the less suicide, consistent with the hypothesis. Population changes of the period, while showing small individual correlations, in toto, add 22 percent with controls. These work toward minimization of black suicide. The period is one of increasing migration and opportunity for blacks in the city, especially during World War II. The percent nonwhite shows a positive correlation (.32), at odds with effects on crime. That is, the more blacks, the more suicide. With controls, little is added to the variance. Throughout this research the percent nonwhite and percent white tend to show spurious relationships (excepting cross-race effects). That is, it is likely that other structural factors associated with the status of black and white groups, mainly ecological-anomie and economic variables, appear to be explaining the relationships found.

1890–1918

In the earliest period, police force size exhibits by far the largest correlations for both racial groups, once again. The correlations are .58 with white suicide, explaining 33 percent of the variance, and .73 for nonwhite, adding 53 percent to the variance. Correlational size of both the economic and population measures is almost comparable. The tax on land measure correlates .51 with white suicide (only 1 percent added to the variance, with controls) and .69 with black (3 percent added). Note that the direction of the relationship for the economic variable is in opposition to that for later time epochs. It can be hypothesized that the proportion of poor in both groups is larger in the earlier than in later time epochs, and therefore the relative deprivation interpretation is more applicable. Alternatively, economic downswings are more critical in this epoch, with fewer social amenities to cushion the impact. It is difficult to test the assumption for changing class status over time with census data. Or, again, there appear to be common sources of variance at work.

SUMMARY

Routing of Theoretical Variables: Dissipation of Effects with Controls

Which factors seem to dissipate in their effects, with statistical controls, and which seem to retain their impact? One variable tends to cancel out the effects of others in numerous tests. A tracing of the histories of the variables through the preceding set of tables yields cues on the nature of their interrelatedness. It is clear that the development of structural equations, that is, specifications of relations between the variables according to a theoretical model (Van de Geer 1971, pp. 210–32) should be nonrecursive. That is, variable A influences variable B, either directly or indirectly, and at the same time B is a direct or indirect determiner of A, and so on. How changes in one variable affect others has been detailed in what has proceeded. Some tentative generalizations may now be hazarded, as a guide to further work on interactions of the independent variables.

Interdependence is almost a constant for the basic theoretical factors investigated over time, namely economic conditions, ecological changes, and police force size. There are indications, however, that the effects of yearly percent population change and rate of change are somewhat independent of others. For example, their variance is not totally eliminated by other variables, notably in the case of

Period III for white rates of homicide, rape, and suicide, as well
as nonwhite rape and suicide. Thus, the change measures appear to
be relatively independent dimensions of the ecological factor, as
compared to population size and to some degree the population ratio
of blacks and of whites.

Scanning of the multiple regression tables on violent crimes
shows that the effects of the police are frequently dissipated, that
is, little variance added, with controls exerted by economic measures.
Note the following examples: nonwhite and white homicide and murder
rates. Conversely, if a police measure is entered at the beginning
of the program, it tends to dissipate a great deal, but not all, of
the variance explained by economic variables. See examples of
white rape in the second period, or white assault and nonwhite and
white suicide in the first, working to minimize the effects of both
economic variables and population size. On the other hand, there
are cases in which the effects of police measures do not dissipate
the effects of other theoretical variables. See, for example, nonwhite
rape in Period III and nonwhite suicide in Period II. Again, population
size does not totally negate the effects of economic measures, in
instances of white assault, nonwhite and white rape, and nonwhite
suicide in Period III. These inter-relationships fluctuate over time,
perhaps reflecting nonconscious political policies. Population size
affects economic conditions and economic conditions, in turn, affect
population size.*

Occasionally the size of the police force does exhibit some
independence from the size of the police per 100,000 population, as
well as variation in direction of the effects. This gives some substance to the rationale used here. That is, absolute size represents
a mass over and beyond the ratio in its effects, especially in high
target parole areas. These are thought to be police districts with
heavy population concentrations of low socioeconomic status.

The impact of the percent nonwhite, or its converse, the percent white, in most time periods seems to be interdependent with
economic conditions, although it is occasionally less affected. For
example, the percent nonwhite tends to show evidence of interactions
with economic and population variables for nonwhite murder and
nonwhite homicide. In at least three instances in which percent nonwhite is working to minimize nonwhite violence, however, the effects

---

*Professor William Agyei, demographer with the Department
of Sociology, Howard University, has suggested that findings tend to
favor economic cycles affecting population cycles, rather than vice
versa (Galbraith and Thomas 1941; Kirk 1942; Easterlin 1962; Stys
1957; Freedman 1963).

are not totally dissipated by economic and population variables. This is so for nonwhite assault, rape, and suicide in Period III, in which a clear black population majority was attained. These findings do not, in their pattern, contribute support to subcultural explanations of violence among blacks.

Nor do the theme of cross-race effects always disappear with controls. For example, economic measures do not dissipate the effects of percent nonwhite on white murder and homicide in Period III: in this instance, the more nonwhites, the less white murder—an unusual case in direction of effects. Or, again, the effects of the percent nonwhite on white assault rates in the third period remain, after controls for population size. In the most recent period, the rate of growth of the total population and the police measures do not remove the apparent stressful effects of nonwhite percent population increases upon white suicide. Nor is the positive effect of percent white upon nonwhite suicide, in the most recent period, canceled out totally by variables of population size and economic conditions.

Increases in the black population in recent years show evidence of tending to ameliorate black violence rates, notably homicide mortality and murder arrests. Again, cross-race effects of these population measures show some tendency to increase white violence rates. These repeated findings in time tests with independently collected data (vital statistics and the police) strengthen an intergroup conflict interpretation. That is, strain is experienced by the group losing numerical strength to the other. The growth of a minority power base, given "colonized" conditions, leads to increased apprehension among the dominant group losing ground.

Differences in Etiology by Violent Crime Type

In summary, it has been demonstrated that over time in Washington, D. C. there are apparent differences in macrostructural etiology of violent crimes by crime type, by race, and by time epoch. These differences appear to be real, and the independent variables in their complexity of interaction demand the context of large social currents in particular historical time periods. A few of these themes will be sketched.

Unanticipated Findings

The strength of the economic variables proved to be greater than anticipated, strongly affecting in frequent tests those measures considered most valid—murder and homicide. Further, the direction of the effects of the economic variable tends to vary for crimes of homicide and murder versus assault and rape. In the tests reported, ecological changes are somewhat more crucial for assault and rape than for murder and homicide. However, when lagged procedures are utilized, as will be reported shortly, the strength of the economic variable increases decidedly for rape and assault. These findings suggest that the economic factor is crucial in the equation of violence for those who become involved in criminal justice processes, typically the economically powerless.

There is more support for the hypothesis of relative deprivation—although the direction of correlations is not consistent through all time epochs studied—than that for direct strain. That is, the noncommonsense notion, once again, that the more prosperity, the more violence, is most commonly found in periods I and III, with the exception of rape. At the same time, the assessment of these findings becomes difficult without sufficient controls for changing class compositions through time in the city.

In Period II the more prosperity there was, the less crime. Perhaps the weight of World War II allowed it to be considered as a period of national cohesion. It seems reasonable to interpret the population changes of the first period as weighted by emigrating whites coming from Europe, and disruptions of social relations among white lives—given a segregated city—adding to the factors maximizing white violence. At the same time, changes of later decades constituted blacks in movement, migrating from the South in large numbers. These movements, in turn, appear to have disrupted social relationships and maximized violent crimes of murder and homicide among blacks.

In both cases, cultural accommodations had to be made in large-scale movements from rural to urban, passing through at least a temporary state of anomie, collective rootlessness, and reorientation. It would seem that the bite of anomie from economic dislocations might be of a somewhat varying collective breed, with festering frustrations accumulating from the failure of the "land of promise" to live up to at least some of its impossible dreams.

Findings on the police show disparate effects, as well, on rape and assault rates, as opposed to homicide and murder. These differences in direction (minimization for the former, and maximization for the latter) may reflect real differences by crime in the impact of the police, that is, deterrence versus structural strains. Alternatively, these results may reflect severe reporting limitations of assault and rape. The more valid indicators of homicide and murder yield findings in opposition to directions of deterrence theory; that is, the more police, the more homicide and murder. The latter findings lead to an interpretation of the police force as a factor—in

the context of a justice system perceived and found to be unjust—adding
to structural strains. This can be considered as affecting blacks in
particular, who, as a group, have been largely outside the power
structure of the city during this period. The strains, then, may work
to magnify anomie and alienation, resulting in displaced aggression
of violence of black on black.

At the same time, gains in the black population ratio in the last
two time periods, and the rates of population change, conversely
accompanied by white losses, serve to add somewhat to structural
strains experienced by whites, evidenced in increased personal
violence perpetrated largely by white on white. Such cross-race
effects were not anticipated in the first stages of the research design.

Findings on percent non-white tend to suggest, consistent with
occasional previous structural research, that the relationship to
crime is spurious. That is, economic and ecological change conditions
associated with race account for the variance. At the same time,
the subculture of violence hypothesis is called into question by the
findings that the more blacks, the less violence, and/or that as blacks
increase in the population in relation to whites, there is less violence.
These relationships suggest real change, as well, by time epoch.
The common research practice of using total crime rates have probably concealed the directions reported here.

Population changes in period III decidedly affect nonwhite suicide
rates. It is a safe assumption that, as population increases, so
does density of population among blacks living in largely segregated
neighborhoods. The unexpected is that ecological changes tend to
show up more strongly than economic changes in explaining the
variance of suicide rates. Both factors in the change process, then,
are suggested as related to anomie.

The police force size tends to maximize suicide rates, as well
as those of homicide and murder. A number of possible interpretations
were offered in the case of homicide for these unanticipated findings.
The same explanations could be applied to suicide. The repetition
of the effect of police force size as a factor adding weight to both
violent crime and suicide levels favors the stress-strain interpretation.
The interaction of independent variables is the major alternative
viable explanation.

Transformations Over Time
of Ecological and Economic Factors

Gould (1969) and Gurr (1976) have discovered shifts in crime
etiology over historical time periods. A major theme here is, as
anticipated, that the effects of any one structural factor on violent

crime and suicide must be inspected within the context of other macro changes for particular epochs. The search for priority of structural variables has led to the affirmation of the contribution of all three factors to the criminogenic processes of the District. However, some are more important than others in specific time periods, with the weights of each appearing congruent with what is known about change processes. Summary correlational findings in Table 6.13 regroup selected independent indicators for murder, homicide, and suicide rates in the three time periods. A purview of the table enables shifts over time to be more rapidly viewed than in the regression tables. For example, the effect of increasing population size on white suicide is positive in the first period, while inverse in later periods, probably influenced by effects of suburban exodus. There are slight inverse effects of population change in Period I and a positive or aggravating effect of total population rate change in Period III, one of strain on whites. Moderately large correlations (.51 to .58) can be seen for all three independent factors with white suicide in Period I. Economic conditions moderate more in Period II and aggravate modestly in Period III. Magnitudes of structural correlations in the first period, are higher, interestingly, for nonwhite suicide rates than for white, with all factors (except percent nonwhite) positively related. Ecological factors (except nonwhite) tend to magnify nonwhite suicide in Period III, and prosperity tends to moderate.

For nonwhite murder, all three structural factors show relatively high positive correlations in Period I (from .57 for police force size, to .66 for taxes on land) except for the moderating influence of percent nonwhite. In the second period, accompanied by some economic gains in World War II, the economic factor shows the highest and moderating correlation (-.56 for the price index), while Period III shifts to a highly aggravating effect of economic conditions (.8 R for the tax measure) and police (.77 R), with moderating effects of population change (percent nonwhite population change -.51; percent white -.58). Similar patterns of change over time tend to be exhibited with the homicide mortality rates and murder arrest rates. Thus, these measures tap the outlines of major macrostructural changes over time that regulate levels of homicide, murder, and suicide.

The Police

There is little evidence in the more valid violent crime indicators that increases in the police force deter crime. In Period I, the more police, the higher are the crime rates. In Period II, however, perhaps with the cohesion exerted by World War II, there is some evidence of inverse correlations for the effects of police size

TABLE 6.13

Correlations for Selected Indicators with Nonwhite and White Murder, Homicide, and Suicide Rates, by Periods

	III MURDER		II MURDER		I MURDER		III HOMICIDE		II HOMICIDE		III SUICIDE		II SUICIDE		I SUICIDE	
	NW	W	NW	W	NW	W	NW	W	NW	W	NW	W	NW	W	NW	W
Population size	-.14	-.53	-.27	-.26	.62	.50	.08	-.46	-.32	-.45	.61	-.26	-.11	-.29	.67	.46
Total percent population change	-.11	.14	.09	.13	.07	.53	-.12	-.13	.08	.13	.26	.31	-.06	-.14	-.06	-.17
Nonwhite percent population change	-.51	-.25	.07	.12	-.13	.35	-.38	-.11	.04	.13	-.13	.26	-.05	-.14	-.31	-.27
White percent population change	.03	-.02	.09	.14	.12	.54	-.04	-.42	.09	.13	.34	-.03	-.07	-.13	.03	-.13
Total rate change	-.04	.28	.15	-.03	.22	.10	.11	.15	.14	.11	.03	.51	-.05	.17	.09	-.08
Nonwhite rate change	-.30	-.07	.15	.02	.12	.06	-.10	-.11	.04	.13	-.08	.28	.08	.09	-.09	-.18
White rate change	.31	.31	.15	-.04	.23	.09	.23	-.42	.09	.11	.07	.17	-.04	.20	.14	-.03
Percent nonwhite	.58	.76	.02	-.20	-.63	-.46	-.26	.65	.05	-.36	-.33	.27	.32	.21	-.69	-.51
Percent white	-.58	-.76	-.02	.20	.63	.46	.26	-.65	-.05	.36	.33	-.27	-.32	-.21	.69	.51
Taxes on land	.80	.84	-.12	-.28	.66	.41	.54	.76	-.13	-.53	-.25	.22	.08	-.04	.69	.52
Price index	.66	.80	-.56	-.28	—	—	.37	.70	-.69	-.20	-.37	.22	-.53	-.71	—	—
Size police force	.77	.71	-.15	-.26	.57	.32	.53	.64	-.12	-.53	-.19	.27	.15	-.02	.73	.58
Police/100,000 total population	.73	.74	.30	.04	.35	.03	.50	.67	.48	-.13	-.25	.30	.56	.61	.60	.54

Note: Period III is most recent.

Source: Compiled by the author.

139

upon murder and homicide rates. Interpretations of Period II are
tenuous because of the cyclical counteracting periods within it. More
detailed work is needed on this period, examining shorter cycles of
economic depression and of affluence, of war and of peace. In Period
III, in which police forces are at all-time high saturation levels, evidence contradicts deterrence theory.

Subculture of Violence

Green (1970) and Flango and Sherbenou (1976) are among those
who find no evidence of a special culture among blacks from aggregate
studies. Inspection of the impact of percent nonwhite and percent
white (the converse) and of changes in the population growth of the
two groups contributes insight into the question. The percent nonwhite can be seen to shift from an inverse correlation with murder
in Period I to a positive correlation in Period III. This last fact
could be interpreted to confirm the subcultural hypothesis: that is,
in recent years the more blacks, the stronger the subculture, and
the more violence. For rape and assault, the percent nonwhite
likewise shows an inverse relationship in the first period, but it
continues through the most recent period. Further, the multiple
regression tables show that the percent nonwhite, when controlled
for population and economic variables, typically adds little to the
variance explanation.

METHODOLOGICAL NOTES

To the best of the writer's knowledge there is little published
work within criminology, with the major exception of Thomas' (1926)
pioneering research, reporting results of time lags. Experimentation
here with 24 or more years, versus 5-, versus 9-year periods, and
so on, suggest that correlational results vary markedly, depending
upon the length of the period chosen for study. Table 6.14 exhibits
the results of correlations using short time periods for selected
independent measures with homicide mortality rates, from 1900 to
1970, for both racial groups. Variations in results found suggest
that seldom are all variables, in fact, constant. For example, it
can be seen that the direction of the correlation and the size of the
correlations between auto registrations and homicide shift markedly
during the period 1929 through 1937 during the Great Depression,
and between 1938 through 1945, which includes World War II.
Constraints on production and sales are likely to have altered this
relationship during World War II, and data for the total period reflect

TABLE 6.14

Correlation of Independent Variables
with Homicide (Mortality) Rates
For Selected Short Time Periods

	1900-09		1910-18		1919-28		1929-37		1938-45		1946-50		1951-55		1956-60		1961-65		1966-70	
	NW	W	NW	W	NW	W	NW	W	NW	W	NW	W	NW	W	NW	W	NW	W	NW	W
Total population	.71	.78	.73	.37	.64	-.70	-.09	.36	-.82	-.70	.66	-.43	.90	.19	-.14	-.66	.55	-.85	.21	-.27
Percent total population change	-.21	-.19	.22	.36	.20	.43	.11	.71	.29	.05	.42	.38	.72	-.06	-.06	-.27	-.76	.07	-.74	-.85
Percent nonwhite population change	.02	.02	.06	.22	.11	.36	.04	.73	.21	.03	.20	.35	-.16	-.67	.39	-.89	-.83	-.23	.88	.77
Percent white population change	-.26	-.24	.24	.36	.22	.43	.13	.70	.31	.05	.57	.35	.90	.14	.34	.47	-.33	.49	-.97	-.95
Size police force	.77	.81	.65	.23	.68	-.65	.12	-.10	-.18	-.16	-.32	-.95	-.88	-.52	.09	.98	.69	-.66	-.70	-.31
Percent nonwhite population	-.72	-.80	-.76	-.23	.46	-.84	.04	.15	-.45	.07	-.79	.39	-.96	-.26	.29	.94	.72	-.44	-.02	.43
Percent white population	.72	.79	.76	.23	-.46	.83	-.03	-.15	.43	-.07	.79	-.39	.96	.26	-.29	-.94	-.72	.45	.02	-.43
Rate of growth total population	-.29	-.26	-.12	-.02	.47	-.08	.14	.36	.25	.31	.17	.96	.20	-.04	-.29	-.11	-.67	.41	-.72	-.57
Rate of growth nonwhite	-.28	-.30	-.40	-.55	-.17	.18	-.01	.85	-.20	-.26	-.37	-.87	-.85	-.64	-.05	-.23	-.83	.08	.94	.78
Rate of growth white	-.13	-.12	.34	.52	.20	-.17	.20	-.82	.14	.07	.48	.85	.91	.67	.10	.25	.84	.00	-.98	-.82
Total auto registrations	—	—	—	—	.40	-.55	-.57	-.38	.90	.71	.82	.30	-.94	-.47	.16	.69	.77	-.15	-.19	.28
Taxes on banks and corporations	—	—	.08	.04	.55	-.59	.25	-.81	-.80	-.48	.62	-.32	-.90	-.03	.27	.95	.66	-.52	-.47	-.46
Taxes on land assessments and improvements	.61	.67	.70	.02	.69	-.78	.74	-.49	-.83	-.66	.63	.41	-.93	-.14	.47	.72	.77	-.25	-.55	-.11
Average consumer price index	.71	.80	.81	.23	-.36	.48	-.74	-.23	-.90	-.69	-.85	-.08	-.76	-.05	.39	.87	.77	-.39	-.51	-.06

Source: Compiled by the author

such discontinuities. Again, the size of the correlations of the size of the police force to homicide is positive during 1956 through 1960, and inverse for the years 1966 through 1970. The reader can observe other examples.

Time Lags

The implication of time lags is that effects are magnified gradually over time. Multiplier effects may take place because (1) action is slow to change because of inertia, or habitual reactions to changes in social structure; or (2) variations in other variables may superimpose themselves, in reaction to change; or (3) stress may be cumulative in effect. An example of (2) and (3) would be that, during periods of depression, unemployment payments run out.

Limited experimentation was undertaken with concurrent, one-, two-, and three-year lags with selected indicators for three sets of independent variables. There is a thread of continuity in the few research efforts utilizing lags for economic indicators. Such experimentation was undertaken here, as well, with the size of population and of the police force. Not as much variation was noted from lagged effects with these measures as with the economic.

Economic indicators (see Table 6.15) show remarkably consistent lagged effects on crimes of assault and rape, with little effect on suicide. Most striking are the effects of a three-year lag upon the rape and assault rates in the most recent time period. Note the jump from a correlation of -.34 to -.85 with the land tax measure, from -.20 to -.88 for the price index for nonwhite rape, and from -.12 to -.52, .03 to -.41 R for white rape rates. These findings, with notably uncertain measures, are found to be repeated with other economic indicators used, as well, raising substantial problems for interpretation. Little, if any, work has been done—to the best of the writer's knowledge—on macrostructural effects upon these violent crimes. On the other hand, a great deal of attention has been given to microstructural interaction patterns (see Wolfgang 1967 on homicide and Viano 1976 on rape). An ex post facto interpretation is that pressures from business cycles exacerbate with time, affecting patterns of microinteraction, triggering violence. This hypothesis should be tested with both macro- and microstructural data in additional cities.

TABLE 6.15

Examples of Correlations
for Lagged Effects of Economic Indicators
with Selected Nonwhite and White Violent Crimes,
by Periods

	YEAR LAG							
	0		1		2		3	
	NW	W	NW	W	NW	W	NW	W
1919-45								
Suicide								
Consumer price index	-.53	.71	-.43	-.44	-.27	-.20	-.17	.01
Land assessments and improvements	.08	-.04	.17	.02	.22	.04	.30	.20
Rape								
Consumer price index	-.04	-.36	-.01	-.27	-.09	-.10	-.17	-.02
Land assessments and improvements	-.13	.03	-.15	.09	-.13	.02	.03	.01
1946-70								
Suicide								
Consumer price index	-.37	.22	-.19	.32	-.17	.33	-.11	.29
Land assessments and improvements	-.25	.22	-.10	.32	-.07	.27	-.07	.21
Assault								
Consumer price index	-.52	.48	-.64	.43	-.83	.26	-.90	.08
Land assessments and improvements	-.62	.32	-.72	.25	-.81	.06	-.84	-.04
Rape								
Consumer price index	-.20	.03	-.30	-.01	-.50	-.11	-.88	-.41
Land assessments and improvements	-.34	-.12	-.44	-.20	-.63	-.33	-.85	-.52

Source: Compiled by the author.

REFERENCES

de Neufville, Judith Innes. 1975. Social Indicators and Policy.
New York: Elsevier.

Doerner, William G. 1976. "The Index of Southernness Revisited:
The Influence of Wherefrom Upon Whodunnit." In Social Systems,
Crime, Delinquency and Deviance: A Reader in Structurally Oriented
Studies, ed. Gloria Count-van Manen. Washington, D.C.: University Press of America.

Durkheim, Emile. 1951. Suicide. Translated by John A. Spaulding and George Simpson. Glencoe, Ill.: Free Press.

Easterlin, Richard. 1962. The American Baby Boom in Historical Perspective. New York: National Bureau of Economic Research.

Feuer, Lewis S. 1975. Ideology and the Ideologists. New York: Harper and Row.

Freedman, Deborah S. 1963. "The Relation of Economic Status to Fertility." American Economic Review 53 (June): 414-26.

Galbraith, Virginia and Dorothy S. Thomas. 1941. "Birth Rates and the Inter-war Business Cycles." Journal of American Statistical Association 36 (December): 465-76.

Gould, Leroy C. 1969. "The Changing Structure of Property Crime in an Affluent Society." Social Forces 48 (September): 1-10.

Gurr, Ted Robert. 1976. Rogues, Rebels, and Reformers: A Political History of Urban Crime and Conflict. Beverly Hills: Sage Publications.

Henry, Andrew F. and James F. Short, Jr. 1954, 1964. Suicide and Homicide. New York: Free Press.

Kirk, Dudley. 1942. "The Relation of Employment Levels to Births in Germany." Milbank Memorial Fund Quarterly 28 (April): 126-38.

Masaryk, Thomas G. 1881, 1970. Suicide and the Meaning of Civilization. Chicago: University of Chicago Press.

Miller, S. M. and Martin Rein. 1966. "Poverty, Inequality, and Policy." In Social Problems—A Modern Approach, ed. Howard Becker. New York: Wiley.

Sheldon, Eleanor Bernert and Wilbert E. Moore, eds. 1968. Indicators of Social Change: Concepts and Measurements. New York: Russell Sage Foundation.

Stys, W. 1957. "The Influence of Economic Conditions on the Fertility of Peasant Women." Population Studies 11 (November): 136-48.

Swigert, Victoria Lynn and Ronald A Farrell. 1977. "Normal Homicides and the Law." American Sociological Review 42 (February).

Thomas, Dorothy Swaine. 1926. Social Aspects of the Business Cycle. New York: Gordon and Breach.

Van de Geer, John P. 1971. Introduction to Multivariate Analysis for the Social Sciences. San Francisco: Freeman.

Viano, Emilio C., ed. 1976. Victims and Society. Washington, D.C.: Visage Press.

Wolfgang, Marvin E. 1967. Studies in Homicide. New York: Harper and Row.

7

PROPERTY CRIMES

HYPOTHESES

There are at least three general classes of hypotheses derivable from varying theoretical positions as to the relationship of economic conditions to property crimes. Two of these conflict with each other in directional outcome (that is, inverse versus positive correlations). One line of reasoning suggests|that economic depressions lead to stress and strain and increases in crime levels, whereas economic prosperity is accompanied by decreases. In this context, the question must be raised as to which classes of people achieve gains and which suffer losses—both relative and absolute—during periods of economic recession and prosperity. Moss (1965, p. 456) reasons as follows:

> Economic growth generally provides growing income for nearly everyone, if the growth is at least as fast as the growth in the number of people available for jobs. In fact, it particularly helps the poor in the sense that a failure of the economy to grow, as in a recession, generally affects the unskilled, uneducated worker more than others. A strongly rising economy benefits the poor more than one rising less strongly.

Crimes committed by the poorest classes, as earlier documented here, are highly represented in official crime data. And relatively large proportions of some minorities, in particular blacks in Washington, live in poverty. If Moss is correct, then street crimes should decrease in prosperous times and increase during periods of recession-depression.

On the other hand, those emphasizing the concept of relative deprivation (Bienen 1968, p. 16) suggest that, while prosperity benefits the poor, improved conditions are often actually accompanied by increasing crime rates. This position links improvements of those in depressed social positions, paradoxically, to periods of civil violence and crime. The crucial intervening variable is posited to be rising expectations and hopes that accompany improved status, where previously there was despair and passivity.

Gould (1969) voices still a third purview: opportunities for the commission of property crimes should be examined. When commodities, such as automobiles and money are scarce, it is more difficult to commit property crimes:

> During a period of abundance, increases in the availability of property would be followed by increases in the rate of theft against that property, while decreases in availability would be followed by decreases in the crime rate. (Gould 1969, p. 58)

Thus, Gould's reasoning agrees with directions indicated by the relative deprivation hypothesis, that is, a positive correlation, or rising property crime should accompany prosperous economic conditions.

Gould's empirical tests with national data on auto theft and bank robbery (uncontrolled, apparently, for changing population and population composition) identified a sharp shift in directions of correlations through time. He found an inverse correlation between registered motor vehicles and motor vehicle theft of -.73 R between 1933 and 1949—encompassed here in Period I—and a positive correlation, .97, from 1950 through 1965—encompassed here in Period III (Gould 1969, p. 52). The author's explanation centered upon the increasing youthfulness and amateurism (assumed) of auto theft over time. In years of affluence, relative deprivation, he conjectured, is experienced most acutely by those groups and individuals not sharing in the ownership of goods that are so conspicuously abundant in life styles of others. Further, periods of greater scarcity in the circulation of goods, as in the 1930s and 1940s, exhibit diminished property ownership and greater efforts for the protection of scarce goods. During scarcity, then, recruits into auto theft and other property crimes are more likely to consist heavily of professional criminals. Such shifts in composition within crime categories over time, then, should be accompanied by changing etiologies. Questions may be raised on Gould's research. First, apparently no controls were exerted on either independent or dependent variables for population, race, or age, in the national counts used. Second, some of his assumptions may be questioned—notably, that protection of goods is greatest in periods of scarcity. No evidence is given, and the writer would raise the opposite hypothesis: that magnitudes of effort for protection

of homes and banks from burglary and robbery, aided by technology,
have been great in recent periods of prosperity. Third, there is
reason to believe that, in Washington at least, burglary involvement
is actually increasing in professional activity, while other crimes
are growing more amateur. The evidence of both Gould and this
writer on the point tends to rest on changing age distributions; that
is, the increasing involvement of youth over time is likely to be
amateur. This assumption is probably, but not necessarily, justified.
The writer suggests an alternative explanation for shifts in correlational directions over time: changing patterns of relationships within
constellations of macrostructural processes identified here. This
alternative proves more consistent with findings to be reported, as
will be explained shortly.

Sutherland (1937) considered professional thieves a genuinely
interactive group, in close communication networks, occupied full
time in crafts demanding rational planning and skills. Professional
criminals are thought to be poorly represented in the criminal justice
processes, in contrast to youthful amateurs. Thus, it is possible
that theoretical perspectives emphasizing rational calculations inherent
in cost-benefit models may be most applicable to group processes for
professional theft, whether of the street or white-collar* varieties.
Little attention has been given to the effects of periods of depression
and of affluence upon the milieus of corporate existence that push
toward crime in greater or lesser degree. A question must at least
be raised when considering the effects of changing macroprocesses.
Is stress experienced more acutely by those who sustain small incre-
mental drops in resources at the bottom, or by those who experience
great drops, from the top? Experientially, any such debate is usually
fired by individuals, each of whom thinks that his or her particular
breed of suffering is unique and greatest. It may prove possible to
explore the possibility of aggregate measurement of white-collar
crime, as affected by macrostructural changes.

---

*The writer is suggesting that white-collar crime may be,
potentially at least, considered to be professional crime. The obvious first question is the degree of involvement in illegality that
should be considered full-time. If price-fixing on goods and services
operates full-time, yet takes a relatively small proportion of
managerial hours, should the effect be considered full-time criminal
activity? If the product instead of the criminal is inspected the answer would be in the affirmative. In contrast, at the other extreme
of social status, part-time involvement in street crime frequently
brands total life chances of individuals.

Interviews with sensitively located police observers[*] in the District tend to confirm, impressionistically, Gould's observations of a shift in the composition of property crimes from professional to amateur among those arrested for property crimes, with the major exception of burglary. It is hypothesized, however, that burglary is an exception in the city: instead of moving toward more amateur involvement over time—contrasting with auto theft, grand larceny, and robbery—it is becoming more professionalized. This line of reasoning, if accurate, may be due to special conditions of the District. As has been detailed, Washington, D.C. exhibits the following characteristics pertinent to this analysis: high saturation of police forces, close coexistence of extreme poverty and extreme wealth, and relatively compact territorial areas with concentrations of wealthy homes and apartments. Street robbery is said to bring relatively small financial returns, while incurring relatively high risks of identification. Burglary, on the other hand, is said to yield relatively high financial rewards, with relatively low risks of detection. These facts, then, fit into an interpretation of that version of economic theory which emphasizes a rational cost-benefit model as potentially applicable to professional theft, but not amateur.

Another interesting line of research that has not been pursued follows from the above: studies of varying crime profiles by city and the special contributions of the ecological and economic conditions of each city to particular patterns of city crime distributions. As will be explained in greater detail in Chapter 8, crime and deviance patterns, themselves, can be considered as systems with regularities, their own rules and regulating mechanisms, and interactions of roles. Why do some cities exhibit high levels of murder and low levels of suicide? high robbery and lower burglary? high alcoholism and low heroin addiction, or vice versa? An accumulation of city profiles of crime and deviance, as recommended here, would be required in order for this order of questions to be examined.

It is hypothesized that rapid change in the constituency and size of population leads to increased anomie and to higher youth-amateur involvement in property crime. Moderate rates of population increase, on the other hand, are thought to be associated with economic well-being (Ogburn 1935) and decreases in property crime rates. Definitions of rapid change have not been achieved (Sheldon and Moore 1968, pp. 4-5). Time series data provide the potential of empirical identification, within the context of measurements in preceding and

---

[*]Informants were the heads of special detachments of the District of Columbia Police Department, such as the homicide, robbery, and burglary squads.

consequent years, for any particular period under examination. The hypothesis on the size or the mass of population of the city posits curvilinearity. That is, up to a point, increased population size is associated with increased anomie and crime. After an unspecified point in size is reached, further increases are expected to have little additional cumulative effect on anomie and crime levels. Expansion into suburban areas in recent years confounds, however, the possibility of tests in this research.

Ecological measures, then, were initially posited as sources of societal strain and anomie. As the research findings began to accumulate, however, in test after test, it became evident that the original hypotheses stemming from the logic of deterrence and some branches of economic theory (pleasure-pain calculations) are not substantiated in numerous tests on specific Class I crime rates. Midway in the research, then, a generalized perspective on macrostructural strain seemed to be more consistent with the findings. That is, all the dimensions identified theoretically and empirically here, including those on economic, ecological, and formal control measures, can be viewed as basic structural processes in society affecting structural strains, anomie, and levels of crime and deviance. This perspective will be developed further in Chapter 8, the Conclusions and Implications.

Findings from Chapters 5 and 6 make feasible refinements of hypotheses by time periods.

1946-70

In the third and most recent time period,

1. Rising expectations, along with general gains in the economy, should work to increase crime rates among low economic-status blacks who do not share in abundance; that is, the higher the price and tax measures, the higher the property crime rates, excluding burglary rates, which should show an inverse relationship to economic conditions.

2. Gains in the population balance of blacks to whites in the central city should minimize personal violent crime rates of blacks and increase those for whites.

3. The more rapid the pace of change in population composition, the higher are the crime rates, especially among youth, for example, for auto theft.

4. All-time-high police saturation in this era should, with deterrence theory, decrease arrest rates, all other factors being equal. Apparent consistency of bias in arrest processes over time, however, suggests that the more police, the greater representation of blacks in arrests for property crimes.

1919-45

Countervailing macrostructural changes in the second period
balance out to minimize overall correlations found; that is, these
will be smaller for the middle than for other time periods.

5. In the years of the Great Depression, the lower the prices
and tax measures, the higher will be the property crime rates (excluding auto theft), especially among the nonwhite group; however, the
preponderant number of years of prosperity (pre-Depression and
World War II) should overbalance the inverse correlations for the
Depression period, and thus exhibit overall moderate positive relationships between property crime rates and business condition indicators.
6. Economic measures should show an inverse correlation to
white property crime rates and positive correlations with black. The
logic of cohesion from a major war effort and absence of young males
from the homefront is thought to apply more to whites than to blacks.

1890-1918

Population gains of whites during Period I are expected to
bring about more anomie and crime among the black population and
less among the white.

7. The greater the population size, the higher will be property
crime rates, especially crimes among the young.
8. The greater the prosperity, the greater will be property
crime rates. High inequalities of wealth and raised expectations are
posited, in the aftermath of the Civil War, to suggest the relative
deprivation logic.
9. The more police, the lower will be property crime rates.
Police increments in this epoch are expected to be at maximum
effectiveness, due to high visibility in a relatively small mass of
population, with relatively rigid role definitions.

OVERVIEW

The order of procedure that follows will be similar to that of
Chapter 6, glimpsing reality from varied angles of the factual presentations, namely, (1) the general configurational predominance of
operationalized concepts, treated with multiple regression control
procedures; (2) correlational and R^2 findings for specific variables;
(3) graphic presentations for a detail not yielded by correlational

treatment; and (4) results of selected methodological experimentation with periods of five- and ten-year duration, and for time lags of the effects of selected macrostructural variables with selected crime rates.

Hirschi and Selvin (1967, pp. 156-159) recommended stepwise multiple regression procedures in preference to factor analysis for causal analysis. Experience here raises a number of problems, for the technique does not result in a totally satisfactory answer to problems of theoretical ordering, using a definition of maximum influence. On the other hand, stepwise multiple regression provides information on the direct and indirect contributions of each new variable added to the equation. The procedure, in principle, should aid in more detailed understanding of how the relationship between one independent and dependent variable may disappear or remain, when other independent variables are held constant.

TYPOLOGICAL PRIORITY: AN OVERVIEW

There is superiority for the economic factor (see Figure 7.1) in seven of twelve tests for black and white burglary and robbery,

FIGURE 7.1

Summary of Percent Variance Explained
by Macrostructural Factors for Property Crimes
by Time Period and Race

Property Type	Crime Period		
	III	II	I
NW Burglary	A 72 E 8 D 3 = 83	E 41 A 18 D 2 = 62	E 58 A 19 D 1 = 78
W Burglary	E 39 A 25 D 11 = 75	E 33 A 20 D 9 = 62	E 56 A 18 D 6 = 81
NW Robbery	A 55 E 25 D 2 = 82	E 32 A 13 D 19 = 64	A 89 D 3 E 0 = 90
W Robbery	A 41 E 15 D 9 = 66	E 67 D 17 A 6 = 90	D 54 A 13 E 0 = 67
NW Larceny	A 80 E 12 D 0 = 92	A 54 E 16 D 2 = 72	A 80 E 12 D 0 = 93
W Larceny	A 92 E 2 D 0 = 94	A 56 E 10 D 4 = 70	D 61 A 14 E 5 = 80
NW Auto Theft	E 64 A 19 D 6 = 89	A 46 D 37 E 7 = 90	—
W Auto Theft	A 45 E 34 D 5 = 84	A 30 D 24 E 22 = 77	—

Note: Rounding of decimal points accounts for the differences between totals.
Source: Tables 7.1-7.6.

confirming the direction of hypotheses for these property crimes.
If burglary alone is examined, the superiority rises to five of six
cases, with the exception for the anomie-ecological measures for
nonwhite burglary in Period III. The degree of population changes
is greatest for both racial groups in the third period, in accord with
the central structural transformation or racial succession that occurs
in the central city in these years.

There is reason to believe that there are real shifts over time
in the constituency of robbery, burglary, and auto theft, as described
earlier, and thus etiology. The ecological-anomie factor proves
somewhat superior in explaining the variance in three of four tests
for auto theft and five of six for grand larceny. Details on grand
larceny, considered a most questionable indicator, are shown in
Tables A.15 and A.16. The two exceptional victories for deterrence
theory are, consistent with hypotheses, for white robbery and white
grand larceny in Period I. However, the inverse relationship expected
is found only for larceny, and not for robbery.

If the regression tables presented in Chapters 6 and 7 are
scanned for ordering of the theoretical complexes of operationalized
measures entered first and second, it can be seen that measures
for two or three of the variable concept sets come into view. For
example, for homicide and murder, it is common that an economic
measure is entered first in multiple regression equations, then an
ecological variable. With assault and rape, the same combination
is common, or population and/or a police variable entered early.
For auto theft the combinations vary: economic and population
measures enter first; or population and police; or, again, in sequence,
one measure from each theoretical complex. For burglary, a frequent
combination is of one or two economic measures entered, followed by
a population measure. Similarly for robbery, a combination is used
of economic variables and the police; or population and the police; or
economic and ecological. Thus, the general theoretical complexes
identified here hold up under repeated tests.

AUTO THEFT

1946-70

Economic measures show the highest correlations and are
entered first for black and white auto theft rates, but with opposite
correlational directions. The taxes on banks measure shows .70 R
with black auto theft and explains 48 percent of the variance, with
other economic measures adding 13 percent, with controls exercised.
In contrast, the taxes on land measure is entered first, with -.48 R,

TABLE 7.1

Multiple Regression of Independent Variables
of Population, Business Cycle, and Police Force Measures
with Nonwhite Auto Theft Rates, by Periods

	Simple R	Multiple R	R^2	Increment in R^2
1919-45				
Police per 100,000 total population	.61	.61	.37	.37
Nonwhite percent population change	.55	.86	.75	.38
Average consumer price index	-.22	.89	.79	.04
Taxes on land assessments and improvements	.09	.90	.80	.02
Total population size	-.03	.91	.83	.03
Percent nonwhite population	.21	.93	.86	.03
Taxes on banks and corporations	.25	.93	.87	.01
Size police force	.25	.93	.87	.00
Rate of growth nonwhite population	.55	.94	.88	.01
Total percent population change	.49	.94	.88	.00
White percent population change	.46	.94	.88	.00
Rate of growth white population	.55	.94	.88	.00
Rate of growth total population	.56	.95	.90	.02
Percent white population	-.21	.95	.90	.00
1946-70				
Taxes on banks and corporations	.70	.70	.48	.48
Average consumer price index	.55	.74	.55	.07
Taxes on land assessments and improvements	.65	.78	.61	.06
Size police force	.46	.81	.65	.04
Rate of growth total population	-.07	.82	.67	.02
Police per 100,000 total population	.46	.83	.69	.01
Total population size	-.21	.85	.73	.04
Vehicle registrations per 100,000 population	.54	.87	.76	.03
Percent white population	-.63	.88	.78	.02
Percent nonwhite population	.63	.90	.81	.04
Rate of growth white population	.02	.91	.84	.02
Nonwhite percent population change	-.12	.93	.87	.03
Total percent population change	.03	.94	.88	.01
Rate of growth nonwhite population	-.13	.94	.88	.00
White percent population change	-.20	.95	.89	.01

Source: Compiled by the author.

TABLE 7.2

Multiple Regression of Independent Variables
of Population, Business Cycle, and Police Force Measures
with White Auto Theft Rates, by Periods

	Simple R	Multiple R	R^2	Increment in R^2
1919-45				
Police per 100,000 total population	.49	.49	.24	.24
Nonwhite percent population change	.40	.67	.45	.20
Rate of growth white population	.31	.69	.47	.03
Rate of growth total population	.33	.71	.50	.03
Taxes on banks and corporations	.02	.72	.52	.02
Taxes on land assessments and improvements	.04	.84	.71	.19
Total population size	-.15	.86	.74	.03
Size police force	.06	.86	.74	.00
Percent white population	-.03	.87	.75	.00
Average consumer price index	-.24	.87	.76	.01
White percent population change	.34	.87	.76	.01
Total percent population change	.36	.88	.77	.01
Rate of growth nonwhite population	.36	.88	.77	.00
Percent nonwhite population	.03	.88	.77	.00
1946-70				
Taxes on land assessments and improvements	-.48	.48	.23	.23
Percent nonwhite population	-.26	.69	.48	.25
Taxes on banks and corporations	-.38	.73	.53	.06
Rate of growth total population	-.22	.76	.58	.04
Vehicle Registrations per 100,000 population	-.37	.79	.62	.04
Nonwhite percent population change	.39	.80	.64	.02
Rate of growth nonwhite population	.05	.84	.71	.07
Total population size	.02	.87	.75	.04
Police per 100,000 total population	-.42	.89	.79	.04
Total percent population change	.02	.89	.80	.01
Percent white population	.26	.90	.80	.00
White percent population change	-.17	.90	.80	.00
Rate of growth white population	-.33	.90	.81	.01
Size police force	-.45	.91	.82	.01
Average consumer price index	-.36	.91	.84	.01

Source: Compiled by the author.

155

and explaining only 23 percent of the variance for white auto theft (see Tables 7.1 and 7.2). Additional economic measures add a further 11 percent, with controls. It is suggested, then, that macroeconomic changes in this time epoch once again exert differential effects by race in the city. Rates of unemployment, it may be recalled, of black youth in inner cities hover between 40 and 50 percent, while the level of education among at least some blacks is rising. The period is one of the black civil rights demands of the sixties, of Watergate, ITT, and other revelations. All could be expected to contribute to heightened anomie among blacks. On the other hand, white youth remaining in the area tend to live in relatively affluent neighborhoods. Thus, the differentiated direction of correlations for the two racial groups appears justified by the macrocurrent processes of the epoch. Additional tests with race-specific auto theft rates for other cities are needed.

The direction of findings on police size measures is positive for black auto theft (.46, with controls entered, adding little or 5 percent to the variance) and inverse for white (-.42 and -.45, adding 5 percent to the variance). Thus, the interpretation applied earlier, which regards the police as an additional source of structural strain[*] among a disadvantaged group, appears warranted. On the other hand, the deterrent effect expected from heavy police saturation in the period for those with vested interests in society, as white youth, should be felt. Previous time epochs (I and II) are thought to have contained larger proportions of lower class, white youth than Period III.

The constellation of ecological measures bears a heavier weight on white auto theft than on black. In the first year of Period III, racial composition is not far from that at the beginning of this study, close to 30 percent of the total black. Racial parity, that is, 50 percent of the population black, is reached by 1957. A more definite black majority of 60 percent is reached by 1962. Are these changes reflected in data here? The ecological variables appear to have relatively little direct effect, once the economic and police variables are entered. However, the direction of the findings on the change measures tends to show some consistency with findings for other measures, insofar as these show inverse effects; that is, the more population change and growth for nonwhites in this period of increase in relation to whites, the less crime. Change towards an increasing numerical

---

[*]Dr. James F. Scott, Chairman of the Department of Sociology, Howard University, has suggested one possible avenue of microeffects of high police saturation. Police disperse black youth who traditionally hang out on the streets and on doorsteps, thus forcing activities back into close and densely occupied quarters.

majority status by a minority can be hypothesized to depress structural
strains and crime rates. In this instance the correlations for nonwhite
percent and rate of change are of relatively low order (-.12 and -.13)
and add little (3 percent) to the variance, after controls. The percent
nonwhite is highly correlated (.63), but adds little to the variance
with controls for business cycles, total population, and total population growth. Thus, on balance, for black youth the favorable aspects
of increasing numbers are not overcome by unfavorable aspects of
continued economic disadvantage in a period of unparalleled affluence.

   With the exception of the rate of growth of the nonwhite population, the ecological measures tend to depress (show inverse relations)
white auto theft rates, including percent nonwhite (-.26, adding 25
percent variance), and decreases in white population. Commonsense
suggests that an increasingly black population offers less opportunity
for car theft in both ratio of cars to population and in constraints of
territory that may result.

1919-45

   The middle period shows no basic realignment in the numbers
ratios of the two racial groups, but there was a good deal of mobility
during the depression years and World War II. It was suggested
earlier that the net effect of the correlations for economic measures
would be minimized by the sharp fluctuations in economic conditions
which work to cancel each other out during this time period. This
appears to be so. Economic variables show relatively low strength as
compared to the ecological and police measures. An inspection of
Figures 5.1 and 5.2 with three-year averages shows that highest
auto theft rates are reached during the Great Depression (as well as
black homicide and white suicide). This suggests the importance of
the factor at work during the period. Business cycles muddy the
waters of this trend-oriented research. The choice of years in this
epoch does not adequately test the economic dimension, unless the
cyclical effects are eliminated. Additional work with this step, or
alternatively using shorter periods with a sample of cities, is
warranted.

   For both groups, the police measure per 100,000 population
is entered first, showing the largest correlations, or .61 and 37
percent of the variance for nonwhite and .49 and 24 percent of the
variance for white. Again, support for the deterrence hypothesis
is not found. Most of the population changes taking place in the
period show positive correlations, serving to uphold the thesis of
increasing change, increasing anomie, and increasing crime levels,
especially among youth. The largest correlation for nonwhite auto

theft is with nonwhite population change, or .55 R, adding 38 percent
to the variance. The finding reflects heavy black migration, and
supports the anomie hypothesis. With this entry, contributions of
other population change variables are indirect and apparently spurious,
showing little additional variance explained, after controls. Similarly,
once the cross-race effects of the nonwhite percent population change
is entered with white auto theft (.40 R, explaining 20 percent of the
variance after the police), little variance is added with additional
entries, except for an economic variable. Again, a conflict-based
hypothesis finds support.

BURGLARY

Hypotheses tend to be confirmed for burglary, with priority
shown for the economic measures. The constituency of burglary
is posited to become more professionalized in the third period, and
should thus show correlational shifts from the first two periods to
the third. This is the case.

1946-70

There are a number of variables exhibiting relatively high
correlations with black burglary rates (see Table 7.3). Note that
all four economic measures show consistent and high correlations,
ranging from -.64 to -.76, with the conditions of prosperity of the
period working to minimize burglary. With controls exerted by the
program for percent white, entered first in the program with a
correlation of .79 R (explaining 62 percent of the variance); however,
the variance explained by each succeeding economic measure is
negligible. The second entry, the price index, adds 6 percent with
a -.68 correlation. The simplest ex post facto interpretation of the
high correlation of percent white to black burglary rates is that the
greater the number of affluent white homes per capita, the greater
the opportunity for burglary. As in previous instances, with the
examination of percent black in the regression tables, however,
economic and ecological interactions are apparent. Common sources
of variance, in this instance, are indicated for both economic
variables and percent white.

Two measures of economic conditions are entered first for
white burglary rates, with moderate inverse correlations (-.44 and
-.20). Together, the two measures account for 36 percent of the
variance. The nonwhite percent population change and the rate of
growth of nonwhite contribute to white burglary rates, but the cross-
race effects add little to the variance.

TABLE 7.3

Multiple Regression of Independent Variables
of Population, Business Cycle, and Police Force Measures
with Nonwhite Burglary Rates, by Periods

	Simple R	Multiple R	R^2	Increment in R^2
1890-1918				
Taxes on land assessments and improvements	.76	.76	.58	.58
Total population size	.65	.84	.70	.12
Rate of growth nonwhite population	.20	.86	.73	.03
Police per 100,000 total population	.20	.86	.74	.00
Percent white population	.71	.86	.74	.01
White percent population change	.13	.87	.75	.01
Rate of growth total population	.17	.87	.76	.01
Rate of growth white population	.14	.88	.77	.01
Total percent population change	.12	.88	.78	.00
Nonwhite percent population change	.03	.88	.78	.00
Size police force	.52	.88	.78	.00
1919-45				
Average consumer price index	-.57	.57	.32	.32
Taxes on land assessments and improvements	.27	.63	.40	.08
Total population size	.11	.66	.44	.04
Nonwhite percent population change	.20	.69	.47	.03
Rate of growth nonwhite population	.05	.75	.57	.09
White percent population change	.19	.77	.59	.02
Taxes on banks and corporations	.30	.77	.60	.01
Size police force	.28	.79	.62	.02
Percent nonwhite population	.44	.79	.62	.00
Total percent population change	.19	.79	.62	.00
Police per 100,000 total population	.35	.79	.62	.00
Rate of growth total population	.07	.79	.62	.00
Rate of growth white population	.07	.79	.62	.00
Percent white population	-.44	.79	.62	.00
1946-70				
Percent white population	.79	.79	.62	.62
Average consumer price index	-.68	.82	.68	.06
Taxes on land assessments and improvements	-.64	.83	.69	.01
Taxes on banks and corporations	-.76	.84	.70	.01
Rate of growth nonwhite population	.12	.84	.71	.01
Nonwhite percent population change	.01	.85	.72	.01
Vehicle registrations per 100,000 population	-.68	.85	.73	.01
Size police force	-.56	.86	.74	.02
Rate of growth total population	.01	.87	.75	.01
Rate of growth white population	-.00	.89	.79	.04
White percent population change	.17	.90	.81	.01
Percent nonwhite population	-.79	.90	.81	.01
Police per 100,000 total population	-.57	.91	.82	.01
Total percent population change	-.16	.91	.83	.00
Total population size	.52	.91	.83	.00

Source: Compiled by the author.

TABLE 7.4

Multiple Regression of Independent Variables
of Population, Business Cycle, and Police Force Measures
with White Burglary Rates, by Periods

	Simple R	Multiple R	R^2	Increment in R^2
1890-1918				
Taxes on land assessments and improvements	.75	.75	.56	.56
Total population size	.64	.81	.66	.10
Rate of growth white population	.17	.82	.68	.02
White percent population change	.07	.83	.69	.01
Percent white population	.70	.84	.71	.01
Size police force	.56	.85	.72	.01
Police per 100,000 total population	.30	.88	.77	.05
Nonwhite percent population change	-.12	.89	.79	.01
Rate of growth nonwhite population	.09	.89	.80	.01
Rate of growth total population	.16	.90	.80	.00
Total percent population change	.03	.90	.81	.00
1919-45				
Taxes on banks and corporations	.51	.51	.26	.26
Police per 100,000 total population	.43	.59	.35	.08
Nonwhite percent population change	.16	.61	.38	.03
Total percent population change	.11	.63	.40	.02
White percent population change	.10	.65	.42	.02
Average consumer price index	-.35	.69	.48	.05
Taxes on land assessments and improvements	.34	.71	.50	.02
Total population size	.16	.72	.52	.02
Size police force	.36	.73	.54	.01
Rate of growth nonwhite population	.17	.74	.55	.01
Percent nonwhite population	.41	.75	.57	.02
Rate of growth white population	.19	.76	.57	.01
Rate of growth total population	.18	.79	.63	.06
Percent white population	-.41	.79	.63	.00
1946-70				
Taxes on banks and corporations	-.44	.44	.20	.20
Vehicle registrations per 100,000 population	-.20	.60	.36	.16
Nonwhite percent population change	.26	.62	.38	.02
Taxes on land assessments and improvements	-.33	.64	.41	.02
Percent nonwhite population	-.39	.66	.43	.03
Total population size	-.02	.71	.51	.07
Rate of growth total population	.04	.75	.56	.05
Size police force	-.37	.77	.60	.03
Police per 100,000 total population	-.32	.82	.68	.08
Percent white population	.39	.85	.72	.04
Rate of growth white population	-.11	.85	.72	.00
Rate of growth nonwhite population	.15	.85	.73	.00
Total percent population change	-.21	.85	.73	.00
White percent population change	-.18	.86	.74	.01
Average consumer price index	-.27	.87	.75	.01

Source: Compiled by the author.

Police variables exhibit modest and inverse correlations, adding little to the variance, with controls exerted by economic measures. The police per 100,000 population adds 8 percent to the variance, with -.32 R with white burglary, and -.57 R for black, adding little to the variance in the last case, after entries of numerous ecological and economic measures. Thus, some deterrence effect may be exerted upon white burglary.

1919-45

Once again, as predicted, the total variance explained for the middle period is somewhat less than for the other two. In this instance, however, it reaches almost 80 percent, as compared to about 90 percent in the first and third periods. Repeated, as well, is the performance of the price index, showing inverse signs as compared to positive signs characteristic of other economic indicators.

For both racial groups, economic measures are entered first. Forty percent of the variance is explained by these measures for nonwhite burglary, with the highest correlation, or -.59 for the price index, explaining 32 percent of the variance. The population upheavals combine to add another 18 percent to the variance, after controls for economic measures. For white burglary, taxes on banks is entered first, with .51 R, explaining 26 percent of the variance.

In this era, the percent white shows inverse correlations in contrast to the first and third period, with a corresponding positive correlation for percent black, or .44 with nonwhite burglary and .41 with white. In the first case, with controls exerted, nothing is added to the variance; in the second case, 2 percent. Thus, once again, the interactions of these measures with economic and ecological variables suggest a spurious relationship.

The modest correlations of police force size (.28 and .35 for nonwhite burglary) tend to be dissipated with controls exerted by economic variables. For white burglary, a police measure is entered second in the sequence, with a correlation of .43, adding 8 percent of the variance after controls exerted by an economic variable. Thus, the effects of the police are somewhat stronger for white than for black burglary activity, but are again inconsistent with a deterrence hypothesis.

1890-1918

A number of findings tend to hold up consistently over the three time periods for burglary rates. Again the highest correlation is

exhibited by an economic measure available, consistent with the
relative deprivation hypothesis, or .76 R for nonwhite and .75 R for
white, with 58 and 56 percent of the variance, respectively, explained.
Total population size is entered second for both groups, again consistent with the hypothesis for this period; that is, the greater the
population size, the greater the social disorganization and crime.
Correlations reach over .65 and .64, but with controls for the economic measure, add 10 and 12 percent of the variance explained to
black and to white rates. In turn, with these two measures exerting
controls, little additional variance is explained by other variables.

In this epoch, once again, the percent white population shows
positive and high correlations (over .70) with both black and white
burglary rates, but again add little to the variance, with controls.
The same finding on controls effects is again true for police measures.
For white burglary, the police size and ratio shows .56 R and .30 R,
with a contribution of 6 percent to the variance, with controls. The
relationships are again contrary to deterrence logic. Likewise,
police size shows a .52 R with black burglary rates, but again adds
nothing to the variance, with controls.

ROBBERY

It is frequent practice to use robbery as an indicator of the
violence of a society. Would not homicide, a more valid measure
as well as a more direct measure of extreme violence, be a more
logical choice? The question is raised, then, does robbery act
etiologically more like the species of violence of murder, widely
considered an effective-emotional type of crime, or is it more akin
to burglary, considered a nonviolent variables suggests that it is
somewhat inbetween the properties of both.

1946-70

Although the total amounts of variance explained by the measures
are fairly large (82 percent for nonwhite robbery and 66 percent for
white robbery), the magnitudes of the correlations tend to be smaller
than for those of burglary and of murder. Further, it can be seen
(Tables 7.5 and 7.6) that, as predicted for violent crimes, the effects
of population upheavals are relatively strong. The size of the correlations of the economic measures with black robbery rates, ranging
from .26 for the vehicle registration measure to .42 for the taxes
on land measure in the last instance, accounts for 17 percent of the
variance. The other economic measures in all, with controls, add

TABLE 7.5

Multiple Regression of Independent Variables
of Population, Business Cycle, and Police Force Measures
with Nonwhite Robbery Rates, by Periods

	Simple R	Multiple R	R^2	Increment in R^2
1890-1918				
Percent nonwhite population	-.88	.88	.78	.78
Total population size	.83	.90	.81	.04
Total percent population change	.03	.92	.84	.02
Rate of growth nonwhite population	-.05	.92	.85	.01
Taxes on land assessments and improvements	.88	.92	.85	.00
Size police force	.81	.93	.86	.01
Police per 100,000 total population	.55	.94	.88	.02
Rate of growth total population	.02	.94	.88	.00
Rate of growth white population	.04	.94	.89	.01
Nonwhite percent population change	-.17	.94	.89	.00
White percent population change	.08	.95	.90	.01
1919-45				
Average consumer price index	-.50	.50	.25	.25
Police per 100,000 total population	-.19	.62	.38	.13
Size police force	.32	.66	.44	.06
Taxes on banks and corporations	.09	.71	.50	.07
Rate of growth white population	-.02	.74	.55	.04
Rate of growth nonwhite population	.06	.77	.59	.04
Rate of growth total population	-.00	.78	.61	.02
Nonwhite percent population change	.31	.79	.62	.01
Total population size	.33	.79	.63	.00
Total percent population change	.31	.80	.64	.01
Percent nonwhite population	.46	.80	.64	.00
White percent population change	.31	.80	.64	.00
Taxes on land assessments and improvements	.16	.80	.64	.00
Percent white population	-.46	.80	.64	.00
1946-70				
Taxes on land assessments and improvements	.42	.42	.17	.17
Percent white population	-.16	.73	.53	.35
Rate of growth nonwhite population	-.04	.75	.56	.04
Nonwhite percent population change	-.34	.76	.58	.02
Average consumer price index	.30	.78	.60	.02
Taxes on banks and corporations	.27	.80	.64	.04
Size police force	.36	.80	.65	.01
Vehicle registrations per 100,000 population	.26	.81	.66	.01
Total population size	-.00	.82	.67	.01
Police per 100,000 total population	.35	.82	.67	.01
White percent population change	.11	.82	.68	.00
Rate of growth total population	.11	.85	.73	.05
Percent nonwhite population	.16	.86	.73	.00
Rate of growth white population	.24	.86	.73	.00
Total percent population change	-.08	.91	.82	.09

Source: Compiled by the author.

TABLE 7.6

Multiple Regression of Independent Variables
of Population, Business Cycle, and Police Force Measures
with White Robbery Rates, by Periods

	Simple R	Multiple R	R^2	Increment in R^2
1890-1918				
Size police force	.72	.72	.52	.52
White percent population change	-.09	.74	.55	.03
Rate of growth total population	.07	.77	.59	.03
Percent nonwhite population	-.65	.77	.60	.01
Total population size	.60	.80	.63	.03
Police per 100,000 total population	.67	.81	.66	.02
Total percent population change	-.12	.81	.66	.00
Rate of growth nonwhite population	.09	.81	.66	.00
Rate of growth white population	.06	.82	.67	.00
Taxes on land assessments and improvements	.63	.82	.67	.00
Nonwhite percent population change	-.21	.82	.67	.00
1919-45				
Average consumer price index	-.79	.79	.62	.62
Size police force	.49	.88	.77	.14
Taxes on banks and corporations	.37	.90	.81	.04
Total population size	.31	.91	.84	.03
Taxes on land assessments and improvements	.29	.92	.85	.01
Police per 100,000 total population	.26	.93	.87	.02
Percent nonwhite population	.68	.93	.87	.00
White percent population change	.39	.93	.87	.00
Total percent population change	.40	.94	.88	.01
Nonwhite percent population change	.42	.94	.89	.01
Rate of growth nonwhite population	.35	.94	.89	.00
Rate of growth total population	.39	.94	.89	.00
Rate of growth white population	.39	.95	.90	.01
Percent white population	-.68	.95	.90	.00
1946-70				
Rate of growth nonwhite population	.47	.47	.22	.22
Size police force	.05	.53	.28	.06
Total percent population change	.25	.54	.30	.02
Taxes on banks and corporations	.05	.57	.32	.02
Average consumer price index	.10	.60	.36	.04
Rate of growth total population	.17	.65	.42	.07
Nonwhite percent population change	.38	.67	.45	.03
Percent white population	-.07	.69	.47	.02
Percent nonwhite population	.07	.71	.50	.03
Total population size	-.07	.72	.51	.01
Police per 100,000 total population	.06	.74	.54	.03
Vehicle registrations per 100,000 population	.08	.76	.58	.04
Taxes on land assessments and improvements	.06	.79	.63	.05
Rate of growth white population	-.22	.80	.64	.01
White percent population change	-.14	.81	.66	.01

Source: Compiled by the author.

seven percent more. The gains in black population again show
moderating effects on black crime (-.34 for nonwhite percent population change, for example), with modest amounts added to the
variance (2 percent), with controls. The percent white is entered
second, with -.16 R, and with the inverse sign adds 35 percent to
the variance. Again, the economic and ecological variables interact.
Also, police force size adds little to the variance, after controls for
economic and ecological variables; and correlations of .35 and .36
for the police measures do not confirm the deterrence hypothesis.

There is a strong case for cross-race stress of population
change on white robbery rates. The rate of growth of the nonwhite
population shows a .47 R, explaining 22 percent of the variance as it
enters first in the program. The second-highest correlation is .38
for NW percent change.

The negligible size of the correlations, constitutes an unusual
case, giving relatively less evidence for the support of macrostructural
effects. Alternatively, robbery was susceptible to reporting manipulation during the Nixon era, and therefore is a less valid index.
Again, the relatively small degree to which the economic measures
correlate and contribute to the variance lends credence to the interpretation that the crime is becoming more youth-amateur in composition, and therefore responds to effects of ecological change, relative deprivation, and anomie.

                              1919-45

For the middle time epoch, robbery—especially the white rates—
tends to respond more to economic conditions than to changes from
ecological measures. This finding is consistent with the idea that
robbery has become more amateur and less professional over time.
The price index shows -.50 R, accounting for 25 percent of the
variance with nonwhite robbery. The direct contribution of the two
police measures with modest correlations holds up better here than
in other tests, with the controls exerted earlier by economic
measures. Note opposite signs of the two measures, which together
add 19 percent to the variance.

A frequent tendency is for the effects of population size to be
dissipated by timing of its entry into the program. For violent
crimes described earlier, as well as here, there is again evidence
that ecological change measures maintain some of their contribution
to the variance in spite of controls. The percent nonwhite shows a
positive correlation of .46 with nonwhite robbers, but is again dissipated in variance explanation by other variables. For white robbery,
the same two variable dimensions, that is the economic and the police,

are entered first. The price index shows -.79 R, explaining 62 percent of the variance. The police, with .49 R, add 14 percent of the
variance, after controls. Population size yields a .31 R, but contributes only 3 percent of the variance, with controls.

The percent nonwhite again shows a cross-race effect on white
robbery, or .68 R, but its effects are again indirect and dissipated
by variables entered earlier.

1890-1918

Unusual effects of the percent nonwhite are evident for this
earliest time period. First, the more nonwhite there were in the
population, the less nonwhite robbery. The high -.88 R accounts
for 78 percent of the variance. There is again consistency in direction of inverse relations found for increases in the nonwhite population.
This theme is interpreted with the vocabulary of strain reduction, in
the context of intergroup relations in the city. Further these findings
are once again inconsistent with subcultural themes of violence.

Second, variance explanation is almost eliminated for other
population and economic variables that display high correlations, by
their late entry into the program. The consistency of the constellations suggest that the first variable entered shows a great deal of
interaction with ecological and economic variables. Thus, total
population size shows .83 R with black robbery, but adds only 4 percent to the variance; taxes on land, .88 R, with no variance; police
size, .81 R and little (1 percent) variance. Substantively, it is hypothesized that police deterrence should work most when the population
mass is at a smaller level, as in Period I. The evidence once again
does not support this hypothesis. In this instance, ecological size,
changes in the white population, police size, and economic conditions
all (except nonwhite) serve to maximize black robbery rates.

The impact of police on white robbery is again positive, even
greater than for the black rate, or with a .72 R and 52 percent of
the variance explained. Again, there are high correlations for other
variables, such as economic, .63, with no variance added; and population size, .60 R, with 3 percent variance added. Logically, again,
the interaction is expected to work from population and economic
conditions to police size rather than vice versa.

SUMMARY THEMES ON THE LIMITATIONS
AND CONSEQUENCES
OF MULTIPLE REGRESSION FOR CAUSAL ORDERING

A few procedural limitations and themes that have repeated
themselves in the analyses of Chapters 6 and 7 will be brought together
here with illustrations. First, it was shown in Chapter 6 that small
inverse correlations, with the procedures of the program, sometimes
appear to exaggerate the amount of variance contributed. A similar
instance is the case of very small positive correlations that may
result in substantial increments in variance explained. Thus, if these
procedures are taken literally, the results suggest that independent
contributions of such measures may operate in the role of catalyst to
the processes at work. An evaluation of such an interpretation can
be aided by both theoretical logic and by the repetitiveness of the
theme in other tests. For example, it can be seen in the table for
nonwhite assault in the middle period (Table 6.7), that the measure
of percent nonwhite is entered late in the program. It shows a correlation of only -.19, but adds 13 percent to the variance after the
controls exerted by entry of a number of previous ecological and
economic variables. measures. With the multiple regression procedures, then, the percent nonwhite adds as much to the variance as
the very first variable entered, the price index, in this instance.
Given the context of the repeatedness of this theme in other tests
with conceptually related measures, such as percent change in nonwhite, the action of the variable is explained by the injection of an
additional explanatory theme, namely, intergroup conflict relations.
Were the correlation positive in direction, a subcultural hypothesis
could be applied. In a number of other instances, however, in which
the direction of nonwhite is positive, the contribution of percent
nonwhite to the variance is erased, when economic and population
change variables are entered first. Indications of a spurious relationship, in repeated tests, tend to negate the logic of subcultural interpretations for most time periods.

The ecological measures contain varied dimensions. Hypotheses
derived from both anomie and social disintegration theory, as well
as conflict and/or intergroup relations theory are consistent with the
findings.

An example of a large increment of variance explained late in
the program may be observed in the table on white murder (Table 6.2)
for the earliest period. In this instance, as well, the ecological
measures appear to tap varied dimensions of change. The percent
white population change enters first into the equation, with a correlation of .54, explaining 29 percent of the variance. Other ecological
change measures, such as rate of growth and nonwhite percent

population change, are entered before the fifth entry is made with total percent population change. The last mentioned explains (with a correlation of .53) an unusual jump in variance, or 28 percent. The procedures, then, suggest that this effect is real and independent of the effects of controls by other ecological and/or economic variables that might have been supposed to be interrelated. Again, white burglary (Table 7.4) for Period III shows moderate correlations on a number of theoretical dimensions. The largest increments in variance are for economic measures. Entered second, the police per 100,000 adds 8 percent to the variance. These findings suggest that the theoretical dimension retains at least some independent contributions of its own, although there are important interactions. Again, the rate of growth of the total population adds 6 percent to the variance, after most of the other ecological and economic measures have been controlled. A similar effect can be noted late in the program for total percent population change in the table on nonwhite robbery (Table 7.5) for Period III.

A second difficulty is in arriving at causal priority for cases in which a number of measures of the varying theoretical factors each exhibit relatively high correlations. Cumulatively, this has been shown to be a problem of interpretation in the literature, as well (see Chapter 3). The solution of the program here is, of course, to take the highest correlation first, and then proceed with controls. For example, in the instance of nonwhite robbery for Period I (see Table 7.5), there are a number of high correlations: for percent nonwhite (-.88); for total population size (.83); for taxes on land assessments (.88); and for the size of the police force (.81). The first variable entered is percent nonwhite, explaining 78 percent of the variance. It is likely, given previous results of additional tests, factors are more truly antecedent in time sequence or in some other aspect of priority. A very small shift in correlation size, then, can radically alter the causal priority mechanism of the program. Again, the repetitiveness of themes and the theoretical rationale must be called into play. In this instance, it looks as if, as a minority group grows in size—within the constellation of social structure of the earliest time period—it becomes less crime prone. The unanticipated theme reoccurs. It is interpreted as a factor contributing to the minimization of structural strains that are a by-product of a population with a strong element of minority-majority group relationships, in this instance racially based. The population ratio at once seems to reflect something about the source of the changing nature of intergroup relationships, as well as its consequences for levels of crime. In this instance, the variance effects of other ecological and economic measures are largely dissipated by controls. More generally, the explanatory value of percent nonwhite (when positive in correlation direction) tends to disappear when the effects of economic and/or ecological variables are controlled by their prior entry into the program. On the other hand, cross-race effects frequently do not dissipate and add to the weight of the conflict theme interpretation.

The procedures, then, cumulatively, help to give insights into direct and indirect contributions of each measure. Each can be followed for its history in the many regression equations, in association with other "independent" measures. The effects of these appear to show real changes over time. For example, correlations in Period I suggest that, the greater the percent nonwhite, the less nonwhite robbery—while the greater the population size, the more robbery. Consistent with this finding, theoretical reasoning for the anomie theme suggests that the larger the population, the more stress and anomie, the more crime. The Ogburn cues are inconsistent: the larger the population, the greater the prosperity, and the less crime. A Gouldian interpretation reads: the more people, the more opportunity for commission of robbery, consistent with the finding on population size.

The procedures, then, help to locate empirical answers to theoretical alternatives. The causal nexus for robbery is seen to vary from that of burglary. Auto theft, in turn, varies from both. These findings reemphasize the strategy used here: each legal crime classification should be inspected separately. Each, in turn, may contain multifaceted types of crime within it, with varying etiologies that may work to change configurations over time.

SUMMARY

The research reported here began with the objective of making repeated tests of competing macrostructural themes with the use of numerous indicators and historical time frames, in search for evidence that would aid in the long-run objective of science, namely, the subjection of competing theories to empiricism and to the weeding out of those approaches that do not survive. With very high levels of variance tending to be explained here, the implication for the task of theory is to call for refinement and/or integration of macrostructural perspectives and for the enunciation of systematic tie-ins with microstructural processes. The preponderant style in American criminology and deviance texts is to list endlessly a series of theories. If an approach to integration is made, it begins with the individual and then sets him in a larger framework. Here the pattern is reversed. Theoretical implications will be elaborated in the upcoming and final Chapter 8.

TABLE 7.7

Correlations for Selected Indicators Arranged by Ecological, Economic, and Police Measures for Nonwhite and White Auto Theft, Burglary, and Robbery Rates, by Periods

	III AUTO THEFT		II AUTO THEFT		III BURGLARY		II BURGLARY		I BURGLARY		III ROBBERY		II ROBBERY		I ROBBERY	
	NW	W	NW	W	NW	W	NW	W	NW	W	NW	W	NW	W	NW	W
Population size	-.21	.02	-.03	-.15	.52	-.02	.11	.16	.65	.64	-.04	-.08	.33	.31	.83	.60
Total percent population change	.03	.02	.49	.36	-.16	-.21	.19	.11	.12	.03	-.08	.25	.31	.40	.03	.12
Nonwhite percent population change	-.12	.39	.55	.40	.01	.26	.20	.16	.03	-.12	-.34	.38	.31	.42	-.17	-.21
White percent population change	-.20	-.17	.46	.34	.17	-.18	.19	.10	.13	.07	.11	-.14	.31	.39	.08	-.09
Total rate change	-.07	-.22	.56	.33	.01	.04	.07	.18	.17	.16	.11	.17	-.002	.39	.02	.07
Nonwhite rate change	-.13	.05	.55	.36	.12	.15	.05	.17	.20	.09	-.04	.47	.06	.35	-.05	.09
White rate change	.02	-.33	.55	.31	-.002	-.11	.07	.19	.14	.17	.24	-.22	-.02	.39	.04	.06
Percent nonwhite	.63	-.26	.21	.03	-.79	-.39	.44	.41	-.74	-.70	.16	.07	.46	.68	-.88	-.65
Percent white	-.63	.26	-.21	-.03	.79	.39	-.44	-.41	.71	.70	-.16	-.07	-.46	-.68	.88	.65
Taxes on land	.65	-.48	.09	.04	-.64	-.33	.27	.34	.76	.75	.42	.06	.16	.29	.88	.63
Price index	.55	-.36	-.22	-.24	-.68	-.27	-.57	-.35	—	—	.30	.10	-.50	-.79	—	—
Size police force	.46	-.45	.25	.06	-.56	-.37	.28	.36	.52	.56	.36	.05	.32	.49	.81	.72
Police/100,000 total population	.46	-.42	.61	.49	-.57	-.32	.35	.43	.20	.30	.35	.06	-.19	.26	.55	.67

Note: Period III is the most recent.

Source: Compiled by the author.

An affirmation of significant contributions of all three factors to levels of crime in the District is the result, not always in accord with the logic of the theories, and usually not equally. There are to be found circumscribed areas of greater and of lesser influence by crime types, by race, by age, and by time periods. The latter tend to be consistent with documentation on changing constellations of macrostructural variables over time.

Table 7.7 presents the Pearsonian correlations, rearranged in order by the three macrostructural factors under consideration, namely, economic, ecological, and police, for selected indicators for the three time periods. The table thus facilitates a highlighting of themes identified. Some of these are held in common with those found for the forms of personal violence discussed in Chapter 6, while others are more peculiar to property crimes.

Changes in Etiology Over Time

A number of examples of changed etiologies over historical time have been remarked here, within the context of previous analyses. These will be summarized with the use of Table 7.7.

Ecological Factors

Note that auto theft, the crime most reflective of a young constituency among the types examined here, is expected to be sensitive to population upheavals as a source of anomie. Indeed, the correlations with ecological variables are strongest for Period II, which showed marked mobility, and somewhat weaker in Period III. The percent nonwhite population change correlates of .55 with nonwhite and .40 with white auto theft in II, while in III it shifts to -.12 with nonwhite and lowers to .39 with white auto theft. Again, the total population rate change in II is .56 with nonwhite auto theft and .33 with white, while nonwhite rate change shows .55 and .36 for white. Thus, ecological changes and the directions expected—that is, the more change, the more crime—are confirmed for Period II, but not for III. Population size, as hypothesized, tends to show strongest correlations in the first period, as compared to the others, or .83 with nonwhite robbery and .60 with white; .65 and .64 with nonwhite and white burglary.

The shift in direction of correlations of percent nonwhite over time, with inverse relationships for nonwhite robbery in the first period, positive ones in the second, and negligible correlations in the third, may be seen. Burglary, on the other hand, moves from inverse in the earliest to positive in the middle, and inverse in the third. This latter unique change in Period III has been interpreted previously as due to increasing professionalism in burglary, as opposed to amateurism in other property crimes over time in the District.

Economic Conditions

There appears to be real directional change over time, as well, in the effects of economic conditions on at least some crimes, and a changing degree in the strength of correlations, as their configurational interrelationships change. Note that the tax on land measure shows a strong relationship to robbery in Period I, at .88 for nonwhite, and .63 for white; much less in Period II, and only a moderate relationship, or .42 with nonwhite robbery in Period III, consistent with the idea of changing etiology of the crime from professional to amateur over time. Again, the direction changes for burglary from .76 and .75 for nonwhite and white, to moderation in II, to inverse in III, with -.64 for nonwhite and -.33 for white. The interpretation is suggested again as due to a shift in constituency of burglary contrasting with other property crimes, notably to increasing professionalism in the first case. The tendency for positive relationships between economic measures and crime throughout the three periods— that is, the greater the prosperity, the greater the crime—allows for two kinds of explanation by economic theories, such as that espoused by Gould—the more goods (opportunity), the more crime— or that which emphasized (but is not inconsistent with Gould) relative deprivation. The measures Gould used of goods in circulation, that is, number of motor vehicles and amount of money, may be viewed as more general barometers of economic conditions. The fact that burglary shows inverse relationships, even when goods are in heavy supply in the affluence of Period III, is inconsistent with Gould's emphasis. Further, decennial data on unemployment (see Table A.17) for the District, 1920-1970, show relatively high and significant relationships between Class I crime and suicide rates. Correlations for nonwhite and white burglary and robbery are, in that order: .70 and .02 significance; .78 and .007 significance; .61 and .04 significance; .79 and .006 significance.

The ambiguity of these results with the overall positive direction of correlations with economic conditions—that is, the higher the prosperity, the more crime—is thought resolved by the inability of economic data used to control for changing class structure and inequality over time. In sum, evidence shows all-time high rates of crime during the Great Depression; high correlations with unemployment, and positive correlations with economic conditions.

The Police

There is little evidence that the police deter crime (for most types of Class I crimes) in these data, including those measures most valid (murder as an indicator of violence and auto theft as an indicator of property crime). In Period I, the more police, the higher were the crime rates. Police size measures tend to correlate most strongly for burglary (.52 and .56) and robbery in Period I (.81 and .72), and inversely only by Period III, in accordance with a deterrence hypothesis, for burglary. If, indeed, crimes are rationally committed, as professional (more than amateur) burglary should be, high saturation of the police, it was reasoned, should perform the expected deterrence function. The failure to do so in other crimes, thought to be highly youthful and amateur in composition, suggests that the police are an additional stress factor. The more general interpretation is that the police or formal controls deter crime among those with vested interests in society, as affluent white youth and among those who carry on crime as a profession. It can be hypothesized, more generally, that the police are most deployed to detain those very groups that are least likely to be deterred by them, while those who might be most deterred, are least detained. Additional research effort would be needed to test this thesis and its assumptions. In the third period, during which the police forces are at all-time high saturation levels, there is little evidence of deterrence for the most valid indicators.

METHODOLOGICAL NOTES

Experimentation results with short cyclical time periods for correlations of the independent variable measures with nonwhite and white auto theft rates is shown in Table 7.8. Once again, the major purpose of the presentation of the table is for cursory insight into cross-currents of directions of correlations for cycles within the larger trend framework of the time periods. Illustrations follow on this point. The reader can discover others. The middle time period, again, shows inverse correlations for the relationship of percent white population in the years 1938-45, with positive correlations for the next five-year period. And again inverse correlations are shown for population change measures to auto theft for 1951-55, while positive correlations are shown for these measures during the five years 1946-50. Data on burglary and robbery during the third time period shows similar results, signaling that greater attention to the total configuration of structural changes over shorter time periods are needed for greater understanding of cyclical fluctuations than the

TABLE 7.8

Correlation of Independent Variables
with Auto Theft Rates
for Selected Short Time Periods

	1910-18		1919-28		1929-37		1938-45		1946-50		1951-55		1956-60		1961-65		1966-70	
	NW	W	NW	W	NW	W	NW	W	NW	W	NW	W	NW	W	NW	W	NW	W
Total population	.92	.81	.80	.66	-.69	.10	.03	.37	.41	.51	-.34	.22	-.09	.46	.86	-.66	-.22	.11
Percent total population change	.55	.24	.12	.08	.38	.72	.74	.66	.77	.29	-.74	-.45	-.64	.08	-.85	.71	-.67	-.85
Percent nonwhite population change	.44	.15	.16	.00	.41	.70	.85	.78	.24	.31	-.30	-.94	.33	.86	-.57	.35	.18	.75
Percent white population change	.56	.23	.12	.10	.37	.74	.69	.61	.83	.29	-.69	-.15	-.98	-.69	.81	.85	-.40	-.90
Size police force	.80	.66	.81	.71	-.83	-.40	.16	.27	-.75	.36	.14	-.57	-.25	-.71	.94	-.71	-.25	-.68
Percent nonwhite population	-.88	-.90	.57	.47	-.78	-.11	.56	.36	-.43	-.38	.52	-.25	-.50	-.87	.98	-.92	.31	.07
Percent white population	.88	.89	-.57	-.47	.75	.11	-.54	-.34	.43	.38	-.52	.25	.50	.87	-.99	.92	-.31	-.07
Rate of growth total population	.16	-.03	-.04	.03	.68	.80	.85	.46	.67	-.34	-.54	-.70	-.52	.18	-.74	.37	-.73	-.90
Rate of growth nonwhite	-.52	-.21	.18	.04	.01	.24	-.16	.26	-.60	.38	.68	-.11	.89	.33	-.39	.06	.15	.78
Rate of growth white	.45	.14	-.19	-.02	.07	.01	.13	-.26	.65	-.38	-.62	.22	-.92	-.38	.38	-.07	-.20	-.83
Total auto registrations	—	.74	.85	.54	.18	-.56	.13	-.18	-.53	-.39	.30	-.47	.04	-.49	.94	-.94	.35	-.04
Taxes on banks and corporations	.72	.72	.56	.39	.12	-.25	-.14	-.02	-.03	-.07	.72	.09	-.55	-.86	.97	-.84	-.12	-.40
Taxes on lands assessments and improvements	.76	.88	.79	.72	.41	.51	-.27	.03	-.37	-.38	.63	-.12	-.47	-.80	.96	-.91	.18	-.38
Average consumer price index	.85	.85	-.10	-.06	.14	-.52	-.13	.16	-.79	-.27	.93	.38	-.63	-.91	.99	-.91	.05	-.41

Source: Compiled by the author.

174

TABLE 7.9

Lagged Effects for Correlations of Selected Ecological and
Economic Measures with Selected Property Crimes

Crime	1946-70								1919-45							
	Non-White				White				Non-White				White			
	0	1	2	3	0	1	2	3	0	1	2	3	0	1	2	3
Auto theft																
Price index	.55	.75	.72	.69	-.36	-.35	-.32	-.25	-.22	-.26	-.16	-.01	-.24	-.28	-.21	-.03
Taxes/land assessments and improvements	.65	.75	.75	.77	-.48	-.47	-.48	-.46	.09	.21	.30	.21	.04	.11	.10	.11
Population size	-.21	-.36	-.33	-.37	.02	.01	-.15	-.19	-.03	-.11	-.12	-.14	-.15	-.21	-.25	-.33
Size police force	.46	.67	.70	.64	-.45	-.51	-.50	-.44	.25	-.08	.10	-.05	.00	-.13	-.01	-.20
Grand larceny																
Price index	-.76	-.81	-.82	-.86	-.85	-.86	-.91	-.92	.32	.42	.42	.44	.13	.30	.33	.38
Taxes/land assessments and improvements	-.69	-.68	-.67	-.67	-.80	-.81	-.80	-.81	-.38	-.35	-.31	-.28	-.41	-.39	-.31	-.28
Population size	.70	.70	.70	-.76	.70	.69	.68	.65	-.63	-.56	-.49	-.53	-.66	-.62	-.57	-.57
Size police force	-.61	-.66	-.57	-.52	-.72	-.70	-.70	-.66	-.58	-.34	-.30	-.18	.53	-.33	-.40	-.28

<u>Source</u>: Compiled by the author.

time frames used. Alternatively, cyclical effects should be statistically removed from the series.

Time Lags

On the basis of experimentation with the effects of short-term time lags (0,1,2, and 3 years) here, further experimentation with the effects of delayed impact of structural variables on crime rates is warranted. It has been observed that lagging procedures for the effect of economic variables markedly affect some of the violent crime rates. This finding is applicable to some cases for Class I property crimes, as well. The effect of lags, while strong, is somewhat less striking. In Period III (see Table 7.9), nonwhite grand larceny moves from -.76 to -.86 with the price index and for white from -.85 to -.92. Similar effects are found for burglary. Again, for Period II, increases for nonwhite grand larceny rise from .32 to .44 and for white larceny from .13 to .38. Similar results are found for robbery and for burglary. These illustrations, then, show some evidence of lagged effects. The amount of change is less notable for other economic measures.

Effects of short lags for population size and police force size on correlations were not found. Experimentation with long time lags, as well, may be warranted. Thus, additional research should pinpoint a choice of lag procedures for each variable. These could then be entered into multiple regression structural equations.

REFERENCES

Bienen, Henry. 1968. Violence and Social Change: A Review of Current Literature. Chicago: University of Chicago Press.

Gould, Leroy C. 1969. "The Changing Structure of Property Crime in an Affluent Society." Social Forces 48 (September): 1-10.

Gurr, Ted Robert. 1976. Rogues, Rebels, and Reformers: A Political History of Urban Crime and Conflict. Beverly Hills: Sage Publications.

Henry, Andrew F. and James F. Short, Jr. 1954, 1964. Suicide and Homicide. New York: Free Press.

Hirschi, Travis and Hanan C. Selvin. 1967. Delinquency Research: An Appraisal of Analytic Methods. New York: Free Press.

Merton, Robert K. 1938. "Social Structure and Anomie." American Sociological Review 3 (October): 672-82.

Moss, Milton. 1968. "Consumption: A Report on Contemporary Issues." In Indicators of Social Change: Concepts and Measurements, ed. Eleanor Bernert Sheldon and Wilbert E. Moore. New York: Russell Sage Foundation.

Ogburn, William. 1935. "Factors in Variation of Crime Among Cities." Journal of American Statistical Association 30 (March): 12-20.

Sutherland, Edwin. 1937, 1963. The Professional Thief. Chicago: University of Chicago Press.

8

CONCLUSIONS AND
IMPLICATIONS

If an agricultural expert were to study only the weather conditions of a particular locale before making recommendations to farmers for fertilizer mix to increase corn yields, the impact on the crop potential would be likely to be ill-aimed. Obviously, the soil characteristics, disease conditions in the area, hardiness of the seed, and the intermix of all of these should enter into his calculations of diagnosis and prescription in order to achieve increased productivity. Yet just such one-sided observation is not uncharacteristic of a good deal of criminological theory and research, as well as citizen belief and social policy for treatment of those human beings identified as the crime problem. To make the connection verbally expeditious through the use of the absurd, it should be obvious, as well, that a farmer would not succeed in cajoling a reluctant or misguided or unsocialized corn seed to grow in ways that are expected through the use of soft words (in spite of beliefs as to the efficacy of human communication on plant life) or by threats of punishment. Yet current treatment modalities rely largely upon counseling and/or punishment to induce individual conformity, with little attention to the conditions that produce the crop. Myths perpetuate the efficacy of these approaches, despite contrary evidence. The disjunction between causation, practice, and beliefs has been identified more completely in Chapter 1. In short, criminological expertise rests not infrequently on theoretical conviction and university socialization. Empirical research fails to test alternative hypotheses, that is, measurement on two or more independent variables. Year after year, decade after decade, textbooks remain catalogues of theories, with little accomplished towards the long-called-for integration of theory, or establishment of linkages. Even those theories that fail tests of empiricism remain on the lists.

The intent here, then, is in contrast. It is one of deliberate perambulation, of moving toward the identification of possible outer boundaries for the establishment of an empirically based, historically oriented macrocriminology, with the end in view of linking these, in turn, to microperspectives that now dominate the field. Toward this end, interdisciplinary explorations were brought to bear both with theoretical leads and methods. Considerable experimentation was undertaken with a number of statistical techniques, and a number of hypotheses were gleaned, especially for those substantive areas in which there has been a paucity of research. These provide a wealth of possible directions for teams of researchers for years to come. It is hoped that verbal critiques on the weaknesses of this work will be sufficiently strong to incite a matching of words with empirical action. Much remains to be done.

A tentative answer is given here to the general substantive question explored: What are the properties of the social system of a city that account for crime and suicide levels? Four independent variables are identified on the basis of theoretical inspection; three of these factors are found testable with time series data; and two[*] are found crucial as antecedents of crime and suicide levels, namely, change processes associated with ecological and economic conditions. These are posited as leading to structural stress and anomie. Both are found, in repeated tests, to explain relatively high levels of variance and to tend toward substantiation of theoretically based hypotheses. Revised formal control hypotheses are constructed and tested, after the findings for violent crimes were reviewed, and before the findings for property crimes were analyzed. Findings on the police, in short, are in the opposite direction posed by deterrence theory. A "strain" vocabulary is suggested instead.

Both the economic and ecological variables are discovered, in repeated tests, to explain relatively high levels of variance. In some 67 tests on Class I crimes and suicide over three time periods, an average of 73 percent of the total variance is explained with measures on the three factors. Of the total 48 tests for specific Class I crimes and suicide, 42 cases explain from 60 to 90 percent of the variance. In 22 cases, over 80 percent of the variance is explained.

---

[*]The two variables exhibit a rough equivalence to two factors, identified by factor analysis in a recent cross-sectional study of cities as urbanization and poverty. It is not clear, however, how these are defined by the authors. The first appears to include population size and to exclude population change. Relatively low levels of variance are explained, averaging 25 percent. It can be speculated that at least part of this result is due to the lack of control for race. See Flango and Sherbenou (1976).

Time series data constitute a potential mechanism for the identification of the dynamic aspects of change in structural configurations and an empirical route for the identification of great change. The impress of the two factors, ecological and economic, are observed to vary over time in accordance with changing profiles of the mix of social structural variables identified here with both qualitative and quantitative observations reported in Chapters 5, 6, and 7. In some time periods, the two factors show relatively balanced weight and interact greatly with each other, as indicated by the limited statistical control cues from the multiple regression analyses; in some periods, and for some crimes, one factor is clearly more explanatory of variance than another; and in some periods one factor is more central for explaining crime rates for one racial social group than another.

Economic conditions—while hypothesized to affect levels of property crimes—are found somewhat unexpectedly to correlate highly with levels of personal violence, as well. Previous studies of violence do not tend to include the state of the economy as a factor associated with aggression (Goldstein 1975). Further, textbooks like Merton and Nisbet (1976), tend to neglect economic theories in macro-structural treatments. Findings on both violent and property street crimes, crimes often described as pushed by the recklessness of desperation, do not fit logically with theories and hypotheses derived from pleasure-pain calculations. Instead reported findings are consistent with a structural strain-anomie interpretation at the macrolevel and stress-alienation at the microlevels. A misguided faith in the degree of man's rationality* in the determination of action by middle-class scholars may be, quite simply, a result of projection. Fairly secure life styles should facilitate rational behavior, but by no means guarantee it.

The second factor, ecological change, was first posited as likely to affect violent crimes to a greater degree than property crimes. Again, there is a great deal of evidence that those macro-conditions affect levels of property crimes, as well as violent crimes, especially among crime arrests of the young and amateur, highly represented in formal control processes. Unanticipated cross-race effects of changes in the majority-minority population ratio show apparent modest effects on street crimes, especially those with a violent component. Intergroup theory, another level of antecedents, (see Figure 8.1, below) is applicable.

---

*At the nonaggregate level of research, there is further evidence that negates the rational model of behavior. A recent in-depth study of the professional fence suggests that "professionals, even learned ones, are not nearly as rational or disciplined . . . as they

The third factor identified here, the police, represents only one arm of the criminal justice system. It is found most frequently, in cases of specific Class I crimes and suicide, to correlate with increases (positive correlations), rather than with decreases, or inverse correlations expected from deterrence theory. The variable is thus interpreted as a factor which, under the historical social conditions encountered, adds to structural strain, tending to exacerbate levels of many Class I crimes and suicide. This is particularly the case for crime rates of the minority group examined in this city. Alternative explanations for these findings would favor differential police deployment and/or the limitations and bias of data. Findings, however, tend to remain consistent for the more valid indicators of crime (murder arrests, homicide mortality, and auto theft arrests), as well as for suicide mortality. At the same time, there is some evidence that the police do play a delimited role of deterrence for some crime types, for some population elements, under some conditions.

As has been emphasized throughout, the concentration here is upon measurement of the so-called major street crimes, or those that largely occupy the attention and thoughts of police, citizens, and politicians. It may well be that these have a more variant structural balance of antecedents than more frequently recurring misdeameanor crimes. The role of economic conditions in pushing towards street crimes, or crimes of desperation, may be more important than strain from anomie posited to result from ecological changes. Ecological-anomie and criminal justice controls are hypothesized to be important structural factors affecting the large bulk of crimes represented by grand and petty larceny, as well as other misdemeanors and other forms of theft such as white-collar crime which are not studied here.

The implication is clear: social ties of individuals are disrupted through strains engendered by macrostructural forces in society, largely beyond the control of any one individual. Yet current policy directions and expenditures aim at the management of individual change. The one focus that has been systemic and that is affected by political-economic processes, that is, the manipulation of the criminal justice system, is misplaced in its attempts to regulate, or lower the levels of specific street crimes.

---

let outsiders believe they are" (Klockars 1974, p. 170). In other areas of behavior, a landmark investigation concluded that learning theories "appear to account for the observed behavior rather better than do the theories of rational behavior . . . postulated in economic theory" (Simon 1957, p. 261).

Although the findings reported provide one tentative step in the directions suggested, a number of theoretical and methodological problems remain in need of refinement. Some of these constitute familiar problems for the criminologists, while others represent relatively new avenues of approach. In theory, there is a call for closer examination of interactions of macrostructural factors; of how these affect the nature of intergroup relations; and how all, in turn, help to regulate or control crime and deviance levels. There is need for studies of the interactions between levels of crime and deviance types, which can be regarded as a system, in itself (more on this shortly). In methods, refinements are needed in work toward structural equations, in further experimentation with techniques for statistical controls and interactions, and for time lags—in short, improvements of multivariate techniques applied to time series. While the general theoretical framework emerging is thought to be applicable to any macrosocial system (see the paradigm below), such as a city, the particular constellation of variables found in Washington, D. C. may or may not be applicable in the same way to other cities in other times. It would be expected that some variations would be found in the patterns of findings, should this research design be applied to other cities with varying economic, political, and social foundations.

TOWARD AN INTEGRATION OF MACRO-
WITH MICROSTRUCTURAL THEORIES

The few previous attempts to link microtheories to macro-theories to macrosituations have aimed largely at the explanation of individual criminal or delinquent or deviant behavior (notably, Yinger's field theory, 1965), rather than levels of these. Figure 8.1 is a mechanism providing routes for the inspection of theoretical and empirical linkages between connecting links to institutional and small group processes, through which the dynamic effects of change are filtered, with consequent ramifications for levels of crime-deviance conformity. As has been suggested in the Preface, an understanding of the reasons for fluctuations in levels of crime and deviance means essentially a diagnosis of the state of society. The question, then, is: How do the dimensions located here calibrate for purposes of hypothesis generation and theory integration? Figure 8.1 represents one visual mode for approaching these questions. The figure can thus serve as a tool or a point of departure for inspecting: (1) points of theoretical interactions, (2) a systemic model with geographies charted, and (3) location of substantive areas in which work in the field has been more and less concentrated. Objectives (1) and (2) will be primary here with the model as a guide, there is a good deal of speculation on theory and empiricism that can be brought to bear.

FIGURE 8.1

Societal Processes, System Elements,
and Crime-Deviance Levels, Schema A

At the outer points of the rim of the Figure 8.1 are located, in somewhat arbitrarily determined compass points, the four variables theoretically identified here. These represent change processes (the wavy lines are a gross attempt with tools at hand to suggest a third dimension of movement) affecting the social system of a city, or other macrosocial unit. At the outer annular boundaries are listed

the factors identified here, both theoretically and empirically, namely:
(1) west: economic instability-stability; (2) north: ecological instability-
stability; (3) east: value dissensus-consensus; (4) south: increasing
or decreasing formal controls. A number of dimensions have been
located within each of these factors; no doubt, others can be added.
For example, the economic factor can be viewed as continuous movement toward recession-depression-prosperity, stagnation-growth,
affluence-poverty, inequality-equality. Ecological changes can be
inspected, as well, along a number of dimensions. Those located
here include sheer mass of size of the population, growth or decline
in population, rate of population change, and size of majority-minority
groups relative to each other. Increases or decreases in formal control efforts are manifest in the changing size and technology of
policing forces, in court processes, in differentiated control of
tactical locations, in degree of punishment, and in the inequities or
equities of the judicial system at each decision point. All are considered points of potential stress(macro)-strain(micro) in the system.
The location of each point, such as the judicial system, may be
debated. It is located in the second ring, south, determined by the
nature of the political-economic system.

There is evidence in findings reported here of real interactions
at all points of the outer boundaries. Crucial are those between
economic and ecological changes. Both appear to interact with police
size. All, in turn, are posited to affect strains, directly and indirectly, in the system that lean to anomie and to the minimization or
maximization of crime and deviance levels. (Feierabend et al. 1969).
Rapid change has long been considered a prime locus for theoretical
emphasis in common for theories emphasizing social disorganization,
anomie, and economics. Their interactions are, at one and the same
time, theoretical, real, and statistical. Path diagrams may prove
to be one technique, among others, that would aid in further refinements of the task.

The outermost ring, then, represents the dynamic aspects of
the macrostructural institutional system, the nature of which both
affects and is affected by the processes of the body politic, and its
organizations and institutions: political organizations and institutions;
businesses and services; educational processes of all of these in the
schools, churches, media, down to small group processes of families
and peers. At this point, learning and socialization theory meshes
with macroprocesses affecting their outcome. For example, fathers
with relatively little social power and economic status in the larger
social system incur difficulty in bringing about socialization of their
children (Count-van Manen 1973). Peer groups have been documented
to supply important social needs in status and emotional supports
(Thrasher 1927; Short and Strodtbeck 1965) that families do not.

At the individual level of internal controls, commonly called conscience, it has been shown that external controls or punishment does not tend to lead to internalized controls and socialization, without rewards experienced within microgroups, notably the family.

Crime and deviance levels are represented here as shunted off from the center location, or conformity levels. The analogy, from the physical sciences, while not originally intended, keeps coming back. It is tempting to think of crime and deviance as being pulled by forces from the nucleus of conformity. Then philosophical questions on the inherent nature of man—evil/good, for example— become evident and will be avoided. If Figure 8.1 could reflect change process, a more unchanging or stable society is predicted to have relatively small levels of crime and deviance, with a larger conformity center. On the other hand, a more changing and unstable society is hypothesized to show greater crime and deviance levels— that is, until new or revised roles and values are incorporated into a transformation of the system. It is at this point, then, that structural theory has been labeled as conservative. Perhaps the price of rapid change is, at least temporarily, uncertainty of values, of expected role relations, and of greater crime and deviance levels. This hypothesis need not be accompanied by a value judgement that change should not take place.

The writer hypothesizes that the most recent epoch of U.S. history is one in which the inner circle of conformity is small and the outer circle of crime very large. That is, as mentioned earlier, there may be rather general agreement to deviate, with the rule, "any means justifies the ends" permeating the system not only at the bottom, where it is more likely to surface, given our system of formal controls, than at the upper reaches of the power structure. Thus, President Richard Nixon was a reflection of a general tendency, further exacerbating it. Such a state, if accurately represented, could help to explain why sociologists, in their naive attempts to empirically capture substantive values in verbal tests, have had little success in differentiating the values of the criminal from those of the noncriminal.

Figure 8.1 demonstrates visually a number of points previously made. Crime and deviance levels, themselves, can be considered as an interacting system. That is, when strain is exerted at one point in the system (unemployment) it affects strains at other points as well (in the family and schools). Increasing police controls, given such circumstances, may only work to displace forms of crime or deviance to other points. More police on the streets, with A (west), B (north), and C (east) constant, is likely to shift crime from assault to bedroom rape, or from robbery to burglary.[*] Control of heroin

---

[*]Interactions between longitudinal crime types in individual criminal careers are reported Wolfgang (1969).

without simultaneous control attempts at other possible points of maneuver may simply shift usage to other drug forms, such as cocaine, methadone, or alcohol. As long, then, as other fulcrums for potential regulation (that is, control) of crime and deviance are not changed simultaneously, the pernicious and complex difficulties in controlling crime are likely to continue to persist.

Another way of stating the above is this: the permeating guidelines of our society—always to consume more and achieve more—were functional goals for a society and its economic base in a pioneering and developing historical stage. The continuing permeation of such goals is now likely to continue in a dysfunctional course for the present and the future, insofar as high levels of crime and deviance are the price of the orientation. Changes being called for by ecologists and some economists are stable growth and limitations on consumption involve a major transformations of the system. Without movement in these directions, however, the seeds of crime are laid at local levels, and of intergroup conflicts at both local and international levels. This aspect of the system of crime and deviance roles may be capable of being encompassed by the rubric of opportunity structures, as suggested in the work of Cloward and Ohlin (1960).

It is possible that in those families in which socialization within the individual has been successfully achieved, structural stress of the outer boundaries is more likely to be manifested in directions of sickness such as deviance, and even early death, which can be considered a form of deviance. The effects of social forces in stress on individuals are moderated, in turn, through small-group learning, labelling, and opportunity processes (Cloward and Ohlin 1960).

Findings on changing number ratios of minority-majority groups in the city suggest, as well, that intergroup power relations (third shell from the center) and/or conflict theory have a place in helping to understand the complexity of social structure, stress, and crime and deviance levels.

An alternative scheme for portraying systemic interactions is presented in Figure 8.2. In this instance, the systemic processes identified are shown in a hierarchy at the top of the page, with their interactions with each other and with institutions within the system, noted below. At the bottom are shown conformity-deviance levels, the products of the interactions of the dynamic process that come from and enter into effects filtered through the political, economic, educational criminal justice, and small-group systems. The crime levels (the last box entries) then are regulated largely by macrostructural factors.

FIGURE 8.2

Societal Processes, System Elements, and Crime-Deviance Levels, Schema B

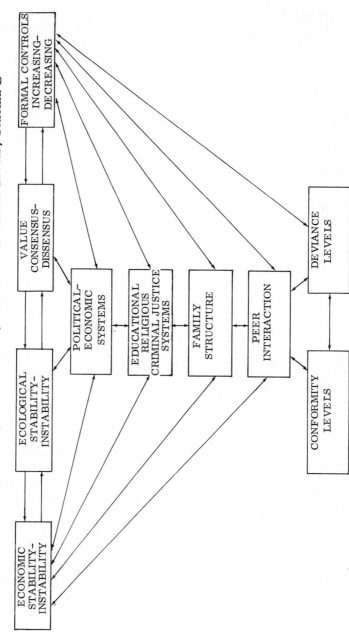

Source: Compiled by the author.

The static versus dynamic problem of social structure, then, here is resolved—consistent with the perspectives of a few others, notably Moore, 1963, and Vogt, 1960[*]—by the identification of stable structural elements of process at the outer rim of Diagram 1 and at the top of Diagram 2 with theoretical leads. These elements should be applicable to any macro area in any time, but the content or weight of each is expected to vary by locality and by historical epoch. Change, then, is encompassed by the changing weights of the elements. These would eventually be reflected in varying structural equations, as theory and technique become more sophisticated. Inherent in this view, as well, is the perspective that macrostructural forces largely control, in the sense of regulate, the size of crime and deviance (and thus conformity) levels, rather than microstructural processes (such as socialization), which have received so much attention in theory, research, and practice. These, in turn, are thought to be affected to a large degree in their outcomes by macrostructural forces.

AN EXAMPLE OF INTERACTIONS OF THEORY, LINKAGES, EMPIRICISM, AND POLICY IMPLICATIONS: SUBCULTURES

One structural theme widely circulated which purports to explain high black homicide rates is the subculture of violence, referred to repeatedly in Chapters 6 and 7. Here, a summary will be made of evidence that can be brought to bear on data from the study; possible interlinkage between macro- and microstructures will be suggested, alternative explanations proposed, and implications for policy drawn.

----

[*]For an excellent summary of the history of thought on social structure and structural analysis, see entries by Edmund R. Leach and Stanley H. Udy, Jr., in: The International Encyclopedia of the Social Sciences (New York: MacMillan, The Free Press, 1968), pp. 482-95. Among the especially pertinent writers for the position above see: Evon Z. Vogt entries, "On the Concept of Structure and Process in Cultural Anthropology," American Anthropologist 62 (1960): 18-33; Wilbert E. Moore, Social Change (Englewood Cliffs, N.J: Prentice-Hall, 1963).

The Evidence

Green (1970) and Flango and Sherbenou (1976) are among those who find no evidence[*] of a special culture among blacks from aggregate studies. How does the evidence look here? An inspection of the impact of percent nonwhite and percent white (the converse), and of changes in the population growth of the two groups, contributes insight into the question. The percent nonwhite can be seen to shift from an inverse correlation with murder in Period I to a positive correlation in Period III. This fact could be interpreted to confirm the subcultural hypothesis: that is, the more blacks, the stronger the subculture, and the more violence. For robbery, the tendency is in the same direction, but the positive correlation is very weak in the third epoch. For rape and assault, the percent nonwhite likewise shows an inverse relationship in the first period, but this continues through the most recent period. Further, the regression tables of previous chapters showed that the percent nonwhite, when controlled for population and economic variables, typically adds little to the explanation of the variance.

The weakest link in the evidence against the subcultural hypothesis is the entrance of percent nonwhite into the stepwise regression for nonwhite homicide in the third period. A modest correlation contributes substantially to the variance. For the nonwhite murder rate, the independent effect of the percentage of nonwhite is dissipated with controls exerted by other economic and population variables.

Further negative evidence is furnished by examination of the effects of nonwhite population increases. For both independent sources of data (murder arrests and homicide mortality), gains in nonwhites tend to ameliorate black violence rates. Further, cross-race effects show some tendency of these nonwhite measures to increase white violence rates. These findings could suggest cross-race socialization in violence, consistent with the subcultural notion. Alternatively, an intergroup-relations-based theory suggests increased strain experienced by the white minority, as it loses numerical strength. Since the same finding is exhibited for the black minority over time; that is, as whites grow in numerical strength, there are higher violence rates for blacks. The interpretation favored is that of strains emanating from the nature of changing intergroup relations.

----

[*]For additional negative evidence and appraisals, see Erlanger (1974, pp. 280-91); Doerner (1976); Cohen and Short (1976).

Macro- and Microstructural Interactions

Possible implications for the findings on the relationship between macrosocial changes and interactional patterns in small groups can be suggested. Economic and ecological changes, as well as increasing formal control mechanisms in the context of minority-majority intergroup relations, are interpreted as leading to structural strains and as raising homicide levels. Such societal conditions, in turn, can be expected to bring about strain in small-group interactions, in families and peer groups. Parents (the unstable poor, for example) who do not share in power have difficulty in socialization of their children (Count-van Manen 1974).

Policy Implications

Although Wolfgang (1967, p. 28) has suggested changes in social structure, he has simultaneously suggested the policy of deliberately "dispersing the group . . . (i.e., blacks) that share the subculture of violence . . . (that) . . . should weaken the value . . ." The evidence here in repeated tests, as in studies of other minorities, suggests to the contrary, that destroying the supportive mechanisms of a subculture would increase anomie and crime. A value of free choice for individuals and groups, should they choose to disperse themselves, can remain.

There is an insidious aspect to the subcultural theory, which has been widely disseminated in the media. It works to reinforce (and perhaps reflects) popular stereotypes, such as "the normal primitive." Core notions of both are similar and their effects on inequities in criminal justice processes have been documented (Swigert and Farrell, 1977). An excellent source bringing together the results of previous research on the relationship between race, crime, and the criminal justice processes, is that of Wolfgang and Cohen (1970).

Alternative policies, then, suggest a reduction of violence in the larger culture, reduction of the sources of structural strain, and/or dissemination of alternative means of dealing with stress. These last appear to accompany improved educational and social status.

Limitations in the Congruence of Vocabularies
of Theory and Measurement

In the natural, as well as in the social, sciences it becomes a necessary procedure to attempt to locate the nature of process by measuring its product. Intervening variables are often not measurable (Hirschi and Selvin 1967, pp. 152-53). Thus, the process of science is forced into inference. We think we know something about the digestive process by its results; about how atoms move, by their traces. Here then is an attempt to learn something about the conditions that are thought to lead to crime through posited processes variously labeled as anomie, stress, and forces. These mental constructs may have more facets in common than originally thought. A force is something that in the natural sciences is thought to push toward or pull or draw apart, as a result of pressures or stress. Such a vocabulary is not literal in either the physical or the social sciences (Jammer 1957). The notion of force, then, can be tested only by its expected effects.

Thus, although the concept of ideology as a force regulating crime is injected into theoretical notions here, there is no measurement instrument that directly links to the concept. This problem has thus far been an insoluble one for structural anomie theory. The attempt here is to locate the kinds of changes within a city that would logically be expected to lead to a decline in the beliefs or values or ideology that are posited to help tie society together. Yet, economic and ecological changes are in a later state of this research process thought to result both in the tearing apart of beliefs and in a loss of social cohesion (not measured). Some social scientists point to the lack of cohesion as ipso facto measured by the extent of deviance, or the "degree to which individuals are unable or unwilling to conform to the normative (or usual) patterns of behavior . . . expected" (Brenner 1973, p. 6). The use of tautology has been one avenue of exit for measurement difficulties in the field.

Nevertheless, a somewhat unusual argument is made here. It is not necessary to test the content of ideology, or of values and norms of behavior. In one sense, at least, it can be argued that these are irrelevant for sociological study. That is, it is the function of ideology in its role as a force binding or splitting apart a particular society that is important, whatever the substance. It is the degree of agreement or disagreement that holds together a group. This does not intend to suggest that the writer does not personally believe content is not important. It may be crucial for global survival. The degree of consensus or dissensus within any one system then, is considered here to push toward or away from deviance—assuming that law and the prosecution of law are consistent with the social values.

Policy Implications

Findings on the importance of macrostructural factors in regulating crime levels refute the myth that street crimes can be controlled by continuing emphasis upon individual treatment forms that have permeated institutional caretaking and action programs for so many decades. The prescriptions are simply not tuned to the diagnosis.

Crime control efforts have, to some degree, changed policies with changing politican incumbancies. Improved police force technology was the goal in the Nixon-Ford eras. The Johnson and Kennedy administrations tended to emphasize local neighborhood community programs. The stance of Jimmy Carter is not yet fully known, but a full employment policy has obtained at least verbal allegiance. Should such a policy be enacted, it would be most important, fitting into the framework of economic forces identified here on the left spoke of Figure 8.1. Any one-sided or purely local effort is foredoomed to continued failure in the control of crime and deviance.

This statement directly contradicts the finding of the U.S. Congress that, according to the Omnibus Crime Control and Safe Streets Act of 1968 (U.S. Department of Justice):

> ... crime is essentially a local problem that must be dealt with by State and local governments if it is to be controlled effectively. It is, therefore, the declared policy of the Congress to assist State and local governments in strengthening and improving law enforcement and criminal justice at every level by national assistance.

As long as the criminal justice nonsystem continues to rest on the unfounded faith (for which social science has accumulated much contradictory evidence, including this effort) that control of crime rests with it, the above article is consistent. When it becomes evident how illusory is this mirage, a changed concept must result. That is, local areas, by themselves, are unlikely to be able to control those facets of the social structure which regulate crime levels, as identified elsewhere and synthesized herein. Efforts to achieve such economic goals as full employment, to reduce inequalities in business, education, jobs, and housing, and to alter perceptions of relative deprivation and consumption goals, or values, are unlikely to succeed without carefully thought-out aims and mechanics at the federal level (see Friedman 1975). A vigorously expanding economy with a simultaneous lowering of delimited squandering of scarce resources, notably energy, represents a combination of transformations which will take the best wills, minds, dedication, and other resources to achieve. An obvious illustration: current movement towards the conversion of a large, luxury automobile from a symbol of status to one of selfish and needless destruction of scarce resources. The goal of transforming the production of built-in obsolescence of material goods to technologically feasible long-run use would simultaneously free armies of bill collectors and debtors (civil crime), and reduce actual and experienced deprivation gaps. The new motto, "small is beautiful" replacing the old, "the biggest is best" is necessary for human survival in a world with awakening desires and demanding equitable distribution of world resources in the context of changing world power balances. Such events appear possible only if short-run corporation profit aims can be subordinated to moderation and change for long-run survival. The real control of crime levels rests simultaneously with such developments. These elements, then, refer to the East (economic) and the West (anomie) theoretical principles in the paradigm presented here.

Policies for the control of elements of the ecological-population balance (the northern fulcrum of the diagram) raise serious philosophical questions for individual liberties. While geographic mobility, for example, has been controlled begnignly in some countries and not so benignly in others, the process would be regarded as undue restraint in this country.

Barring any further radical population redistributions of populace such as have taken place with large movements of Europeans to America, from southern agriculture areas to northern cities by Afro-Americans, and from cities to suburbs, the impact of migration on crime levels is close to spending its course. The major possible migratory push of the future would occur if total financial and social disaster overtake our cities. With this eventuality, a major deurbanization process is likely, and would again represent major transformation.

Nevertheless, some questions may be at least raised concerning population balances and movements which are found to affect crime rates. What is the ideal size of a city for its financial solvency, for human habitat, and for the minimization of crime levels? Just how much migration and immigration represent a high price to pay in crime for a city? If majority-minority relationships continue to be painful realities, what is the ideal ratio or mix of group constituency from the perspective of crime minimization? The deliberately designed architecture of human relationships is as necessary as that of spatial-aesthetic plans.

As to the fourth, or southern fulcrum point for the macrostructural factors, the elements of formal control: In this and other research findings, there is quite consistent evidence that the criminal justice system is not the source of regulation or control of crime, at least not for specific Class I street crimes studied here and of concern to citizens and politicians. Although the police and other elements of the judicial system are necessary components of modern society, and although these should become as impartial, fair, and just as possible, their effects in past years have been both to maximize strain-anomie effects, and to exacerbate crime levels. Formal control efforts represented by the criminal justice system must be divested of direct responsibility for crime regulation. In addition to its stated dysfunctional effects, it in practice teaches the police how to become better deviants in reporting crime, which in turn makes the work of structural research more difficult. It is at the same time possible that increased efforts at the policing of crimes committed by professional criminals, including those who pursue conventional professions and jobs, (white collar crime) might result in the achievement of a deterrence function.

In sum, the major foci of real control efforts to reduce crimes most feared rest with those elements of the social structure identified as interacting here, namely the economic and value systems. It may well be that the major pressures for such transformations will originate outside the local city and outside the United States.

With this thought, a major weakness inherent in the concept of system, as it has been delineated in the past, becomes apparent. Its dimensions have included those of interaction, wholeness, transformation, and self-regulation (Piaget 1970). It is the last-mentioned point which is brought into question. The old warning of the wise poets that "no man is an island unto himself" appears to have become increasingly applicable to systems as well. No system is a system unto itself. This limitation is, perhaps, most apparent for the field of crime in acts of terrorism, not under investigation here. Such crimes appear to be bewildering nightmares, without sense. But they are suggested here as frequently the result of interactions between systems boundaries.

For purposes of hypothetical application of the theoretical paradigm presented here, the species of political terrorism will serve as an illustration, especially since such a case recently occurred in Washington, D.C. The theoretical frame may of course, be applied to other places and times as well. For example, it appears relevent for a recent study of nineteenth century crime in England (see Tobias 1972).

Application of the elements of Figure 8.2 would suggest a structural hypothetical equation of elements that would fit into, again, the four spokes, with weight upon the economic and anomie.

More specifically, terrorist groups that are organized tend to have political-economic aims related to some reallocation of power resources, accompanied by a deep sense of group injustice (anomie) and individual alienation. These occur just as a particular group and its members achieve gains in education and status, but serve in the interim stages to increase their sense of relative deprivation. The violence potential is reinforced by intergroup struggles within and between system borders and by rigid, competing ideologies which flourish in a rapidly changing, uncertain, and seemingly unjust situation.

These factors—mass structural variables—appear to permeate in common far-flung manifestations of organized violence, whether in bombs exploding in exclusive London department stores, in Irish pubs, in mails and airways, in killings at the Olympic games, in assassinations of world leaders, or in sabres and machetes on Sixteenth Street in Washington, D.C. Blood is erased from the streets and cleaned from the floors. Fears are momentarily pushed back. Sales of security mechanisms soar. And the "experts" continue to debate the efficacy of police tactics for the so-called control of the next incident.

As the author reflects on the existential meaning of what has been attempted here in the cold vocabulary and measurement of science, it seems that no better translation could be made than with the ingredients of the life-death drama that recently took place in the streets and buildings of the nation's capital. Knife-wieldings and shoot-outs were part of the scenario that was played in the corridors and offices of City Hall on Pennsylvania Avenue (not far from the offices of the U.S. Department of Justice and the Federal Bureau of Investigation), in a Muslim mosque on Embassy Row of Massachusetts Avenue (not far from the assassination of a former Chilean diplomat a few months preceding), and in the offices of B'nai B'rith (located in an upper-middle class, white business neighborhood). At the three locations were the combined representatives of the forces of the District of Columbia Police Department, the Federal Bureau of Investigation, the President's special security forces, and the U.S. Department of Justice—all joining, in the somewhat festive spring days, with tight-lipped efforts to control the situation. As the Pakistani, Iranian, and Egyptian ambassadors joined the scene in the mosque for negotiations, threats of efficiently chopped heads rolling onto the city streets hung in the fresh March air.

It happened that, as the drama unfolded for all to safely view on their television sets, a local educational television station had also scheduled a program on an obscure Australian head-hunting tribe, thought to be responsible for the killing of young

Michael Rockefeller. After seeing the customs of the tribe, it was remarked by the announcer that oil, coincidentally perhaps, had been discovered near the villages. The television then flashed a new development in native life. The undressed black natives were now dressed, under the tutelage of a local priest teaching them not to kill neighboring tribes. They were then shown working together nearby to clear the forest for a new airstrip. The payment for their labors: cigarettes, added to their group customs, the gift of civilization. Some might regard it as a handy form of addiction to help bridge the tensions and stress sure to follow in the transition.

Back in Washington, the police were being congratulated on their excellent handling of the tense situation. Traffic began to return to the streets that had been emptied. District of Columbia citizens would no longer need to resent the traffic tieups. Those who couldn't see Bully, the dramatic enactment of Teddy Roosevelt's life, could surely get new tickets from the National Theater. Newspapers began to report the latest pronouncements (in a line or two) of expert criminologists as the reasons for the episode. When the smoke and blood had cleared, the toll looked like this:

1. The narrow escape from death of Marion Barry, the local black council member and city leader, with a bullet lodged close to his heart. Barry had some years ago pioneered an anticrime program with sizable funds and no strings attached, the finding granted by the then head of the U.S. Department of Labor, Wilbur Cohen.

2. The death of young Maurice Williams, a local WHUR radio announcer. Williams was a recent graduate of Howard University's new communications school. WHUR is Howard University's recently acquired FM station, a gift of Mrs. Katharine Graham, publisher of The Washington Post.

3. The paralysis from the waist down of Robert Pierce, an Antioch law school intern.

4. An unknown number of people with stab wounds, a few causing paralysis, among the 134 hostages. Some have undergone surgery at George Washington Hospital Medical Center. Among the hostages were those who were reminded of their previous experiences in Nazi Germany. Mayor Walter Washington, the original target of the Hanafi gunmen, was safe. The Muslims made the wrong turn as they ran for his office.

Incidents of terrorism, such as reported here, expose the weakness of the maxim that has dominated criminological thought for the last half century at least (see F. Thrasher, 1927, a leading exponent of this theory), mainly: crime and its control are local problems. Inherent in this belief, which still exerts profound influence on institutions currently dedicated to crime control, are a

series of unwarranted assumptions that are seldom questioned and
that have failed the tests of time. Police activities, for example, are
locally administered, but there is increasing evidence that local
police do not control street crime levels. Informal community controls appear to be largely nonoperative, or ineffectual. In scattered
incidences of victory, aroused citizen groups have installed street
lights or initiated interpersonal alert systems. While lowering crime
in one community, the effects have been to raise crime incidence in
adjacent areas. At the level of individual therapy, the pervasive goal
has been to bring about attitudinal change as a prerequisite to rehabilitation. The embarassing record of failure of counseling programs
has furnished some stimulus for a shift to the alternative view that
structural positions of individuals (as social class, ethnicity, and
so on) help to predetermine attitudes. But the programs remain.

On the other hand, recent empirical results, such as those
reported and reviewed here, are cumulative in demonstrating that
it is feasible to identify a few factors of the macrosystem that do
regulate street crime levels. Moreover, it is self-evident that
these elements—as business cycles and demographic balances—are
less affected by local than by national and even international policies.
Unfortunately, the social lag that exists between sociological findings
and policy formation remains. Current efforts at crime control remain
geared to the wisdom of earlier epochs of research. Simply put, we
continue to put the cart before the horse, or the microlevels before
the macro.

REFERENCES

Brenner, Meyer Harvey, 1973. Mental Illness and the Economy.
Cambridge, Mass.: Harvard University Press.

Cloward, Richard A. and Lloyd E. Ohlin. 1960. Delinquency
and Opportunity: A Theory of Delinquent Gangs. Glencoe, Ill.: Free
Press.

Cohen, Albert K. and James F. Short, Jr. 1976. In Contemporary Social Problems, ed. R. K. Merton and Robert Niobet. New
York: Harcourt Brace.

Comer, James P. 1969. "The Dynamics of Black and White
Violence, " in Violence in America, Vol. 2, Staff report to the
National Commission on the Causes and Prevention of Violence by
Hugh Davis Graham and Ted Robert Gurr. (Washington, D.C., U.S.
Government Printing Office).

Count-van Manen, Gloria and Cecil Josiah. 1974. "Person and Property Crimes as Etiological Types: Some Empirical Evidence for the District of Columbia, 1890-1970." Unpublished paper delivered at the Annual Meetings of the International Sociological Society, 1974, Toronto, Canada.

Doerner, William G. 1976. "The Index of Southernness Revisited." In Social Systems, Crime, Delinquency, and Deviance: A Reader in Structurally-Oriented Studies, ed. G. Count-van Manen. Washington, D.C.: University Press of America.

Erlanger. Howard S. 1974. "The Empirical Status of the Subculture of Violence Thesis." Social Problems 22: 280-91.

Ezekial, Mordecai and Karl A. Fox. 1959. Methods of Correlation and Regression Analysis. New York: Wiley.

Feierabend, Ivo K., Rosalind L. Feierabend, and Betty A. Nesvold. 1969. "Social Change and Political Violence: Cross-National Patterns." In Violence in America, Vol. 2. Staff Report to the National Commission on the Causes and Prevention of Violence, by Hugh Davis Graham and Ted Robert Gurr. Washington, D.C.: U.S. Government Printing Office.

Flango, Victor Eugene and Edgar L. Sherbenou. 1976. "Poverty, Urbanization, and Crime."

Friedman, Robert. 1975. "Institutional Racism: How to Discriminate Without Really Trying." In Racial Discrimination in the United States, ed. T. F. Pettigrew. New York: Harper and Row.

Goldstein, Jeffrey H. 1975. Aggression and Crimes of Violence. New York: Oxford University Press.

Green, Edward. 1970. "Race, Social Status, and Criminal Arrest." American Sociological Review 35 (June): 476-90.

Gurr, Ted Robert. 1976. Rogues, Rebels, and Reformers: A Political History of Urban Crime and Conflict. Beverly Hills: Sage Publications.

Hirschi, Travis and Hanan C. Selvin. 1967. Delinquency Research: An Appraisal of Analytic Methods. New York: Free Press.

Jammer, Max. 1957. Concepts of Force: A Study in the Foundations of Dynamics. Cambridge: Harvard University Press.

Klockars, Carl B. 1974. The Professional Fence. New York: Free Press.

Merton, Robert K. and Robert Niobet. 1976. Contemporary Social Problems. New York: Harcourt Brace.

Piaget, Jean. 1968, 1970. Structuralism. Translated and edited by Chaninah Maschler. New York: Harper and Row.

Rao, Potluri and Roger LeRoy Miller. 1971. Applied Econometrics. Belmont, Calif.: Wadsworth.

Short, James F. Jr., and Fred L. Strodtbeck. 1965. Group Process and Gang Delinquency. Chicago: University of Chicago Press.

Simon, Herbert H. 1957. Models of Man. New York: Wiley.

Swigert, Victoria Lynn and Ronald A. Farrell. 1977. "Normal Homicides and the Law." American Sociological Review 42: 16-32.

Thrasher, Frederic M. 1927. The Gang. Chicago: University of Chicago Press.

Tobias, J. J. 1972. Urban Crime in Victorian England. New York: Schocken Books.

Tobin, James. 1975. "The Negative Income Tax." In Racial Discrimination, in the United States, ed. T. F. Pettigrew. New York: Harper and Row.

U. S. Department of Justice. Program Plan for Statistics, 1977-81 (Washington, D.C.: Government Printing Office).

Wolfgang, Marvin E. 1967. Studies in Violence. New York: Harper and Row.

_____.1969. "Recidivism Over the Criminal Career." In Crimes of Violence, Vol. 12 (December), pp. 525-61 Report to the National Commission on the Causes and Prevention of Violence. Washington, D.C.: Government Printing Office.

Wolfgang, Marvin E. and Bernard Cohen. 1970. Crime and Race. New York: American Jewish Committee.

Yinger, Milton J. 1965. Toward a Field Theory of Behavior: Personality and Social Structure. New York: McGraw-Hill.

TABLE A.1
Size of the Police Force per 100,000 Population, and Nonwhite
and White Arrests per 100,000 Population for Homicide and for
Robbery, District of Columbia, 1890-1970

Year	Actual Police Force Size	Per 100,000 Population	Nonwhite Arrest Rates		White Arrest Rates	
			Homicide	Robbery	Homicide	Robbery
1890	320	138.9	.2	3.9	2.6	.6
1891	376	156.9	7.7	16.6	.6	—
1892	408	164.3	6.2	24.9	5.4	1.2
1893	418	162.5	9.7	12.1	6.3	5.2
1894	433	163.2	10.5	8.2	2.2	1.7
1895	449	161.6	4.5	14.7	3.1	2.6
1896	464	166.9	10.1	11.2	3.3	3.1
1897	475	170.8	10.1	3.3	.5	1.5
1898	525	180.6	14.5	4.4	2.6	3.1
1899	544	195.3	17.8	6.7	2.6	6.8
1900	560	200.9	9.3	—	9.1	—
1901	571	200.5	6.8	—	3.1	—
1902	590	203.3	15.7	—	1.5	—
1903	626	211.9	8.9	—	2.9	.9
1904	641	212.1	9.9	18.0	1.4	18.0
1905	686	222.5	5.4	14.8	3.7	14.8
1906	694	222.3	11.9	45.2	5.1	10.4
1907	731	230.4	8.6	63.1	6.3	4.7
1908	731	227.4	16.0	49.0	2.2	14.0
1909	731	223.5	7.4	37.0	2.6	7.3
1910	732	220.8	14.7	78.9	5.1	7.6
1911	732	212.8	11.4	81.8	4.8	10.5
1912	735	216.2	17.0	108.9	3.7	10.5
1913	722	201.8	19.5	73.8	6.1	15.7
1914	715	194.5	11.1	54.6	2.6	8.5
1915	715	197.9	13.5	112.3	7.2	12.8
1916	807	222.4	28.5	137.3	3.0	26.8
1917	807	209.5	23.1	91.2	7.0	9.4
1918	821	196.6	23.0	107.5	5.1	7.9
1919	854	191.8	37.8	254.8	6.3	11.9
1920	899	205.5	32.5	177.0	7.6	8.5
1921	935	209.4	34.4	113.8	10.2	12.9
1922	935	208.0	30.3	117.5	8.7	10.1
1923	960	212.0	27.3	128.6	4.5	11.3
1924	968	212.2	32.8	124.5	5.0	20.4
1925	1152	249.8	30.1	102.4	6.7	24.0
1926	1281	273.1	34.8	139.9	7.2	13.3
1927	1284	269.8	31.9	142.0	6.1	29.7
1928	1285	268.3	25.7	183.1	6.0	21.9
1929	1261	261.2	39.8	110.1	4.5	24.9
1930	1262	259.2	25.6	124.9	5.7	19.7
1931	1281	254.0	42.6	107.6	9.6	36.8
1932	1341	261.4	43.2	200.3	10.8	33.8

(continued)

200

Year	Actual Police Force Size	Per 100,000 Population	Nonwhite Arrest Rates		White Arrest Rates	
			Homicide	Robbery	Homicide	Robbery
1933	1316	248.6	46.4	255.6	7.3	55.3
1934	1316	231.8	44.4	261.6	2.9	57.2
1935	1341	220.6	40.1	211.7	11.1	37.1
1936	1366	217.1	27.2	364.7	5.1	46.6
1937	1500[a]	243.4	32.8	271.6	5.1	49.0
1938	1500[a]	235.2	31.6	308.9	2.6	45.7
1939	1500	228.0	27.3	173.7	3.1	50.9
1940	1422	214.5	26.1	225.6	2.1	26.3
1941	1800[a]	235.6	21.8	240.4	4.8	55.6
1942	2300[b]	470.0	24.5	187.7	3.9	27.0
1943	1711	190.1	24.7	200.3	2.6	20.9
1944	1836	208.4	15.9	190.4	2.1	27.1
1945	1836	193.5	21.3	157.9	1.3	22.6
1946	1739	193.4	21.1	239.3	3.4	28.9
1947	2500	281.5	26.7	215.5	2.1	40.6
1948	2500	297.6	21.9	290.0	1.1	27.5
1949	1954	242.1	25.7	245.5	2.4	41.1
1950	1895	236.2	21.5	300.7	2.7	40.1
1951	2073	252.3	20.0	205.9	4.2	39.4
1952	2088	255.4	16.7	262.9	3.6	36.1
1953	2064	253.1	16.0	341.6	12.9	44.0
1954	2142	268.2	20.1	254.7	3.2	37.5
1955	2248	283.7	12.2	221.1	2.1	28.7
1956	2226	285.7	15.2	172.5	2.5	29.9
1957	2293	291.1	13.9	143.8	3.8	34.5
1958	2310	292.8	14.8	209.9	2.4	37.0
1959	2507	323.1	12.4	171.9	4.5	33.5
1960	2536	332.0	18.9	232.6	3.5	25.9
1961	2579	329.4	16.1	261.2	4.4	48.6
1962	2757	348.2	17.2	256.9	5.0	46.8
1963	2827	352.1	19.0	263.5	2.8	48.9
1964	2902	357.8	22.1	209.4	2.2	25.4
1965	2915	363.5	27.9	255.4	5.0	37.3
1966	2885	361.5	33.0	259.2	5.1	31.1
1967	2758	347.6	27.5	308.2	7.3	38.9
1968	2958	382.6	29.8	268.5	5.0	28.4
1969	3535	469.0	29.8	291.2	6.9	47.9
1970	4436	586.4	38.0	360.9	8.1	33.9

[a] Actual numbers in the police force not available. Data used are those of the authorized size of the force. Typically, the authorized numbers run somewhat higher than the size of the actual force.

[b] The number of the police in 1942 is inflated by a volunteer auxiliary police force of 4,000 members who averaged 10 hours of work per week.

Source: Annual Reports, District of Columbia Police Force.

TABLE A.2

Pearson Product-moment Correlations of Class I Crimes Against Every Other
Class I Crime for Nonwhite and Whites,
District of Columbia,
1890–1970

	Larceny		Robbery		Auto Theft		Assault		Rape		Homicide (Mortality)		Homicide (Arrest)	
	NW	W	NW	W	NW	W	NW	W	NW	W	NW	W	NW	W
Burglary	.50	.07[a]	.76	.69	.69	.74	.54	.55	.34	.49[c]	.60	.07[a]	.66	.33
Larceny			.22[c]	.02[a]	.35	.22[c]	.26[c]	.14[a]	-.02[a]	-.10[a]	.45	.23[c]	.40	-.01[c]
Robbery					.68	.75	.59	.51	.46	.33[c]	.55	.05[a]	.57	.11[a]
Auto theft							.31[b]	.40	.20[c]	.37	.70	.19[c]	.68	.42
Assault									.86	.73	.04[a]	-.08[a]	.09[a]	.19[c]
Rape											-.10[a]	-.11[a]	-.08[a]	.06
Homicide (mortality)													.81	.35
Homicide (arrest)													—	—

a Not significant
b Significance .002–.005.
c Significance .02–.10.
Note: Significance .001 except where otherwise noted
Source: U.S. Office of Vital Statistics and Annual Reports, District of Columbia Police Force.

TABLE A.3

Correlations of Types of Crime and Suicide for Nonwhites and Whites, 1890–1918

	Burglary NW	Burglary W	Larceny NW	Larceny W	Robbery NW	Robbery W	Auto Theft NW	Auto Theft W	Assault NW	Assault W	Rape NW	Rape W	Homicide (Mortality) NW	Homicide (Mortality) W	Suicide NW	Suicide W	Homicide (Arrest) NW	Homicide (Arrest) W
Burglary NW		.7417 (.001)	-.0293 (.880)	-.2007 (.297)	.7183 (.001)	.5107 (.005)	.5899 (.001)	.7786 (.001)	.3711 (.047)	.0060 (.975)	.0289 (.882)	-.0492 (.800)	.7319 (.001)	.3416 (.070)	.3454 (.067)	.2624 (.109)	.6211 (.001)	.3702 (.048)
Burglary W			-.2760 (.147)	-.4153 (.025)	.7117 (.001)	.5041 (.005)	.4227 (.022)	.6316 (.001)	.1672 (.386)	-.2153 (.262)	-.0522 (.788)	-.1025 (.597)	.4793 (.009)	.3221 (.088)	.5665 (.001)	.4733 (.010)	.6153 (.001)	.4314 (.019)
Larceny NW				.8123 (.001)	-.3383 (.073)	-.4319 (.019)	.1409 (.466)	.0292 (.880)	.4586 (.012)	.4905 (.007)	-.0180 (.926)	-.4274 (.021)	-.0520 (.789)	.0760 (.695)	-.4461 (.015)	-.4157 (.025)	-.1833 (.341)	-.2560 (.180)
Larceny W					-.4106 (.027)	-.4400 (.017)	-.1728 (.370)	-.2175 (.257)	-.4378 (.018)	-.6308 (.001)	-.1273 (.511)	-.2126 (.268)	-.3121 (.099)	-.0907 (.640)	-.4487 (.015)	-.2834 (.136)	-.3304 (.080)	-.3022 (.111)
Robbery NW						.7631 (.001)	.5392 (.003)	.6499 (.001)	.0243 (.901)	-.3796 (.042)	-.3235 (.087)	-.2495 (.192)	.6157 (.001)	.2508 (.189)	.6499 (.001)	.6349 (.001)	.8531 (.001)	.7003 (.001)
Robbery W							.2214 (.248)	.3889 (.037)	-.2095 (.275)	-.3885 (.037)	-.4348 (.018)	-.4063 (.029)	.5103 (.005)	.1009 (.603)	.5336 (.003)	.6241 (.001)	.6125 (.001)	.5845 (.001)
Auto theft NW								.8773 (.001)	.3034 (.110)	-.1034 (.594)	-.0192 (.921)	-.1189 (.539)	.6019 (.001)	.2131 (.267)	.2909 (.126)	.0008 (.997)	.6613 (.001)	.4541 (.013)
Auto theft W									.3730 (.046)	-.0955 (.622)	-.0684 (.724)	-.0022 (.991)	.6357 (.001)	.2059 (.284)	.4029 (.030)	.1086 (.575)	.7275 (.001)	.5188 (.004)
Assault NW										.7238 (.001)	.1872 (.331)	-.3871 (.038)	.1495 (.439)	.2737 (.145)	-.2556 (.181)	-.3041 (.109)	.0451 (.816)	-.4730 (.369)
Assault W											.2976 (.117)	.1360 (.482)	-.1264 (.513)	-.3268 (.084)	-.5101 (.005)	-.4123 (.026)	-.3554 (.058)	-.4524 (.014)
Rape NW												.3751 (.045)	-.0331 (.865)	.0827 (.670)	-.2183 (.225)	-.4159 (.025)	-.2980 (.116)	-.3851 (.039)
Rape W													-.1811 (.347)	.0792 (.683)	-.1526 (.430)	-.2655 (.164)	-.7393 (.471)	-.2013 (.295)
Homicide NW (mortality)														.1168 (.546)	.3787 (.082)	.1822 (.344)	.6639 (.007)	-.4899 (.007)
Homicide W (mortality)															.0073 (.970)	-.0277 (.887)	.3525 (.061)	.2730 (.152)
Suicide NW																.7570 (.001)	.6573 (.001)	.6920 (.001)
Suicide W																	.4807 (.008)	.5313 (.003)
Homicide NW (arrest)																		.9205 (.001)

Note: Figures in parentheses indicate levels of significance.

Source: U.S. Office of Vital Statistics and Annual Reports, District of Columbia Police Force.

TABLE A.4

Correlations of Types of Crime and Suicide for Nonwhites and Whites, 1919-45

	Burglary NW	Burglary W	Larceny NW	Larceny W	Robbery NW	Robbery W	Auto Theft NW	Auto Theft W	Assault NW	Assault W	Rape NW	Rape W	Homicide (Mortality) NW	Homicide (Mortality) W	Suicide NW	Suicide W	Homicide (Arrest) NW	Homicide (Arrest) W
Burglary NW		.3627 (.063)	-.0509 (.801)	-.0376 (.852)	.5404 (.004)	.6803 (.001)	.3764 (.053)	.6101 (.001)	-.3641 (.062)	.0743 (.713)	-.1987 (.320)	.2626 (.186)	.3642 (.062)	.0010 (.996)	.4083 (.035)	.5041 (.007)	.5969 (.001)	.1860 (.353)
Burglary W			-.2006 (.316)	-.1621 (.419)	-.0687 (.733)	.3565 (.068)	.4641 (.015)	.3234 (.100)	-.3414 (.081)	-.2539 (.201)	-.1714 (.393)	.3160 (.608)	.2517 (.205)	.0859 (.670)	.3208 (.103)	.4531 (.018)	.4933 (.009)	.2124 (.287)
Larceny NW				.8332 (.001)	-.2789 (.159)	-.4060 (.036)	.1118 (.579)	.1105 (.583)	.0317 (.875)	-.3676 (.059)	-.2069 (.300)	.0036 (.986)	.3058 (.121)	.4265 (.027)	.1724 (.390)	.1201 (.551)	-.0806 (.689)	.3368 (.086)
Larceny W					-.3260 (.097)	-.2345 (.239)	.1917 (.338)	.1440 (.474)	.0315 (.876)	-.1958 (.328)	.0053 (.979)	-.0678 (.737)	.4034 (.037)	.4436 (.020)	.2658 (.180)	.2898 (.143)	.0033 (.987)	.2917 (.140)
Robbery NW						.6174 (.001)	.0588 (.771)	.1184 (.556)	-.4086 (.035)	-.2165 (.278)	.1188 (.555)	-.1163 (.563)	-.0337 (.867)	-.2710 (.172)	.2130 (.286)	.1224 (.543)	.2819 (.154)	.1918 (.338)
Robbery W							.3506 (.073)	.4153 (.031)	-.4927 (.009)	.0887 (.660)	.1042 (.605)	.1942 (.332)	.2209 (.268)	-.1839 (.358)	.4159 (.031)	.5494 (.003)	.4898 (.010)	.0657 (.745)
Auto theft NW								.7088 (.001)	.0020 (.992)	-.1307 (.516)	-.0541 (.789)	.4189 (.030)	.2066 (.301)	.1726 (.389)	.4008 (.038)	.2590 (.192)	.2766 (.163)	.0015 (.994)
Auto theft W									-.1662 (.407)	-.2694 (.174)	-.2926 (.139)	.4374 (.023)	.3763 (.053)	.2674 (.178)	.1732 (.388)	.2945 (.136)	.4823 (.011)	.1255 (.533)
Assault NW										.2260 (.257)	.0189 (.925)	-.1865 (.352)	-.4181 (.030)	-.3198 (.104)	-.2840 (.151)	-.5065 (.007)	-.5814 (.001)	-.1796 (.370)
Assault W											.1908 (.340)	-.2674 (.177)	-.2574 (.195)	-.0559 (.782)	.0543 (.788)	-.2639 (.184)	-.2207 (.269)	-.1015 (.614)
Rape NW												-.0773 (.720)	-.2153 (.281)	-.1240 (.538)	-.0815 (.686)	.0406 (.841)	-.2340 (.240)	-.0803 (.690)
Rape W													.2078 (.298)	.2822 (.154)	.3303 (.092)	.5280 (.005)	.5231 (.005)	-.0700 (.729)
Homicide NW (mortality)														.5864 (.001)	.3663 (.060)	.5911 (.001)	.7076 (.001)	.6447 (.001)
Homicide W (mortality)															.2725 (.169)	.2930 (.138)	.3948 (.042)	.3745 (.054)
Suicide NW																.5823 (.001)	.4558 (.017)	.1017 (.614)
Suicide W																	.7374 (.001)	.1890 (.345)
Homicide NW (arrest)																		.2439 (.220)

Note: Figures in parentheses indicate levels of significance.

Source: U.S. Office of Vital Statistics and Annual Reports, District of Columbia Police Force.

TABLE A.5

Correlations of Types of Crime and Suicide for Nonwhites and Whites, 1946-70

	Burglary		Larceny		Robbery		Auto Theft		Assault		Rape		Homicide (Mortality)		Suicide		Homicide (Arrest)	
	NW	W	NW	W	NW	W	NW	W	NW	W	NW	W	NW	W	NW	W	NW	W
Burglary NW		.4951 (.012)	.7155 (.001)	.6578 (.001)	.1054 (.616)	.0239 (.910)	-.3045 (.139)	-.0082 (.969)	.4923 (.012)	-.2994 (.146)	.1459 (.487)	-.0906 (.667)	-.0961 (.648)	-.3840 (.058)	.1401 (.504)	-.2599 (.210)	.0967 (.646)	-.1566 (.455)
Burglary W			.3372 (.127)	.3133 (.127)	.0854 (.685)	-.0472 (.823)	-.1181 (.574)	.3643 (.073)	.5148 (.008)	.1347 (.521)	.4041 (.045)	.3059 (.137)	-.2742 (.185)	-.2064 (.322)	-.0581 (.783)	-.1506 (.472)	.0059 (.978)	-.0602 (.775)
Larceny NW				.9388 (.001)	.0908 (.666)	.0752 (.721)	-.5209 (.008)	.0105 (.960)	.5802 (.002)	-.4999 (.011)	.1199 (.568)	-.2060 (.323)	-.0935 (.657)	-.4891 (.013)	.2714 (.189)	-.2782 (.178)	.2663 (.198)	-.2154 (.301)
Larceny W					.0443 (.833)	-.0159 (.940)	-.5933 (.002)	.1563 (.456)	.5979 (.002)	-.4783 (.016)	-.1241 (.555)	-.1489 (.478)	-.2592 (.214)	-.6022 (.001)	.3217 (.117)	-.3109 (.130)	.2323 (.264)	-.3137 (.127)
Robbery NW						.2606 (.208)	.2584 (.212)	-.5661 (.003)	-.0056 (.979)	.1228 (.559)	-.2058 (.324)	-.2760 (.182)	.5500 (.004)	.4021 (.046)	-.0155 (.941)	-.1543 (.462)	.1015 (.629)	.1969 (.345)
Robbery W							-.1947 (.351)	-.0093 (.965)	.0982 (.640)	.2941 (.154)	.1759 (.400)	-.0692 (.743)	-.0238 (.910)	.2256 (.278)	-.1047 (.618)	.2785 (.178)	.0847 (.687)	.3264 (.111)
Auto theft NW								-.1870 (.371)	-.5919 (.002)	.0098 (.963)	-.2983 (.147)	-.1182 (.574)	.4102 (.042)	.4830 (.014)	.0444 (.833)	.0085 (.968)	.2029 (.331)	.3935 (.052)
Auto theft W									.0342 (.871)	-.1631 (.436)	.0934 (.657)	.1417 (.499)	-.6959 (.001)	-.3745 (.065)	-.0760 (.718)	.0867 (.680)	-.0834 (.692)	-.1319 (.530)
Assault NW										.2899 (.160)	.7463 (.001)	.3582 (.079)	-.4255 (.034)	-.4920 (.012)	-.0917 (.663)	-.3652 (.073)	-.1311 (.532)	-.2775 (.179)
Assault W											.5370 (.006)	-.5786 (.001)	-.1378 (.511)	.2544 (.220)	-.4058 (.044)	-.0283 (.893)	-.2617 (.206)	-.2259 (.278)
Rape NW												.6735 (.001)	-.3985 (.049)	-.2317 (.265)	-.1541 (.402)	-.2413 (.245)	-.2377 (.253)	-.1487 (.478)
Rape W													-.3894 (.054)	-.2390 (.250)	-.1294 (.538)	-.3038 (.531)	-.3038 (.140)	-.0491 (.816)
Homicide NW (mortality)														.5762 (.003)	.1330 (.526)	-.0593 (.778)	.2133 (.308)	.2576 (.214)
Homicide W (mortality)															-.1121 (.594)	.2912 (.158)	.0089 (.966)	.4099 (.042)
Suicide NW																-.1164 (.580)	.2896 (.160)	-.1924 (.357)
Suicide W																	-.0733 (.728)	.2181 (.295)
Homicide NW (arrest)																		.7053 (.001)

Note: Figures in parentheses indicate levels of significance.
Source: U.S. Office of Vital Statistics and Annual Reports, District of Columbia Police Force.

TABLE A.6

Correlations of Independent Variables with Each Other, 1890–1918

	2 (2)	3 (3)	4 (4)	5 (5)	6 (6)	7 (7)	8 (8)	9 (9)	10 (10)	11 (11)	12 (12)	13 (13)	14 (14)	15 (15)	16 (16)
1. Total population (1)	.29	.06	.36	.92	-.98	.98	.13	-.10	-.00	.96	1.0	—	.92	.97	.68
2. Percent total population change (2)		.93	.99	.12	-.26	.26	.69	-.25	.09	.23	.29	—	.18	.20	.33
3. Percent nonwhite population change (3)			.90	-.11	-.02	.02	.65	-.21	-.00	.03	.05	—	-.03	-.01	.16
4. Percent white population change (4)				.18	-.33	.33	.66	-.25	.10	.30	.36	—	.24	.27	.36
5. Size police force (5)					-.91	.91	.10	-.04	-.00	.93	.92	—	.92	.86	.50
6. Percent nonwhite population (6)						-1.0	.14	.08	-.01	-.89	-.99	—	-.96	-.98	-.69
7. Percent white population (7)							.14	-.08	.01	.89	.99	—	.96	.98	.69
8. Rate of growth total population (8)								-.47	-.15	.08	.14	—	.12	.11	.22
9. Rate of growth nonwhite population (9)									-.09	-.10		—	-.06	-.07	.43
10. Rate of growth white population (10)										-.03	-.00	—	-.01	-.01	.04
11. Density nonwhite population (11)											.95	—	.84	.88	.52
12. Density white population (12)												—	.93	.97	.69
13 Auto registration per 100,000 population (13)													—	—	—
14. Taxes on banks and corporations (14)														.93	.55
15. Taxes on land assessments and improvements (15)															.73
16 Average consumer price index (16)															—

Source: Compiled by the author.

TABLE A.7

Correlations of Independent Variables with Each Other, 1919–45

	1	2	3	4	5	6	7	8	9	10	11	12	13	14	15	16
		(2)	(3)	(4)	(5)	(6)	(7)	(8)	(9)	(10)	(11)	(12)	(13)	(14)	(15)	(16)
1. Total population (1)		.32	.30	.32	.71	.80	-.80	-.09	-.08	.09	1.0	1.0	.16	.67	.85	.03	—
2. Percent total population change (2)			.98	1.0	.47	.27	-.27	-.54	-.15	.18	.32	.32	.14	.03	.02	-.30	—
3. Percent nonwhite population change (3)				.96	.39	.27	-.27	-.61	-.04	.06	.30	.29	.15	.04	.02	-.30	—
4. Percent white population change (4)					.49	.25	-.25	-.52	-.19	.22	.32	.32	.12	.01	.02	-.30	—
5. Size police force (5)						.58	-.58	-.41	.43	.71	.71	.23	.47	.47	-.01		—
6. Percent nonwhite population (6)							-.99	.13	-.22	.21	.84	.78	.61	.81	.78	-.46	—
7. Percent white population (7)								-.13	.22	-.21	-.84	-.78	-.61	-.81	-.78	.46	—
8. Rate of growth total population (8)									-.24	.21	-.06	-.10	.15	.08	-.12	-.36	—
9. Rate of growth nonwhite population (9)										-.98	-.09	-.07	-.17	-.21	-.03	.21	—
10. Rate of growth white population (10)											.10	.08	.15	.19	.03	-.19	—
11. Density nonwhite population (11)												1.0	.21	.70	.85	-.02	—
12. Density white population (12)													.14	.66	.84	.06	—
13. Auto registration per 100,000 population (13)														.62	.36	-.60	—
14. Taxes on banks and corporations (14)															.84	-.20	—
15. Taxes on land assessments and improvements (15)																.02	—
16. Average consumer price index (16)																	—

Source: Compiled by the author.

TABLE A.8

Correlations of Independent Variables with Each Other, 1946-70

	1 (2)	2 (3)	3 (4)	4 (5)	5 (6)	6 (7)	7 (8)	8 (9)	9 (10)	10 (11)	11 (12)	12 (13)	13 (14)	14 (15)	15 (16)	16
1. Total population (1)	.14	.10	.23	-.51	-.73	.73	-.14	.26	-.16	-.67	.80	-.83	-.57	-.61	-.76	—
2. Percent total population change (2)	.38	.57	-.04	.08	-.08	.60	-.20	.16	.10	-.04	-.09	.09	.00	.00	—	
3. Percent nonwhite population change (3)	-.37	-.43	-.16	.16	.21	.63	-.66	-.15	.13	-.17	-.21	-.33	-.25	—		
4. Percent white population change (4)	.05	-.20	.20	.39	-.72	.79	-.19	.23	-.25	-.14	-.10	-.14	—			
5. Size police force (5)	.82	-.82	-.04	-.36	.45	.81	-.77	.76	.82	.91	.88	—				
6. Percent nonwhite population (6)	-1.0	.03	-.19	.14	1.0	-.99	.92	.96	.93	.96	—					
7. Percent white population (7)	-.03	.19	-.14	-1.0	.99	-.92	-.96	-.93	-.96	—						
8. Rate of growth total population (8)	-.34	.23	.01	-.04	.06	-.02	.07	.03	—							
9. Rate of growth nonwhite population (9)	-.93	-.17	.19	-.22	-.18	-.31	-.29	—								
10. Rate of growth white population (10)	.13	-.12	.18	.16	.32	.28	—									
11. Density nonwhite population (11)	-.98	.90	.98	.92	.94	—										
12. Density white population (12)	-.94	-.93	-.89	-.95	—											
13. Auto registration per 100,000 population (13)	.88	.91	.96	—												
14. Taxes on banks and corporations (14)	.94	.93	—													
15. Taxes on land assessments and improvements (15)	.96	—														
16. Average consumer price index (16)	—															

Source: Compiled by the author.

TABLE A.9

Correlations of Nonwhite and White Males Age 15-29 Years With Nonwhite and White Crime Rates, 1890-1970

Crime	Nonwhite		White	
	Correlation	Significance	Correlation	Significance
Auto theft	.97	.001	.71	.02
Burglary	.97	.001	.84	.003
Robbery	.99	.001	.75	.01
Grand larceny	.49	.09	.71	.02
Homicide arrests	.98	.001	.17	.33
Rape	.68	.02	.44	.12
Assault	.73	.01	.24	.26
Suicide	.93	.001	.74	.01

Source: U.S. Census Bureau, Census of Population, 1890 through 1970.

TABLE A.10

Consumer Price Index for Urban Wage Earners and Clerical Workers for Washington, D.C., Maryland, and Virginia, 1914-73
(All Items—Series A; 1967 = 100)

Year	Average	Year	Average	Year	Average
1914	.0	1934	42.3	1954	81.1
1915	31.3	1935	43.1	1955	81.0
1916	33.6	1936	43.3	1956	81.9
1917	40.8	1937	44.4	1957	84.4
1918	48.1	1938	43.4	1958	86.4
1919	52.6	1939	43.1	1959	86.8
1920	59.1	1940	43.3	1960	87.7
1921	52.1	1941	45.3	1961	89.0
1922	49.2	1942	50.3	1962	89.8
1923	50.0	1943	53.4	1963	91.3
1924	49.9	1944	54.2	1964	92.8
1925	51.1	1945	55.8	1965	94.1
1926	51.7	1946	60.7	1966	97.3
1927	50.3	1947	68.6	1967	100.0
1928	49.9	1948	72.7	1968	104.7
1929	49.7	1949	72.6	1969	111.2
1930	48.8	1950	73.6	1970	117.6
1931	45.8	1951	78.5	1971	122.7
1932	42.3	1952	80.7	1972	126.9
1933	40.9	1953	81.1	1973	135.0

Source: U.S. Department of Labor, Bureau of Labor Statistics.

TABLE A.11

Paid Civilian Employment of the Federal Government,
Washington, D. C. Metropolitan Area,
1816-1973

Year	Total	Year	Total
1816	535	1936	122,937
1821	603	1937	117,020
1831	666	1938	120,744
1841	1,014	1939	129,314
1851	1,533	1940	139,770
1861	2,199	1941	190,588
1871	6,222	1942	276,352
1881	13,124	1943	284,665
1891	20,834	1944	276,758
1901	28,044	1945	264,770
1908	34,647	1946	242,263
1909	35,936	1947	213,515
1910	38,911	1948	214,544
1911	39,782	1949	225,901
1912	38,555	1950	223,312
1913	38,975	1951	265,980
1914	40,016	1952	261,569
1915	41,281	1953	242,678
1916	41,804	1954	228,501
1917	48,313	1955	231,873
1918	120,835	1956	232,707
1919	106,073	1957	236,330
1920	94,110	1958	230,271
1921	82,416	1959	234,358
1922	73,645	1960	239,873
1923	70,062	1961	246,266
1924	68,000	1962	257,350
1925	67,563	1963	266,737
1926	64,722	1964	269,993
1927	63,814	1965	279,997
1928	65,506	1966	299,429
1929	68,266	1967	318,608
1930	73,032	1968	329,879
1931	76,303	1969	328,077
1932	73,455	1970	327,369
1933	70,261	1971	334,250
1934	94,244	1972	334,617
1935	108,673	1973	334,809

Note: Prior to 1941, figures are for the District of Columbia only; for 1941-49 only parts of Fairfax, Montgomery, and Prince Georges counties were included; beginning with 1950, District of Columbia, Arlington and Fairfax counties, Falls Church and Alexandria cities (Virginia), and Montgomery and Prince Georges counties, (Maryland) included; beginning with 1964, Fairfax City, Virginia, included; beginning with 1967 Loudoun and Prince William Counties, Virginia, included.

Figures are of June 30, except for 1920 and 1921 which were as of July 31, and 1919 which was as of November 11. Data prior to 1948 are partially estimated.

Figures include employees exempted from personnel ceilings in the Youth Programs, Public Service careers, and Worker Trainee Opportunities Program.

Source: U.S. Civil Service Commission, Manpower Statistics Division.

TABLE A.12

Motor Vehicle Registration, District of Columbia, 1926–70
(per 100,000 total population)

Year	Number	Year	Number
1926	28,464.8	1949	23,682.4
1927	27,640.4	1950	25,724.1
1928	32,233.6	1951	24,611.1
1929	36,939.9	1952	25,053.9
1930	35,877.4	1953	24,959.5
1931	32,707.0	1954	25,887.1
1932	31,193.6	1955	27,276.7
1933	28,710.2	1956	26,606.9
1934	28,890.8	1957	26,040.2
1935	29,287.1	1958	25,941.9
1936	30,317.5	1959	26,949.2
1937	31,483.7	1960	27,933.8
1938	26,687.0	1961	27,544.1
1939	26,095.5	1962	27,567.1
1940	26,228.2	1963	28,276.2
1941	23,924.2	1964	29,070.7
1942	19,618.2	1965	30,397.9
1943	15,800.3	1966	31,990.4
1944	14,936.5	1967	32,408.8
1945	13,843.5	1968	34,707.2
1946	15,521.5	1969	35,706.6
1947	18,710.8	1970	35,483.4
1948	21,259.3		

Source: Auto License Office of the District of Columbia.

TABLE A.13

Taxes on Banks and Public Service Corporations
Calculated as Percent of Gross Earnings, 1900-70
(dollars)

Year	Total	Year	Total
1900	$ 1,595.00	1936	$ --- ---
1901	3,287.50	1937	2,081,352.00
1902	29,226.00	1938	2,150,725.00
1903	340,437.57	1939	2,136,897.00
1904	398,422.05	1940	2,210,100.00
1905	401,875.12	1941	2,207,967.00
1906	442,243.22	1942	2,123,294.00
1907	495,182.00	1943	2,473,841.00
1908	527,837.00	1944	2,536,987.00
1909	567,352.00	1945	2,678,859.00
1910	629,137.00	1946	2,645,571.00
1911	676,280.00	1947	2,244,000.00
1912	687,799.00	1948	3,066,782.00
1913	713,219.00	1949	2,578,606.00
1914	745,296.00	1950	1,496,273.00
1915	757,864.00	1951	3,682,644.00
1916	792,713.00	1952	4,165,464.00
1917	796,624.00	1953	4,562,000.00
1918	835,182.00	1954	4,869,000.00
1919	951,234.00	1955	5,034,920.00
1920	1,118,389.00	1956	5,280,000.00
1921	1,472,028.00	1957	5,842,000.00
1922	1,560,075.00	1958	6,010,000.00
1923	1,596,262.00	1959	6,320,000.00
1924	1,078,903.00	1960	6,547,000.00
1925	1,732,330.00	1961	7,293,407.00
1926	1,999,093.00	1962	8,507,777.00
1927	2,043,923.00	1963	9,668,381.00
1928	2,115,697.00	1964	10,125,840.00
1929	2,146,440.00	1965	10,911,085.00
1930	2,228,531.00	1966	11,739,234.00
1931	2,215,140.00	1967	13,060,228.00
1932	2,094,084.00	1968	11,636,096.00
1933	1,650,280.00	1969	11,916,000.00
1934	1,841,408.00	1970	12,955,149.00
1935	1,937,670.00		

Source: Reports of the Government of the District of Columbia.

TABLE A.14

Taxes on Land Assessments and Improvements,
District of Columbia, 1890-1970
(dollars)

Year	Total	Year	Total
1890	$137,626,419.00	1931	$1,211,162,618.00
1891	141,609,891.00	1932	1,226,691,948.00
1892	145,481,278.00	1933	1,229,359,566.00
1893	147,024,276.00	1934	1,168,252,220.00
1894	191,417,804.00	1935	1,132,827,649.00
1895	192,555,046.00	1936	1,131,798,384.00
1896	188,922,343.00	1937	1,144,457,153.00
1897	180,376,908.00	1938	1,171,330,921.00
1898	181,256,284.00	1939	1,193,499,086.00
1899	183,156,371.00	1940	1,211,208,484.00
1900	176,567,549.00	1941	1,237,937,085.00
1901	180,334,641.00	1942	1,267,288,429.00
1902	182,525,608.00	1943	2,210,461,712.00
1903	208,519,436.00	1944	2,255,452,295.00
1904	213,250,418.00	1945	2,281,120,810.00
1905	217,608,296.00	1946	2,304,571,601.00
1906	239,461,985.00	1947	2,324,783,379.00
1907	247,306,494.00	1948	2,592,154,983.00
1908	255,324,834.00	1949	2,645,282,928.00
1909	277,570,952.00	1950	2,716,581,906.00
1910	285,153,771.00	1951	2,764,366,557.00
1911	294,767,547.00	1952	2,831,811,765.00
1912	330,322,487.00	1953	2,944,063,417.00
1913	339,198,990.00	1954	2,988,079,000.00
1914	345,124,144.00	1955	3,075,496,339.00
1915	390,309,278.00	1956	3,148,440,611.00
1916	394,209,904.00	1957	3,216,205,213.00
1917	402,099,232.00	1958	3,275,621,105.00
1918	410,173,609.00	1959	3,312,198,062.00
1919	414,610,691.00	1960	3,964,048,487.00
1920	426,623,630.00	1961	4,146,689,294.00
1921	437,794,768.00	1962	4,277,504,787.00
1922	472,874,209.00	1963	4,463,971,748.00
1923	723,199,268.00	1964	4,653,581,031.00
1924	778,860,673.00	1965	5,010,196,446.00
1925	891,625,572.00	1966	5,261,012,451.00
1926	900,749,812.00	1967	5,544,999,077.00
1927	946,367,422.00	1968	6,520,333,649.00
1928	1,118,093,162.00	1969	6,755,064,338.00
1929	1,138,057,905.00	1970	7,698,774,990.00
1930	1,182,463,345.00		

Source: Reports of the Commissioners of the District of
Columbia.

TABLE A.15

Multiple Regression of Independent Variables
of Population, Business Cycle, and Police Force Measures
with Nonwhite Larceny Rates, by Periods

	Simple R	Multiple R	R^2	Increment in R^2
1890-1918				
Police per 100,000 total population	-.75	.75	.56	.56
Size police force	-.58	.76	.57	.01
Percent white population	-.38	.81	.66	.09
Total population size	-.35	.86	.74	.08
Rate of growth white population	.03	.86	.75	.01
White percent population change	.20	.87	.75	.00
Taxes on land assessments and improvements	-.28	.87	.76	.01
Nonwhite percent population change	.33	.88	.77	.00
Total percent population change	.25	.89	.79	.02
Rate of growth total population	.02	.89	.79	.00
Rate of growth nonwhite population	-.02	.89	.79	.00
1919-45				
Total population size	-.63	.63	.40	.40
Average consumer price index	.32	.72	.52	.12
Percent nonwhite population	-.56	.79	.62	.10
Rate of growth white population	-.20	.80	.64	.02
Rate of growth total population	-.18	.81	.66	.02
Taxes on land assessments and improvements	-.38	.82	.67	.01
White percent population change	-.49	.83	.69	.01
Size police force	-.58	.84	.70	.02
Taxes on banks and corporations	-.31	.85	.72	.02
Police per 100,000 total population	.28	.85	.73	.00
Rate of growth nonwhite population	-.11	.85	.73	.00
Nonwhite percent population change	-.43	.86	.73	.00
Total percent population change	-.48	.86	.74	.00
Percent white population	.56	.86	.74	.00
1946-70				
Percent white population	.87	.87	.76	.76
Taxes on land assessments and improvements	-.69	.93	.86	.10
Rate of growth white population	-.10	.94	.88	.02
Taxes on banks and corporations	-.82	.94	.89	.01
Total percent population change	-.12	.95	.90	.01
Average consumer price index	-.76	.95	.91	.01
Total population size	.70	.95	.91	.00
Vehicle registrations per 100,000 population	-.74	.96	.92	.01
Nonwhite percent population change	.07	.96	.92	.00
Rate of growth total population	.00	.96	.93	.01
Rate of growth nonwhite population	.17	.96	.93	.00
White percent population change	.13	.96	.93	.00
Police per 100,000 total population	-.65	.97	.93	.00
Percent nonwhite population	-.87	.97	.93	.00
Size police force	-.61	.97	.93	.00

Source: Compiled by the author.

TABLE A.16

Multiple Regression of Independent Variables
of Population, Business Cycle, and Police Force Measures
with White Larceny Rates, by Periods

	Simple R	Multiple R	R^2	Increment in R^2
1890-1918				
Police per 100,000 total population	-.68	.68	.46	.46
Rate of growth white population	-.14	.69	.48	.02
Percent white population	-.50	.70	.49	.01
Taxes on land assessments and improvements	-.40	.73	.54	.05
Total percent population change	.04	.76	.58	.04
Total population size	-.49	.77	.60	.02
Size police force	-.63	.86	.75	.15
White percent population change	-.01	.87	.76	.01
Nonwhite percent population change	.22	.87	.76	.00
Rate of growth total population	-.14	.88	.77	.01
Rate of growth nonwhite population	-.08	.89	.80	.03
1919-45				
Total population size	-.66	.66	.43	.43
Taxes on land assessments and improvements	-.42	.70	.50	.07
Average consumer price index	.13	.72	.52	.02
Percent nonwhite population	-.49	.75	.56	.04
White percent population change	-.31	.77	.59	.03
Taxes on banks and corporations	-.26	.77	.59	.01
Police per 100,000 total population	.42	.78	.61	.02
Rate of growth white population	.05	.79	.62	.01
Size police force	-.53	.80	.64	.02
Nonwhite percent population change	-.27	.82	.67	.03
Rate of growth total population	.07	.83	.68	.01
Rate of growth nonwhite population	.10	.83	.69	.01
Total percent population change	-.31	.84	.70	.00
Percent white population	.49	.84	.70	.00
1946-70				
Percent white population	.92	.92	.85	.85
Taxes on land assessments and improvements	-.80	.93	.87	.02
Rate of growth white population	-.13	.94	.88	.01
Nonwhite percent population	.02	.94	.89	.01
Rate of growth total population	-.04	.95	.89	.01
Average consumer price index	-.85	.95	.90	.01
Total percent population change	-.13	.96	.91	.01
Taxes on banks and corporations	-.88	.96	.92	.00
Rate of growth nonwhite population	.12	.96	.92	.00
Vehicle registrations per 100,000 population	-.84	.96	.92	.00
White percent population change	.17	.96	.93	.01
Police per 100,000 total population	-.75	.97	.94	.01
Total population size	.70	.97	.94	.00
Percent nonwhite population	-.92	.97	.95	.00
Size police force	-.72	.97	.95	.00

Source: Compiled by the author.

TABLE A.17

Correlations of Unemployment Status
With Nonwhite and White
Class I Crime Rates 1920-70
(Decennial)

Crime	Non-White		White	
	R	Significance	R	Significance
Auto theft	.59	.05	.51	.08
Burglary	.70	.02	.78	.007
Robbery	.61	.04	.79	.006
Grand larceny	.51	.08	.43	.13
Homicide arrests	.55	.06	-.30	.22
Assault	.54	.07	.31	.21
Rape	.45	.11	.52	.08
Suicide	.68	.02	.86	.001

Note: The basis for unemployment classifications has not been consistent over time. For example, in 1940 those seeking work prior to March 30, 1940 were included, as well as those on public emergency projects. In 1950, these were included as well as those who believed no work was available in their community, or their line of work. In 1960, a person was considered to be looking for work if he had made such efforts in the past 60 days and was awaiting results from those efforts.

Source: for Unemployment Data: U.S. Census Bureau, Census of Population, 1920-70.

NAME INDEX

Abrahamson, Mark, 38, 39, 40
Anderson, T. W. , 53
Angell, Robert C. , 35, 36, 37, 38, 39, 81
Antunes, George, 28

Barnett, Jean T. , 52
Bauer, Raymond A. , 55
Beasley, Ronald W. , 28
Becker, Gary S. , 30
Bell, Daniel, 72
Bellah, Robert N. , 18
Bent, Dale H. , 64
Berman, Yitzchak, 36
Biderman, Albert D. , 55
Bienen, Henry, 146
Bierstedt, Robert, 13
Black, Donald J. , 56
Blau, Peter M. , 4
Bogen, David, 26
Boggs, Sarah L. , 39, 40
Bogue, Donald J. , 81
Bonger, William Adrian, 7, 11, 14, 16, 18, 23, 26, 31, 32
Bottomore, T. B. , 15, 17, 52
Brenner, Meyer Harvey, 8, 53, 58, 191
Burgess, Ernest W. , 5, 6, 19

Chambliss, William J. , 14
Clark, Kenneth B. , 6
Clark, Terry N. , 73
Clinard, Marshall B. , 18, 38
Cloward, Richard A. , 6, 20, 186
Cohen, Albert K. , 6, 189
Cohen, Bernard, 190

Conrad, John P. , 41
Count-van Manen, Gloria, 25, 26, 28, 29, 42, 50, 52, 53, 54, 55, 60, 73, 83, 184, 189, 190
Couzens, Michael, 55, 56, 75
Cressey, Donald R. , 83

Darlington, Richard B. , 65, 66
Davis, Nanette J. , 14
DeGrazia, Sebastian, 17
de Neufville, Judith Innes, 106
Denisoff, R. Serge, 14
Doerner, William G. , 30, 189
Duncan, Otis Dudley, 7
Dunham, H. Warren, 40
Durkheim, Emile, 1, 4, 5, 12, 13, 17, 18, 19, 38, 53, 71, 72, 126, 127

Easterlin, Richard A. , 77, 134
Engels, Friedrich, 13
Ennis, Philip H. , 55
Erikson, Kai T. , 49
Erlanger, Howard S. , 6, 189
Ezekiel, Mordecai, 63, 65, 66

Faris, Robert E. L. , 18
Farrell, Ronald A. , 108, 130, 190
Feierabend, Ivo K. , 184
Ferdinand, Theodore N. , 33, 34, 49
Feuer, Lewis S. , 103
Flange, Victor Eugene, 140, 179, 189
Fleisher, Belton M. , 26, 27, 29, 30, 32, 34
Fox, Karl A. , 3, 50, 63, 65, 66
Franklin, John Hope, 26
Freedman, Deborah S. , 134
Freud, Sigmund, 1, 13
Friedman, Robert, 192, 193

Quetelet, L. A. J. , 16
Quinney, Richard, 14, 27, 30, 31, 37, 38

Reasons, Charles E. , 7
Rein, Martin, 117
Reiss, Albert J. , Jr. , 55
Rice, Kent, 26, 28, 32, 33, 34, 53
Rosenbaum, Betty B. , 26, 27, 61
Ross, Marvin, 26, 29, 31, 32, 33, 34, 35

Schuessler, Karl, 27, 36, 37, 39
Seidman, David, 54, 56, 75
Sellin, Thorsten, 54
Selvin, Hanan C. , 38, 52, 152, 191
Shaw, Clifford, 81
Sheldon, Eleanor Bernert, 146, 149
Sherbenou, Edgar L. , 140, 179, 189
Short, James F. Jr. , 24, 31, 32, 34, 53, 54, 55, 127, 189, 190
Simmel, Georg, 53, 78
Simon, Herbert A. , 181
Simpson, Ray Mars, 34
Slatin, Gerald, 27, 36, 37, 39
Sonquist, John A. , 64, 66
Sorokin, Pitirim A. , 1, 12, 13, 14
Spector, Paul E. , 31, 34, 36, 40
Spier, Rosalind B. , 37, 38
Strodtbeck, Fred L. , 190
Stys, W. , 134
Sullivan, Richard F. , 19, 30
Sutherland, Edwin H. , 83, 148
Swigert, Victoria Lynn, 108, 130, 190

Swimmer, Gene, 27, 28, 29, 31, 32, 34, 43, 44

Tarde, Gabriele, 11, 18, 73
Taueber, Irene, 27, 86
Thomas, Dorothy Swaine, 24, 27, 28, 29, 31, 32, 34, 53, 58, 65, 134, 140
Thomas, W. I. , 18
Thrasher, Frederic M. , 6, 7, 190
Tobias, J. J. , 49, 192
Tobin, James, 192
Traub, Stuart H. , 18
Turk, Austin T. , 14

Udy, Stanley H. Jr. , 188

Van de Geer, John P. , 133
Veblen, Thorstein, 15
Viano, Emilio, 42, 83, 142
Vogt, Evon Z. , 188
Vold, George B. , 14, 28, 34, 55
Voss, Harwin L. , 25, 81
Votey, H. , 42

Waugh, Frederick V. , 65
Weber, Max, 1
Wellford, Charles F. , 26, 28, 30, 33, 34, 36, 42, 43, 52
Wiers, Paul, 26, 31, 32, 34
Wilkins, Leslie T. , 59
Willbach, A. , 52
Wirth, Louis, 40, 78
Wolfgang, Marvin E. , 6, 41, 54, 142, 186, 190, 191

Yablonsky, Lewis, 81
Yinger, Milton J. , 182

Zimring, Franklin E. , 19, 41, 42
Zito, George V. , 8
Znaniecki, Florian, 18

ABOUT THE AUTHOR

Gloria Count-van Manen is Associate Professor of Criminology in the Department of Sociology and Anthropology at Howard University. Dr. Count-van Manen's training and experience are interdisciplinary, crossing the borders of criminology and deviance, economics, psychology, and psychoanalysis. She has recently edited a volume, Social Systems, Crime, Delinquency, and Deviance: A Reader in Structually Oriented Studies. She has published articles, chapters in other volumes, and monographs on crime, family socialization, and social economics.

Dr. Count-van Manen has served in the capacity of consultant for numerous projects, including ones at the University of Chicago and Howard University. Under President John F. Kennedy and Mayor Richard Daley, she served as research associate and worked in the planning of delinquency control projects. Earlier, she worked: at the Family Study Center of the University of Chicago; in the Chief Examiner's Office there; at the United States Department of Labor as a labor economist at the bureau of Labor Statistics; and for the Marshall Plan, in the central office in Paris.

Dr. Count-van Manen obtained her Ph.D. degree from the University of Chicago, with a special field of competence in criminology and deviance in the Department of Sociology. Three fellowships at this institution allowed for interdisciplinary training in psychology, as well. Earlier, she studied at the Washington School of Psychiatry. Her M.S. was obtained at Louisiana State University, with a major in sociology and a minor in economics, her B.S. at the University of Minnesota. As a Fulbright scholar, she studied in Southeast Asia.

ALIENATION IN CONTEMPORARY SOCIETY: A Multidis-
ciplinary Examination
> edited by
> Roy S. Bryce-Laporte
> Claudewell S. Thomas

CRIMINAL RECIDIVISM IN NEW YORK CITY: An Evaluation
of the Impact of Rehabilitation and Diversion Services
> Robert Fishman

THE EFFECTIVENESS OF CORRECTIONAL TREATMENT:
A Survey of Treatment Evaluation Studies
> Douglas Lipton
> Robert Martinson
> Judith Wilks

ISSUES IN CRIMINAL JUSTICE: Planning and Evaluation
> edited by
> Marc Riedel
> Duncan Chappell

TOWARD A JUST AND EFFECTIVE SENTENCING SYSTEM:
Agenda for Legislative Reform
> Pierce O'Donnell
> Michael J. Churgin
> Dennis E. Curtis
> Foreward by
> Senator Edward M. Kennedy

VICTIMS, CRIME, AND SOCIAL CONTROL
> Eduard A. Ziegenhagen